T0330345

The Heritage Turn in China

Publications

The International Institute for Asian Studies (IIAS) is a research and exchange platform based in Leiden, the Netherlands. Its objective is to encourage the interdisciplinary and comparative study of Asia and to promote (inter)national cooperation. IIAS focuses on the humanities and social sciences and on their interaction with other sciences. It stimulates scholarship on Asia and is instrumental in forging research networks among Asia Scholars. Its main research interests are reflected in the three book series published with Amsterdam University Press: Global Asia, Asian Heritages and Asian Cities. IIAS acts as an international mediator, bringing together various parties in Asia and other parts of the world. The Institute works as a clearinghouse of knowledge and information. This entails activities such as providing information services, the construction and support of international networks and cooperative projects, and the organization of seminars and conferences. In this way, IIAS functions as a window on Europe for non-European scholars and contributes to the cultural rapprochement between Europe and Asia.

IIAS Publications Officer: Paul van der Velde
IIAS Assistant Publications Officer: Mary Lynn van Dijk

Asian Heritages

The Asian Heritages series explores the notions of heritage as they have evolved from European based concepts, mainly associated with architecture and monumental archaeology, to incorporate a broader diversity of cultural forms and value. This includes a critical exploration of the politics of heritage and its categories, such as the contested distinction 'tangible' and 'intangible' heritages; the analysis of the conflicts triggered by competing agendas and interests in the heritage field; and the productive assessment of management measures in the context of Asia.

Series Editors
Adèle Esposito, CNRS-IRASEC, Bangkok, Thailand
Michael Herzfeld, Harvard University, U.S.A., and Leiden University, the Netherlands

Editorial Board
Sadiah Boonstra, 2019-2020 Asia Scholar, The University of Melbourne/Curator of Public Programs Asia TOPA, Australia
Min-Chin Chiang, Taipei National University of the Arts, Taiwan
Yew-Foong Hui, Hong Kong Shue Yan University
Aarti Kawlra, IIAS, the Netherlands
Ronki Ram, Panjab University, India

The Heritage Turn in China

*The Reinvention, Dissemination
and Consumption of Heritage*

*Edited by
Carol Ludwig, Linda Walton
and Yi-Wen Wang*

Amsterdam University Press

International
Institute for
Asian Studies

Publications

ASIAN HERITAGES 5

Cover illustration: Traditional Association Performance at Miaofengshan Pilgrimage, May 2000
Source: Florence Graezer Bideau

Cover design: Coördesign, Leiden
Lay-out: Crius Group, Hulshout

ISBN   978 94 6298 566 7
e-ISBN   978 90 4853 681 8 (pdf)
DOI   10.5117/9789462985667
NUR   694

Printed and bound by CPI Group (UK) Ltd, Croydon, CR0 4YY

To Jack, whose birth took place together with the birth of this book

Table of Contents

Section 1   (Re)constructions, (Re)inventions, and Representations of Heritage

Section 2   Creating Identities: Constructing Pasts, Disseminating Heritage

List of Figures

Acknowledgments

This edited volume is one of the products of an international collaboration between Xi'an Jiaotong-Liverpool University (XJTLU), the University of Liverpool, UK, the Suzhou University of Science and Technology, China, and the World Heritage Institute of Training and Research for the Asia and Pacific Region (WHITRAP Suzhou) under the auspices of UNESCO. We are grateful to all these institutions, faculty, and staff for their support.

We would also like to specifically thank the following people:

The two co-Editors of the Asian Heritages Series, Professor Michael Herzfeld and Dr Adèle Esposito for their invaluable feedback on the manuscript;

The three anonymous reviewers, who provided helpful and insightful comments;

The International Institute for Asian Studies (IIAS), particularly Dr Paul van der Velde, the IIAS Publications Officer, and Mary Lynn van Dijk, the Assistant Publications Officer; and

The Amsterdam University Press (AUP), specially, dr Saskia Gieling, the Asian Studies Commissioning Editor, and drs Jaap Wagenaar, the AUP's Production Editor.

Introduction

(Un)Authorised Heritage Discourse and Practice in China

Carol Ludwig and Linda Walton

This edited volume focuses on heritage discourse and practice in China today as it has evolved from the 'heritage turn' that can be dated to the 1990s (Madsen 2014; Denton 2014). Using a variety of disciplinary approaches to a broad range of case studies, the contributors to this volume show how particular versions of the past are selected, (re)invented, disseminated and consumed for contemporary purposes. These studies explore how the Chinese state utilises heritage not only for tourism, entertainment, educational and commercial purposes, but also as part of broader political strategies on both the national and international stage. Together, they argue that the Chinese state employs modes of heritage governance to construct new modernities/identities in support of both its political legitimacy and its claim to status as an international superpower.

Both before and after the founding of the People's Republic of China (PRC) in 1949, views of cultural heritage changed dramatically, from preservation to targeted destruction to reconstruction. Although the Cultural Revolution (1966-1976) is well-known for violent attacks on people, places, and things associated with the 'feudal' past, in fact much earlier in the twentieth century, especially during the May Fourth Movement (1919), aspects of China's cultural heritage were critiqued and rejected as a source of political weakness in the modern era (Ip, Hon & Lee 2003). During the first 30 years of the People's Republic, while the pre-revolutionary past was for the most part vilified, revolutionary events, people, and places were celebrated with the building of the Yan'an Museum of Revolution in 1950, for example, although 'Red Tourism' to sites of revolutionary history did not become a phenomenon until the 1990s (Wang 2012; Denton 2014: 214-242). The pre-revolutionary past, however, drew positive attention from policymakers in the 1980s, when they began to see China's cultural heritage primarily as an asset to be managed and utilised in the interests of the nation. State support

Ludwig, Carol, Linda Walton, and Yi-Wen Wang (eds), *The Heritage Turn in China: The Reinvention, Dissemination and Consumption of Heritage.* Amsterdam: Amsterdam University Press 2020
DOI: 10.5117/9789462985667_INTRO

and regulation of cultural heritage consequently became a prominent aspect of governance. Since the 1990s, however, in tandem with efforts to practice heritage conservation, both urban development and massive public works projects such as the Three Gorges Dam have frequently derailed the protection of cultural heritage sites (Demattè 2012). Such projects have also displaced local communities, reflecting conflicts between the goals of economic prosperity (including profits for the powerful) and the preservation of cultural heritage (Shepherd 2016: 91-120). In the 2000s, tensions between conflicting national goals have intersected with international pressures to maintain global standing as a world power, one aspect of which is China's contribution to world cultural heritage, recognised through soaring numbers of UNESCO-designated World Heritage Sites (Shepherd 2009; UNESCO 2019a; Silverman & Blumenfield 2013: 5).

Positioned within current international trends in heritage discourse, in particular the global spread of Western[1] approaches to heritage conservation, the studies presented here contribute to understanding this new and historically significant phase in how heritage conservation is framed, conceptualised, and practiced in China. This 'turn' in how heritage is imagined, disseminated and consumed has important implications for the international practice of heritage conservation and management over the coming decades (Winter 2014a). As Western conceptions and practices of heritage have themselves been questioned and revised, it is imperative to consider how their global spread has begun to reshape them through translation to vastly differing geographic, political, and cultural spaces (Winter 2014b; Winter 2014c). In China and across the globe, the intersection of local, national, and international interests has brought new agency to a wider range of actors who participate in the construction of modernities/identities through the heritagisation process and raised new questions about the meaning and practice of heritage in a global setting (Askew 2010).

What is Heritage and Heritagisation?

The studies in this book are grounded in the understanding of heritage as a mutable, multifaceted construct, which is produced at any given point in

1   The term 'Western' is used throughout this volume to refer to people, objects, ideas or methods originating from Europe or the United States. We fully acknowledge the ambiguity and generalising nature of the term, yet consider it to be the most appropriate, given its frequent usage and acceptance in academic circles.

time, and is accessed and consumed in the present (Ludwig 2016). Rather than a fixed tangible object, heritage is a set of values that are meaningful to different people, at different times, in different contexts and for different reasons (Ludwig 2013). Because heritage is constantly changing, it is useful to envision it as a process – heritagisation – as well as a construct, a verb rather than a noun (Harvey 2001; Smith 2006; Maags and Svensson 2018). To understand heritage as a subject of critical enquiry, it is useful to explore its discourse across scalar boundaries (Harvey 2015: 579) and through the conceptual lens of the authorised heritage discourse (AHD). The AHD is an uncritical, naturalised, and deeply embedded 'way of seeing', centred on the material nature of heritage defined by 'experts' (Smith 2006). With its origins in the Western nineteenth-century birth of the conservation ethic, it excludes 'all dissonant, conflicted or non-core accounts of heritage' (Smith 2006: 11). Its exclusionary nature reinforces ideological representations of heritage that focus on elite/consensus history, nationalism, tangibility, age and aesthetics. Moreover, it is described as a 'self-referential' discourse that, 'privileges monumentality and grand scale, innate artefact/site significance tied to time depth, scientific/aesthetic expert judgement, social consensus and nation building' (Smith 2006: 11). The AHD is therefore underpinned by a powerful set of ideas about what heritage is, and these ideas act as orientation points for expert decision-making and adaptation (Ludwig 2016). In contrast to the AHD and in line with recent critical scholarship, we perceive heritage to be complex, multilayered and closely tied to ascribed social meanings, associations and emotions. It therefore encompasses the tangible, built heritage 'objects', as well as the intangible heritage and its 'affective registers' (Waterton & Watson 2013).

The notion of intangible heritage was officially recognised by UNESCO as a separate category of heritage in 2003, with the Convention for the Safeguarding of Intangible Cultural Heritage. It emerged as a result of growing criticism fuelled by questions that both affected communities and heritage scholars have raised about UNESCO's focus on the traditional, elitist and tangible vision of heritage described above, and the consequent closing down of marginal voices (Smith and Waterton 2009; Bortolotto 2007). UNESCO (2019b) defines Intangible Cultural Heritage as 'traditions or living expressions inherited from our ancestors and passed on to our descendants, such as oral traditions, performing arts, social practices, rituals, festive events, knowledge and practices concerning nature and the universe or the knowledge and skills to produce traditional crafts'. The inclusion of intangible cultural heritage on the international conservation agenda therefore means 'conceiving heritage not only as a consecrated masterpiece of the past to be venerated and preserved, but also as a symbolic and living space' (Bortolotto 2007: 21).

Intangible heritage, therefore, is human activity. This understanding of heritage encompasses reproduction and the transmission of practices, and stands in stark contrast to the naturalised, and deeply embedded 'way of seeing' born out of the nineteenth century conservation ethic described above. As such, this interpretation has serious implications for the continued application of traditional conservation criteria used to identify heritage. One obvious issue is that of authenticity, for example. Whether heritage is deemed authentic traditionally relates to its genuineness, determined by experts, examining scientific evidence to establish whether the original fabric is sufficiently 'intact' (Taylor 2004: 430), as opposed to a form of 'fake' restoration (Larkham 1996; Hobson 2004; Pendlebury 2009). There are generally many problems with this positivist approach to the legitimisation of heritage assets (Ludwig 2016) and these are particularly exacerbated in the context of the Asia Pacific region (Verdini et al. 2017), where, in contrast to Europe, for example, architecture is 'essentially made of perishable and fragile materials, such as timber … [requiring] frequent rebuilding' (Zhu 2015: 597). The Nara Document on Authenticity (1994) arguably goes some way to address this problem by acknowledging the plurality of cultural traditions and calling for more flexible criteria in regard to authenticity (Verdini et al. 2017); however problems remain in trying to shoe-horn the idea of intangible heritage into the long-established model (operations and rational mindsets) of traditional heritage practice and its deeply embedded conservation philosophy (Ludwig 2016; Also see Delafons 1997 and Jokilehto 1999). Indeed, several scholars are deeply critical about the very separation of the material from the symbolic, the tangible from the intangible (Byrne 2011: 147). Herzfeld (2014: 48), for instance, argues that such a separation assumes that these are 'two clearly defined and mutually opposed entities', which he considers to be not only unhelpful, but also ontologically impossible (Byrne 2011: 155). Indeed, he argues that the very act of reificating (documenting, creating a book, etc.) is textual and thus creates tangibility. Other scholars have also argued that there is 'no such thing as heritage' '(Smith 2006: 11) or in other words all heritage is subjective, socially-constructed and intangible, existing only because of the values people attribute to it.

The initial inclusivity and openness created by UNESCO's official division of the tangible and intangible therefore swiftly evaporated into a problematic and confusing dichotomy. Moreover, if it is a question of ontology, i.e., what *is,* then just as for tangible heritage, Herzfeld argues that the important question is 'who gets to define what is' (Byrne 2011: 156). This is, of course, subject to much contestation, simply because people value things in different ways, for different reasons. Herzfeld (2004) explains this through what he terms a 'global hierarchy of value', where only the 'officially acceptable' [heritage] get reified'- not the folklore or traditions which make up a country's' 'cultural intimacy' (those uncomfortable or embarrassing jokes, songs or stories perceived as a potential source of national ridicule) (Byrne 2011: 148). As the conceptual heir of colonialisation, the global hierarchy of value therefore determines 'how seriously different traditions and intellectual cultures will be taken' (Herzfeld 2010: 296) and just like the conflict surrounding tangible heritage, the addition of intangible heritage provides merely an additional layer of subjectivity and 'vagueness' to this value system, which Herzfeld argues is the very essence of its authority. While the global shift from a tangible, archival approach to an intangible, process-oriented approach to heritage thus marks a change in direction for the AHD (Bonnici 2009; Meyer-Bisch 2009; CoE 2011; Sykes & Ludwig 2015; Ludwig 2016; Svensson & Maags 2018), and has 'paved the way' for a new perspective and appreciation of many cultural practices in China as elsewhere (Svensson and Maags 2018: 23), there is yet to be a fundamental shift in the underlying power of the AHD (Smith 2006: 106-114). Moreover, the case for heritage still needs to be made using an appropriate heritage discourse that is recognised within an ambiguous framework of heritage values and, perhaps more importantly, is complementary to contemporary national interests and priorities.

Despite its complex and controversial nature and history, the AHD therefore still provides a useful theoretical entry point, and several studies have adopted it as a heuristic device for international analysis (Waterton 2010; Högberg 2012; Mydland & Grahn 2012; Harvey 2015; Ludwig 2016). But others have also identified conceptual limitations of the AHD, arguing that its use as a critical theoretical device has diverted attention from the continuing significance and political role of nation states – not just simply professional elites – as stakeholders in the construction of it (Svensson & Maags 2018: 16; Herzfeld 2004; Askew 2010; Meskell 2013). This is an especially important consideration in understanding the theory and practice of the AHD in China, while documenting and analysing its practice in China promises to further complicate theoretical perspectives.

Rooted in a Western material understanding of heritage, the AHD is therefore a helpful construct to unravel nationalistic discourses in, of and for heritage (Waterton & Watson 2013) and to unpack consequent tensions between state-led and bottom-up celebrations of culture and identity (Svensson & Maags 2018). In the case of the UK, for example, it is relatively straightforward to identify the AHD, as it is consistently written into official policy and law. It therefore provides a distinct contrast to the 'unauthorised' (alternative, minority or subaltern) versions of heritage, which subsequently may become marginalised and excluded. Indeed, the AHD is traditionally based on a deeply embedded conservation philosophy, which despite nuances, and claims of adjustment (Pendlebury 2013) remains pervasive in Western conservation practice (Ludwig 2016). Applying the AHD to the Chinese context is more complex, in part because of its size and regional diversity. Nonetheless, since the very beginning of the People's Republic of China, there have been a series of state agencies responsible for developing and implementing official policies toward the protection and preservation of China's cultural heritage. Currently, the State Administration of Cultural Heritage (SACH) manages heritage sites and museums at national, provincial, and county levels throughout the country, and it also oversees nominations for World Cultural Heritage Site status at the global level. Since 2004, all construction- and heritage-related activities at national and provincial levels must follow a process of approval, planning, and construction under the authority of SACH. Although the bureaucrats and experts who constitute SACH can be said to represent a governmentally endorsed AHD, the chapters in this collection illuminate the diversity of institutional and non-institutional heritage definitions and approaches across China, reflecting both geographical scale and regional difference. These studies point to what could be better defined as, to borrow the term from Pendlebury (2013), an 'assemblage' of AHDs. In the absence of a singular, rigidly defined AHD, the plurality of interpretation and representation from local and non-elite groups may alter the version of AHD as conceived and intended by SACH and its regional counterparts. In other words, we suggest that the AHD in China is characterised by a relatively high degree of variability and fluidity.

While one of the underlying messages conveyed in the chapters is a 'collective' endeavour (or strong drive) to conserve, reconstruct and even reinvent heritage in China at all spatial scales, the campaign for heritage conservation has been driven and orchestrated by the state for clear purposes (discussed in more detail below) and such state-driven heritage management remains largely top-down and undemocratic. However, we show that tensions between stakeholders emerge, providing examples to demonstrate that spontaneous enthusiasm and initiatives undertaken from the bottom-up or grassroots level in many cases have been equally important, illustrating that other actors are very much involved in the heritagisation process and in creating a continuously developing AHD assemblage for China.

The nature and meaning of heritage continue to be a topic of intense debate, and its contemporary *use* is the subject of an expanding field of academic enquiry. This expansion includes the 'critical heritage studies' movement 'to promote heritage as an area of critical enquiry', developed in part in response to the growth of a global 'heritage industry' (www. criticalheritagestudies.org; Maags & Svensson 2018: 11-12). A mounting number of studies show that heritage forms part of the overall 'territorial capital' of a place (Sykes & Ludwig 2015: 9) and plays a core role in legitimising and mobilising current identities (Massey 1995). The elements of history chosen for reproduction, dissemination and consumption reveal much about the social, economic and political power/influence of heritage in the contemporary world. More specifically with regard to China, researchers have asked questions about the uses of history, nostalgia and heritage by the post-Mao state in the construction of Chinese identities and subjectivities (Wu 2006; Blumenfield & Silverman 2013; Maags & Svensson 2018). The chapters in this book address questions related to the production and practice of an AHD in China, its social, political and economic impacts, as well as conflicts between the goals and priorities of state authorities, experts, and local communities through several key interconnected themes: concepts of power and legitimacy, (re)claiming identity, public pedagogy/moral education, urbanisation, and economic development.

Meanings and Uses of Heritage in Early and Imperial China

Prior to the twentieth century, conceptions and displays of heritage played important roles in the state's assertion of its legitimacy and power in China as elsewhere (Harvey 2001). As early as the Zhou era (1045-256 BCE), for example, the development of urban space in the capital projected the ruler's authority. Like the Zhou capital, succeeding dynastic capital cities all followed the same general arrangement: a rectangular walled city, centrally located palace, north-south orientation and central axis. Both the buildings themselves and the layout of the city were designed to reflect the centrality of the ruler and his power (Sit 2010: 95-101). Cultural artefacts also assumed an important symbolic role. Rulers asserted their legitimacy by displaying 'bronze and jade ritual objects, court seals, scrolls and tax records of either ancestors or those whom they had defeated' in order to illustrate their triumph and/or legitimise their new status of power/authority (Shepherd & Yu 2013: 5). For example, when the founder of the Ming Dynasty (1368-1644), Zhu Yuanzhang, conquered the Mongol Yuan Dynasty (1279-1368), an imperial collection of artefacts dating from the ninth century was seized (Shepherd & Yu 2013: 5). These were proudly displayed as a symbol of the power and legitimacy of the new regime.

Cultural artefacts were valued in the private, as well as public, realm. During the Song (960-1279) era private scholarly interest in remnants of the past blossomed, especially the study of bronze and jade ritual objects. While differing political and cultural agendas motivated scholars to collect antiquities and compile catalogues of them, all shared a belief in the contemporary relevance of the relics of the past (Hsu 2010). Rubbings of ancient texts were also collected and catalogued because determining the authenticity of the textual tradition was an important undertaking with deep political significance. For these reasons, cultural heritage, in the form of ancient relics, was the object of profound concern not only for emperors intent on confirming the legitimacy of their rule but also for the educated elite who sought continuity with antiquity, both as a source of classical ideals and as a link to their own ancestors (Wang & Rowlands 2017: 261).

Throughout the history of imperial China, from the Han Dynasty (207 BCE-225 CE) to the early twentieth century, conceptions of cultural heritage were closely tied to Confucianism. A primary example is the performance of Confucian rites and the transmission of these rites through texts as well as practice. Both Confucian texts and ritual vessels embodied the ideals of antiquity and the moral values of the sages who created them, as the practice of rites making use of both texts and vessels performed this cultural heritage. The preservation and transmission of cultural heritage were driven by a desire to access the accurate record of the past in order to use it as a model for correct behaviour in the present (although not necessarily to apply it in a literal sense). Moral and pedagogical uses of the past did not disappear after the demise of imperial China, although the influence of Confucianism was drastically curtailed until its official renaissance in the post-Mao era (Billioud & Thoraval 2015).

Heritage Conservation and the Modern Nation State in China

While both urban space and ancient relics were used by China's dynastic rulers to legitimise their authority, a modern conception of heritage conservation in the public realm and as an aspect of governance only began to emerge in the late Qing era (1644-1911). Along with other elements of 'modernity', the idea of heritage conservation as a domain of state authority was introduced into China from the West. Imperialist exploitation and plunder of historic sites such as the Buddhist cave-temples of Dunhuang by European nations and Japan spurred the Qing government to take steps to protect and preserve China's cultural heritage, beginning with *Measures for the Protection of Ancient Sites* in 1909. The growth of public awareness and legislation to protect cultural heritage were tied to the building of a modern nation state in China, as the idea of heritage had evolved in tandem with the rise of the nation state in Europe (Meskell & Brumann 2015: 23; Evans & Rowlands 2014: 276; Lai 2016: 50-51). After the fall of the Qing Dynasty and the revolutionary upheavals that followed, however, it was not until 1930 that a second policy statement on the protection of cultural heritage was adopted by the Nationalist government (Lai 2016: 72-78). The *Law on the Preservation of Ancient Objects* was quickly followed in 1931 with further conservation-related legislation, including the *Statute for the Preservation of Scenic Spots, Points of Historical Importance*, and *Articles of Historical, Cultural, and Artistic Value* (Gruber 2007). In 1948, an attempt was made to categorise China's material heritage with the listing of 450 sites in the publication *A Brief List of Important Architectural Heritages in China* (Shepherd & Yu 2013: 10). This inventory, the first of its kind in China, was compiled only a short time before the collapse of the Nationalist government following civil war with the Communists. Political and military turmoil disrupted the prior momentum for heritage conservation and thus had a profound effect on the development of heritage policy in China (Lew 2009).

Following the defeat of the Nationalists in 1949, heritage conservation was not an immediate priority for the Communist government, given the more urgent military, political, and economic demands of establishing a new nation. Once power was consolidated and their rule stabilised, the new government supported archaeological work to salvage artefacts of Chinese antiquity while both utilising and altering cultural monuments inherited from the past. The Gate of Heavenly Peace at the entrance to the Forbidden City was used purposefully by the victorious Communists for their triumphal announcement of the founding of the People's Republic of China on 1 October 1949. Standing on this symbolic monument of the Qing and earlier dynasties, Chairman Mao Zedong waved to the cheering masses, showing that the previously Forbidden City, accessible only to the rulers, had become a public space open to the people and that China now belonged to them. While such monuments from the past were used in this way to legitimise Communist power and authority, the new government also permitted the destruction of cultural sites for the purpose of constructing new monuments and public spaces. The historic areas south of the Forbidden City were demolished in 1958-1959 to build the Great Hall of the People and to expand Tiananmen Square (Shepherd & Yu 2013: 15). Destruction also occurred in the course of urban development undertaken to fulfil the regime's promise to meet the daily needs of the masses. For example,

Beijing's Ming-era walls were destroyed during the construction of a new subway system in the mid-1960s (Shepherd & Yu 2013: 15).

One of the first indications of the Communist leadership giving serious attention to heritage management as a domain of state power and a potent political and cultural resource was the 1961 adoption of the PRC's first official policy on the protection and management of cultural heritage, the *Provisional Regulations on the Protection and Administration of Cultural Relics*. Only a year later, in 1962, the Cultural Relics Bureau within the Ministry of Culture published a list of national cultural sites (Shepherd & Yu 2013: 15). Together, these changes represented an attempt to form a national cultural heritage system for China. This momentum was disrupted by the Cultural Revolution, characterised by Mao's encouragement of an unprecedented attack on the 'four olds' – customs, culture, habits, and ideas (Dikötter 2016). The decade between 1966 and Mao's death in 1976 saw the consequent destruction and vandalism of many historic sites, including temples, churches, and mosques, as a means of eradicating all evidence of 'old thinking' and 'old culture'. Despite prevalent images of destruction and desecration during the Cultural Revolution, however, both official and private efforts succeeded in protecting many sites and relics by promoting their value as instruments of revolutionary nationalism (Ho 2011; Evans & Rowlands 2014: 276-277). State interest in China's cultural heritage surged in the 1980s, in tandem with the political and economic 'opening' that took place in the aftermath of the Cultural Revolution. In 1982 China published its first *Law on the Protection of Cultural Heritage of the People's Republic of China*, and three years later it ratified the 1972 UNESCO Convention on the Protection of World Cultural and Natural Heritage.

During the 1980s, as China adapted to UNESCO-based global values and language, the term 'cultural relic' (*wenwu* 文物) was replaced by 'heritage' (*yichan* 遗产), which originally referred to inherited family property. The compound '*wenhua yichan*' (文化遗产) thus came to be used for public historical remains or 'cultural heritage', a seemingly better fit with the universalistic language employed by UNESCO's member states (Wang & Rowlands 2017: 268; Fiskejö 2015: 100). Once China's participation in the global heritage community was formally established, the Chinese government sought to inscribe sites such as the Great Wall, Beijing's Forbidden City and the nearby Peking Man archaeological site at Zhoukoudian on to the World Heritage List (Shepherd & Yu 2013: 19). UNESCO (2019a) lists 55 Chinese cultural, natural and mixed heritage assets currently inscribed on the World Heritage List. The Chinese government now claims these and other sites to be of 'World Heritage value', despite the fact that some had been attacked and discredited in the recent past. The fluidity of values ascribed to such sites over time – from negative associations with 'feudal' culture to proud reminders of a glorious past – is compounded by the ambiguity surrounding UNESCO's European-derived universalistic conceptualisation of heritage coupled with the claims of the modern Chinese nation state to represent the legacy of an ancient and unique civilisation (Evans and Rowlands 2014: 273). This dilemma is not unique to China, but it is nonetheless a crucial framework for understanding how Chinese state authorities negotiate China's position in the global hierarchy of value (Herzfeld 2004; Meskell & Brumann 2015). International recognition and accolades are useful marketing tools to highlight what China's cultural heritage has to offer the world and to enhance its value as an economic asset. Following the embrace of heritage in China, the tourism industry has boomed, drawing both domestic and foreign tourists to these and other sites (Sofield & Li 1998; Ryan & Gu 2009; Bao, Chen & Ma 2014). However, a number of questions concerning this 'heritage turn' remain to be answered: how did domestic and global strategic purposes evolve and align, whose and what interests did processes of selectivity in heritagisation serve, and what were the consequences of the ensuing (re)invention, dissemination and consumption of heritage?

Content and Contributions of this Book

From the perspective of the state, heritage is viewed in contemporary China as a vehicle for the rebuilding of moral values and as a tool to cultivate shared national identity in the face of widespread disaffection from Marxism and cynicism about the Communist Party (Madsen 2014). Set within the historical context briefly outlined above, this book draws attention to the ways in which sanitised historical discourses of nostalgia and heritage (carefully controlled, selective narratives of the past) are used to cultivate a form of cultural nationalism by (re)claiming past identities, how these discourses can be understood as a tool of power/knowledge and governance (Foucault 1991; Johnson 2016; Wu & Hou 2015), and how they can be used to assert political authority by leaders at all levels (Barr 2011). In doing so, the chapters present a variety of case studies to illustrate how versions of the past are selected, (re)invented, disseminated and consumed for contemporary purposes. Each chapter raises complementary questions about which parts of the past are included in such narratives, whose pasts are (re)presented and for what purposes, who is involved and how does the Chinese notion of heritage drive the (re)invention process? Finally, they ask what are the implications of the above for place-making and conservation of the built environment, and what are the effects of the consumption of such sanitised forms of heritage for China, as well as for the rest of the world?

By addressing these questions, the chapters in this book explore the strategies of cultural heritage management that political leaders in China and elsewhere use to represent their national identities on the world stage. Indeed, there is increasing recognition that 'shared' cultural heritage can play an important role in promoting international cooperation, and simultaneously enhance a nation's global reputation (Winter 2015). While the values of culture, science, and education have been seen as critical indicators of the success, civility and development of nations, using heritage as a mechanism to promote such 'achievements' has become a popular contemporary political strategy (Winter 2014a). Scholars such as Nye (2004) refer to this as a diplomatic strategy of 'soft power', arguing that China and other nations invest in the enhancement of their country's 'soft power' to achieve broader nationalist aims, including national security and peace-keeping. Robert Albro (2012) describes this as 'cultural display' and Winter (2014a: 335) explains that such cultural display is used, 'to convey affinities, bonds, dialogue, mutuality, and other such values in the international diplomatic arena'. The complexities that can arise in the nationalistic asser-tion of cultural heritage ownership in the international setting have been revealed, for example, in the 'Zodiac saga' concerning Chinese demands for the return of bronze-plated animal figures stolen from the ruins of the Summer Palace in Beijing in 1860 (Fotopoulos 2015). The irony here is that these figures were of European manufacture in imitation of Chinese style, presented to the Chinese court, then reportedly looted by Westerners. At the beginning of the twenty-first century when these objects began to appear on the international art market, the Chinese government demanded their repatriation as part of its cultural heritage stolen by Europeans. Given the questionable provenance of these figures as 'Chinese', claims to them as part of China's cultural heritage are rooted more in a rhetorical narrative of national humiliation than in verifiable cultural patrimony (Fiskesjö 2010).

The chapters presented here contribute to the growing body of literature on China's appeal to the exposition of its traditional values and cultural heritage after rising to the status of a global economic power, as suggested by the cultural politics of the 'Zodiac saga'. While Winter (2014a: 326), for example, draws on the recent book by Natsuko Akagawa (2014) to explain how Japan is using cultural display to advance a foreign policy built on 'nar-ratives of peace', other scholars have suggested that China has also embraced and invested in heritage for international diplomatic purposes. Since the re-awakening of interest in the country's heritage in the 1980s following the widespread destruction of historical sites, particularly during the Cultural Revolution, heritage has been linked closely to Chinese nationalism and shaped by a desire to restore a strong sense of the historical standing of China's 'great' civilisation. In other words, China is eager to portray itself externally as a country 'with a rich cultural past' and as 'a civilization that has influenced other countries and cultures' (Winter 2014a: 328). Such claims are supported by China's evident 'stepping up [of] its heritage diplomacy efforts' (Svensson & Maags 2018: 17; Winter 2015), including its active involvement since the 1980s with UNESCO World Heritage initiatives. The process of heritage-making is used as a mechanism through which 'soft power' can be enhanced and modern identities can be crafted, interpreted and consumed.

The chapters in this collection are the product of an international symposium on heritage held in April 2016 in Suzhou, Jiangsu, China. The combination of expertise in the fields of history, anthropology, ethnography, urban planning and design, politics, critical theory, literary and visual culture casts a vital multidisciplinary lens on the discourse and practice of heritage in China, enabling a nuanced and comprehensive perspective on this complex topic. Papers were invited around three themes: 'Sanitised narratives of heritage', 'Politics of heritage' and 'Commodification of heritage'; they were selected based on their fit within these topic areas, together with their theoretical contributions and positioning within the wider literature. The papers chosen for publication in this book draw upon established theoretical discourse in heritage studies, as well as more recent developments in the critical heritage studies movement. This book builds on and expands two related collections on China: *Cultural Heritage Politics in China* (Blumenfield & Silverman 2013) and *Chinese Heritage in the Making: Experiences, Negotiations and Contestations* (Maags & Svensson 2018). The studies presented here ask complementary theoretical, socio-political, ethical and geographical questions about the management and politics of heritage governance in China in an age of shifting global power, introducing new topics, areas of research, and disciplinary perspectives.

Section 1 looks at processes of reconstruction, reinvention, and representation of heritage in different settings. In Chapter 1 Florence Graezer Bideau (Ecole Polytechnique Fédérale de Lausanne, Switzerland) presents a conceptual introduction to many issues addressed throughout the book. She uses the disciplinary lens of anthropology to focus on two case studies, a sacred mountain near Beijing and an urban district in Beijing, highlighting the implementation of institution-driven policies as well as the agency of affected communities, and conflicts that erupt among them. From the perspective of state policy, Chapter 2 argues that the restoration and reconstruction of traditional Confucian academies as cultural heritage sites represent a sanitised Confucian past used to cultivate cultural identity and foster bonds of nationalism. Linda Walton (Portland State University, USA) shows that state investment in such heritage-making is crucially about more than simply extracting the profit from heritage and that it is instead better understood as promoting public pedagogy through the use of the traditional academy as a model of moral education deeply rooted in Confucian values.

Yingjie Guo (University of Sydney) builds on this in Chapter 3, analysing the restoration of sites at Confucius's birthplace to show how China's position in relation to heritage has transformed from neglect to an unprecedented commitment to heritage conservation. He illustrates the close linkage between conservation and nationalism, as well as the primacy of identity politics in decision-making for major Confucian sites. In doing so, he draws attention to the official ideology of state socialism, national self-identity and China's vision of its place in the world. Kristin Bayer's (Marist College, USA) Chapter 4 deals with a universally recognised feature of the Chinese landscape, the Great Wall, through its literary representations in works by William Edgar Geil (1865-1924) and more recently by William Lindesay (b.1956). She traces how the Wall's meanings and symbols have been manufactured to fit both non-Chinese and Chinese imaginings, suggesting that the Great Wall is a malleable symbol of cultural heritage that can serve multiple – and even conflicting – interests, including foreign as well as Chinese.

The above chapters pave the way for Section 2 'Creating Identities: Constructing Pasts, Disseminating Heritage'. In Chapter 5 Carol Ludwig (University of Liverpool) and Yi-Wen Wang (Xi'an Jiaotong-Liverpool University) examine the selective usage of memory and practice to reconstruct specific versions of the past. Beamish open-air museum, Durham, UK and the theme park Song Dynasty Town in Hangzhou are presented as comparative case studies. The authors use education, tourism and the creation of new identities as an analytical framework to understand the different ways in which the dissemination and consumption of cultural heritage take place. They show that the 'unauthorised' heritage, such as the commercial heritage presented in these cases, which was not necessarily intended by the state to be a part of the AHD, can become a part of it, revealing a blurring between authorised and unauthorised heritage.

Chapter 6 by Patrick Wertmann (Institute of Asian and Oriental Studies, Zurich) similarly addresses the dissemination and consumption of cultural heritage by showing how the popularisation of cultural heritage is part of government strategies to foster common cultural identity, social unity, and patriotism among different groups and levels of society in China. The author provides examples of how the achievements of Chinese civilisation are glorified through entertainment, education (edutainment), the creation of 'unforgettable experiences' and initiatives such as the mobile museum. He argues that such initiatives have successfully popularised heritage while simultaneously enabling its transmission to wider audiences. Finally in this section, focusing on the creation, dissemination, and consumption of heritage through museums, Chapter 7 by Kenny K. K. Ng (Hong Kong Baptist University) surveys several museums in Nanjing to show how museums in this former imperial and modern capital contribute to the construction of local identities through (re)creations of the past in place. He thus addresses the theme of place-making in the creation, dissemination, and consumption of heritage.

Section 3 on 'History, Nostalgia and Heritage: Urban and Rural', picks up the idea of place, beginning with Andrew Law's (University of Newcastle) Chapter 8, which reveals how selective discourses of history and nostalgia are used as part of place-making and place-branding strategies for urban growth, as well as for constructing Chinese modern identities. He draws on contemporary examples from the cities of Shanghai, Wuhan and Xi'an to argue that histories and imaginaries of the Republican 1920s-1930s, Ming (and Qing) era mercantile capitalism and the earlier Tang Dynasty imperium, have all played important parts in the construction of indigenous urban histories and identities of Chinese modernity and capitalism. These real or imagined heritages, he argues, serve as crucial marketing instruments in the branding of Chinese cities, but perhaps more importantly are also 'used to actualise imaginaries in the present'. Turning to the role of nostalgia and history in heritage-making in a rural environment, Marina Svensson (Lund University, Sweden) analyses in Chapter 9 the ways in which heritage is constantly (re)imagined in Xinye village and how, in particular, performance and entertainment have become crucial and normalised aspects of China's heritagisation process.

Section 4, 'Appropriations and Commodifications of Ethnic Heritage', addresses the utilisation of ethnicity by the state for the definition and construction of heritage as a means of social and political control, and by ethnic groups themselves as a means of resistance. The latter is demonstrated by Joseph Lawson (University of Newcastle) in Chapter 10 on the Yi ethnic group's reappropriation of their alcohol-related culture as heritage, in opposition to Han Chinese perception and interpretation of it as simply the excessive consumption of alcohol (criticised by both health researchers and government officials). It explores various historical narratives and the influence these have on discourses and practices of heritage in the present-day. This is complemented in Chapter 11 by Melissa Shani Brown and David O'Brien's (University of Nottingham) study of the idealisation and commodification of ethnicity and the past in Xinjiang. The chapter focuses on the utilisation of a traditional Kazakh village to present an idealised depiction of national ethnic harmony – images of ethnicity reiterated, represented and disseminated, as well as commodified and consumed.

While aspects of the heritage 'turn' in China are well-documented elsewhere (Blumenfield & Silverman 2014, Maags & Svensson 2018), this book pays particular attention to this (re)awakening in a discursive and global context. It argues that heritage is being (re)invented, disseminated and consumed in ways that diverge from, and even challenge, Western understanding and practice of heritage. Moreover, the role and purpose of heritage (re)invention, dissemination and consumption are expanding into new arenas. These relate not only to the economic value of heritage, or to the public pedagogy/reclamation of traditional moral values and ideals, but also to the fostering of bonds of national identity, purifying and strengthening the 'spirit' of citizens and cultivating cultural nationalism. In China as elsewhere, heritage has also become a useful political strategy for wider international diplomacy and power relations on the world stage (Winter 2015). The purpose of this book is to advance understanding of heritagisation in China at the intersection of the local, national, and international arenas, tracking the dynamics of this process as it unfolds in diverse settings, the stakeholders and actors who carry it out, and its dissemination and consumption.

References

Akagawa N. (2014), *Heritage Conservation and Japan's Cultural Diplomacy: Heritage, National Identity and National Interest*. London: Routledge.

Albro, R. (2012), 'Cultural Diplomacy's Representational Conceit', 12 March 2012. [Online]. Available from: http://uscpublicdiplomacy.org/index.php/newswire/cpdblog_detail/cultural_diplomacys_representational_conceit (accessed 13 June 2017).

Askew, M. (2010), 'The Magic List of Global Status: UNESCO, World Heritage and the Agendas of States', in Labadi, S. & C. Long (eds.), *Heritage and Globalisation*, 19-44. London: Routledge.

Bao, J., G. Chen, & L. Ma (2014), 'Tourism Research in China: Insights from Insiders', *Annals of Tourism Research* 45: 167-181.

Barmé, G. (2009), '1989, 1999, 2009: Totalitarian Nostalgia', *China Heritage Quarterly* 18: 1-10.

Barr, M. (2011), *Who's Afraid of China? The Challenge of Chinese Soft Power*. London and New York: Zed Books.

Billioud, S. & J. Thoraval (2015), *The Sage and the People: The Confucian Revival in China*. Oxford: Oxford University Press.

Blumenfield, T. & H. Silverman (2014), *Cultural Heritage Politics in China*. New York: Springer.

Bonnici, U. (2009), 'The Human Right to the Cultural Heritage – The Faro Convention's Contribution to the Recognition and Safeguarding of This Human Right', in CoE (ed.), *Heritage and Beyond*, 53-59. Strasbourg: CoE Publishing.

Bortolotto, C. (2007), 'From Objects to Processes: UNESCO's Intangible Cultural Heritage', *Journal of Museum Ethnography* 19: 21-33.

Byrne, D. (2011), 'Archaeological Heritage and Cultural Intimacy: An interview with Michael Herzfeld', *Journal of Social Archaeology* 11 (2): 144-157.

CoE (2011), *Action for a Changing Society, Framework Convention on the Value of Cultural Heritage for Society*. Strasbourg: CoE Publishing.

Delafons, J. (1997), *Politics and Preservation: A Policy History of the Built Heritage 1882-1996*. London: Spon Press.

Demattè, P. (2012), 'After the Flood: Cultural Heritage and Cultural Politics in Chongqing Municipality and the Three Gorges Areas', *Future and Anterior* 9 (1): 48-64.

Denton, K. (2014), *Exhibiting the Past: Historical Memory and the Politics of Museums in Postsocialist China*. Honolulu: University of Hawai'i Press.

Dikötter, F. (2016), *The Cultural Revolution: A People's History, 1962-1976*. London: Bloomsbury.

Evans, H. & M. Rowlands (2014), 'Reconceptualizing Heritage in China: Museums, Development and the Shifting Dynamics of Power', in Basu, P. & W. Modest, (eds.), *Museums, Heritage and International Development*, 272-294. London: Routledge.

Fiskesjö, M. (2010), 'Politics of Cultural Heritage', in Hsing, Y. & C. Lee (eds.), *Reclaiming Chinese Society: The New Social Activism*, 225-245. London: Routledge.

Fiskesjö, M. (2015), 'Review Essay: The Museum Boom in China and the State Efforts to Control History', *Museum Anthropology Review* 9 (1-2): 96-105.

Fotopoulos, A. (2015), 'Understanding the Zodiac Saga in China: World Cultural Heritage, National Humiliation, and Evolving Narratives', *Modern China* 41 (6): 603-630.

Foucault, M. (1991), 'Governmentality', in G. Burchell, C. Gordon, P. Miller (eds.), *The Foucault Effect: Studies in Governmentality*, Chicago, IL: University of Chicago Press.

Graham, B., G. Ashworth, & J. Tunbridge (2000), *A Geography of Heritage: Power, Culture and Economy*. London: Arnold.

Gruber, S. (2007), 'Protecting China's Cultural Heritage Sites in Times of Rapid Change', *Asia Pacific Journal of Environment and Law* 253 10: 253-301.

Harvey, D. (2001), 'Heritage Pasts and Heritage Presents: Temporality, Meaning and the Scope of Heritage Studies', *International Journal of Heritage Studies* 7 (4): 319-338.

Harvey, D. (2015), 'Heritage and Scale: Settings, Boundaries and Relations', *International Journal of Heritage Studies* 21 (6): 577-593.

Herzfeld, M. (2004), *The Body Impolitic: Artisans and Artifice in the Global Hierarchy of Value*. Chicago and London: The University of Chicago Press.

Herzfeld, M. (2010), 'Purity and Power: Anthropology from Colonialism to the Global Hierarchy of Value', *Reviews in Anthropology* 39 (4): 288-312.

Herzfeld, M. (2014), 'Intangible Delicacies: Production and Embarrassment in International Settings', *Ethnologies* 36 (1-2): 47-62.

Hewison, R. (1987), *The Heritage Industry: Britain in a Climate of Decline*. London: Methuen.

Ho, D. (2011), 'Revolutionizing Antiquity: The Shanghai Cultural Bureaucracy in the Cultural Revolution, 1966-1968', *The China Quarterly* 207: 687-705.

Hobson, E. (2004), *Conservation and Planning: Changing Values in Policy and Practice*. London: Spon Press.

Högberg, A. (2012), 'The Voice of the Authorized Heritage Discourse: A Critical Analysis of Signs at Ancient Monuments in Skåne, Southern Sweden', *Current Swedish Archaeology* 20: 131-167.

Hsu, Y. (2013), 'Antiquaries and Politics: Antiquarian Culture of the Northern Song, 960-1127', in A. Schnapp (ed.), *World Antiquarianism: Comparative Perspectives*, 230-248. Los Angeles: Getty Research Institute.

Ip, H., T. Hon & C. Lee (2003), 'The Plurality of Chinese Modernity: A Review of Recent Scholarship on the May Fourth Movement', *Modern China* 29 (4): 490-509.

Johnson, I. (2016), 'China's Memory Manipulators', *The Guardian* 8 June 2016. [Online] Available from: https://www.theguardian.com/world/2016/jun/08/chinas-memory-manipulators (accessed 12 July 2016).

Jokilehto, J. (1999), *A History of Architectural Conservation*. Oxford: Butterworth Heinemann.

Lai, G. (2016), 'The Emergence of Cultural Heritage in Modern China: A Historical and Legal Perspective', in A. Matsuda & L.E. Mengoni (eds.), *Reconsidering Cultural Heritage in East Asia*, 47-85. London: Ubiquity Press.

Larkham, P.J. (1996), *Conservation and the City*. London: Routledge.

Lew, C. (2009), *The Third Chinese Revolutionary Civil War, 1945-49: An Analysis of Communist Strategy and Leadership*. London: Routledge.

Ludwig, C. (2013), 'From Bricks and Mortar to Social Meanings: An Examination of Local Heritage Designation in England', PhD diss., Northumbria University.

Ludwig, C. (2016), 'From Bricks and Mortar to Social Heritage: Planning Space for Diversities in the AHD', *International Journal of Heritage Studies* 22 (10): 811-827.

Maags, C. & M. Svensson (eds.) (2018), *Chinese Heritage in the Making: Experiences, Negotiations, and Contestations.* Amsterdam: Amsterdam University Press.

Massey, D. (1995), 'Places and their Pasts', *History Workshop Journal* 39 (1): 182-192.

Matsuda, A. & L.E. Mengoni (eds.) (2016), *Reconsidering Cultural Heritage in East Asia.* London: Ubiquity Press.

Meskell, L. (2013), 'UNESCO's World Heritage Convention at 40: Challenging the Economic and Political Order of International Heritage Conservation', *Current Anthropology* 54 (4): 483-494.

Meskell, L. & C. Brumann (2015), 'UNESCO and New World Orders', in L. Meskell (ed.), *Global Heritage: A Reader*, 22-42. Somerset, UK: John Wiley & Sons.

Meyer-Bisch, P. (2009), 'On the "Right to Heritage" – The Innovative Approach of Articles 1 and 2 of the Faro Convention', in CoE (ed.), *Heritage and Beyond*, 59-67. Strasbourg: CoE Publishing.

Mydland, L. & W. Grahn (2012), 'Identifying Heritage Values in Local Communities', *International Journal of Heritage Studies* 18 (6): 564-587.

Nye, J. (2004), *Soft Power: The Means to Success in World Politics.* New York: Public Affairs.

Pendlebury, J. (2009), *Conservation in the Age of Consensus.* London: Routledge.

Pendlebury, J. (2013), 'Conservation Values, the Authorised Heritage Discourse and the Conservation-Planning Assemblage', *International Journal of Heritage Studies* 19 (7): 709-727.

Oakes, T. (2012), 'Heritage as Improvement: Cultural Display and Contested Governance in Rural China', *Modern China* 39 (4): 380-407.

Ryan, C. & H. Gu (2009), *Tourism in China: Destinations, Cultures, and Communities.* New York & London: Routledge.

Shepherd, R. (2009), 'Cultural Heritage, UNESCO, and the Chinese State: Whose Heritage and for Whom?', *Heritage Management* (2.1): 55-80.

Shepherd, R. (2016), *Faith in Heritage: Displacement, Development, and Religious Tourism in Contemporary China.* London & New York: Routledge.

Shepherd, R. (2017), 'UNESCO's Tangled Web of Preservation: Community, Heritage and Development in China', *Journal of Contemporary Asia* 47 (4): 557-574.

Shepherd, R. & L. Yu (2013), *Heritage Management, Tourism, and Governance in China: Managing the Past to Serve the Present.* New York: Springer.

Silverman, H. & T. Blumenfield (2013), 'Introduction', in Blumenfield, T. & H. Silverman (eds.), *Cultural Heritage Politics in China*, 3-22. New York: Springer.

Sit, V. (2010), *Chinese City and Urbanism: Evolution and Development*. Hackensack, NJ: World Scientific.

Smith, L. (2006), *Uses of Heritage*. London: Routledge.

Smith, L. & E. Waterton (2009), *Heritage, Communities and Archaeology*. London: Gerald Duckworth & Co.

Sofield, T. & F. Li (1998), 'Tourism Development and Cultural Policies in China', *Annals of Tourism Research* 25 (2): 362-392.

Svensson, M. & C. Maags (2018), 'Mapping the Chinese Heritage Regime', in Maags, C. & M. Svensson (eds.), *Chinese Heritage in the Making: Experiences, Negotiations, and Contestations*, 11-37. Amsterdam: Amsterdam University Press.

Sykes, O., & C. Ludwig (2015), 'Defining and Managing the Historic Urban Landscape: Reflections on the English Experience and Some Stories from Liverpool', *European Spatial Research and Policy* 22 (2): 9-35.

Taylor, K. (2004), 'Cultural Heritage Management: A Possible Role for Charters and Principles in Asia', *International Journal of Heritage Studies* 10 (5): 417-433.

UNESCO (2003), *Convention for the Safeguarding of the Intangible Heritage*. Paris: UNESCO.

UNESCO (2019a), *'China'*. [Online]. Available from: http://whc.unesco.org/en/statesparties/cn (accessed 22 July 2019).

UNESCO (2019b), *'What is Intangible Cultural Heritage?'* [Online]. Available from: https://ich.unesco.org/en/what-is-intangible-heritage-00003 (accessed 12 August 2019).

Verdini, G.F., Frassoldati, & C. Nolf (2017), 'Reframing China's Heritage Conservation Discourse. Learning by Testing Civic Engagement Tools in a Historic Rural Village', *International Journal of Heritage Studies* 23 (4): 317-334.

Wang, H. (2012), 'War and Revolution as National Heritage: "Red Tourism" in China', in Daly, P. & T. Winter (eds.), *Routledge Handbook of Heritage in Asia,* 218-233. London: Routledge.

Wang, S., & M. Rowlands (2017), 'Making and Unmaking Heritage Value in China', in J. Anderson & H. Geismar (eds.), *The Routledge Companion to Cultural Property,* 258-276. London: Routledge.

Waterton, E. (2010), *Politics, Policy and the Discourses of Heritage in Britain*. Basingstoke: Palgrave Macmillan.

Waterton, E., & S. Watson (2013), 'Framing Theory: Towards a Critical Imagination in Heritage Studies', *International Journal of Heritage Studies* 19 (6): 546-561.

Winter, T. (2014a), 'Heritage Conservation Futures in an Age of Shifting Global Power', *Journal of Social Archaeology* 14 (3): 319-339.

Winter, T. (2014b), 'Heritage Studies and the Privileging of Theory', *International Journal of Heritage Studies* 20 (5): 556-572.

Winter, T. (2014c), 'Beyond Eurocentrism? Heritage Conservation and the Politics of Difference', *International Journal of Heritage Studies* 20 (2): 123-137.

Winter, T. (2015), 'Heritage Diplomacy', *International Journal of Heritage Studies* 21 (10): 997-1015.

Wright, P. (1985), *On Living in an Old Country*. London: Verso.

Wu, J. (2006), 'Nostalgia as Content Creativity: Cultural Industries and Popular Sentiment', *International Journal of Cultural Studies* 9 (3): 359-368.

Wu, Z. & S. Hou (2015), 'Heritage and Discourse', in E. Waterton & S. Watson (eds.), *The Palgrave Handbook of Contemporary Heritage Research*, 37-51. New York: Palgrave Macmillan.

Zhu, Y. (2015), 'Cultural Effects of Authenticity: Contested Heritage Practices in China', *International Journal of Heritage Studies* 21 (6): 594-608.

About the Authors

CAROL LUDWIG is a Chartered Member of the Royal Town Planning Institute (RTPI) and Honorary Research Fellow at the University of Liverpool. Her research interests include the theorisation of heritage, the cultural process of identity formation, and community mobilisation in local conservation planning processes.

LINDA WALTON is Professor Emerita of History at Portland State University and Visiting Professor at Hunan University Yuelu Academy Research Institute. A historian of Song and Yuan China, especially academies, she has recently been studying the revival of Song-era academies in contemporary China and their role as sites of cultural heritage tourism.

Section 1

(Re)constructions, (Re)inventions,

and Representations of Heritage

1 The Social Life of Heritage-Making

Cultural Representations and Frictions

Florence Graezer Bideau

Abstract

This chapter adopts an anthropological perspective to explore the role played by institutions in the social and historical construction of heritage. Since member states ratified the UNESCO Conventions, national inventories have been collated so that candidacies can be submitted to international lists for recognition and, in turn, return the benefits of this cultural showcase to the nation. Based on ethnographic fieldwork in China and Switzerland, this chapter focuses on the logic underlying processes of selection, which involves both political and administrative bodies. How cultural heritage is interpreted by various stakeholders will be outlined, along with an analysis of practices and narratives that almost inevitably produces friction. The case studies presented here highlight the complexity of cultural meanings and frictions among stakeholders at all levels who claim their 'rights to cultural heritage'.

Keywords: anthropology, state regime, heritage-making, identity, Miaofengshan, Gulou

Introduction[1]

This chapter will discuss various interpretations of stakeholders involved in the heritage-making processes. Its purpose is to explore the social and historic construction of heritage and the role played in this by institutions,

[1]   I would like to thank the organisers (Pierre-Alain Croset, Yi-Wen Wang, Carol Ludwig and Yiping Dong) of the 'Reclaiming Identity and (Re)Materialising Pasts: Approaches to Heritage Conservation in China' International Symposium for offering me the opportunity to give a keynote speech at the conference on 6 April 2016.

Ludwig, Carol, Linda Walton, and Yi-Wen Wang (eds), *The Heritage Turn in China: The Reinvention, Dissemination and Consumption of Heritage*. Amsterdam: Amsterdam University Press 2020
DOI: 10.5117/9789462985667_CH01

from an anthropological perspective. Nations have long undertaken the process of heritage-making but, since they ratified the UNESCO Conventions, this has taken on a new dimension. National inventories have been collated so that candidacies can be submitted to international lists and, in turn, the benefits of this cultural showcase return to the nation. This chapter takes a comparative perspective, looking at China and Switzerland. It also focuses on the logic underlying processes of selection, which involves both political and administrative bodies. The evaluation of how cultural heritage acts, and is interpreted by various stakeholders, is based on ethnographic fieldwork, which will be outlined along with an analysis of which practices and narratives almost inevitably produce friction. The case studies presented highlight the complexity of cultural meanings and frictions among multi-layered stakeholders who claim their 'rights to cultural heritage' and, in doing so, challenge the norms and values that it carries which, they feel, must be transmitted to the next generation.

When I arrived at Peking University in 1995 and began fieldwork in a small neighbourhood between Beida and Tsinghua, the notion of heritage principally referred to the past built environment (beautiful historic buildings of classical/imperial China), which contrasted sharply with ordinary mixed habitations from the Mao era (*dazayuan*) in very bad conditions. Participant observations within a local residential association that had revived popular dance introduced me to the notion of living culture. This led to a study of popular culture and its significant relationship to the occupation of public spaces and landmarks in the historic landscape. My regular visits to China have given me the opportunity to observe rapid change in the understanding of heritage issues in China, where attachment to past heritage – and the will to enhance tangible and intangible culture heritage as a whole – are clearly expressed. The ethnographic fieldwork[2] presented in this chapter, undertaken mostly in China and Switzerland, illustrates these heritage dynamics, which play a fundamental role in the construction of local and national identity. These dynamics can be used as a popular political strategy to promote national branding within a country or

2   Several different grants enabled the author to conduct research in China (State grant and SNSF Grant for young scholars between 1995 and 2000; Swiss Network for International Studies (SNIS) between 2015 and 2017) and in Switzerland (SNSF Grant for senior scholars, Interdivision coordination and cooperative research between 2009 and 2014). Collected data are based on ethnographic observations and interviews that were carried out with heritage stakeholders (civil servants, cultural cadres, scholars, local communities and practiioners, heritage preservationists, etc.). They were completed by scientific literature and other sources (policies, newspapers, photography, etc.) bringing a better understanding of the contours and the issues of developed themes.

on the world stage (Winter 2015). As will be shown below, this is something of which China appears to have been cognisant. Its application of this knowledge, however, has played a role in producing tensions, which will be highlighted.

The social life of heritage-making refers explicitly to Arjun Appadurai's book *The Social Life of Things. Commodities in Cultural Perspective* (1986). His principal idea was to highlight the complexity of values attributed to objects and the multiplicity of social meanings that they carry. Appadurai introduces a new perspective on the circulation of objects in social life that goes beyond strictly economic values of commodities. Within a framework of exchange of goods, he describes commodities at different moments of their social life and in different situations and he demonstrates how they enter a circle of selection and competition according to their associated practices and social classification, embedded within time and place. I do not seek to add another interpretation of this much discussed perspective, but Appadurai's work represents a solid foundation for the arguments presented below. He offers trans-historic and transcultural reflections, and his extension in the definition of things offers a germane framework for describing the extension of definitions that have fundamentally changed the notion of heritage.

The Social and Historic Construction of Heritage

The construction of identity has been central to anthropology from the start. Initially anthropologists observed ways or processes through which individuals identify with a group and described how a community stands together. Decades ago, however, a paradigm was introduced in anthropology that analyses the notion of identity as a social and historical construction. Rather than being a fixed, pre-determined, essentialised notion, scholars understand this as both relational – act of classifying self and others – and contextual – dynamics of local realities, set of institutions that provide norms and values. This approach enhances the universal structures or similar patterns found in many contexts (the unity of the global) and particularities, or differences, which separate each case from the others (the diversity of the local). In no way should this endeavour consider groups, communities or nations as homogenous entities. On the contrary, diversity of population, blurring of borders, extension of global cultural flows and multiple identities provide complexities that scholars need to consider in their analyses.

References to the past play an important role in this process of identification. The power of memory is an element of negotiation between the multilayered actors involved in defining history. Conserving the past is crucial for under-standing the present. Most of the time heritage is used as concrete facts to explain the present, which legitimises a sense of history that should be shared by all. The built environment, remains or archives are major traces of the past and the interpretations of them need to be perpetuated in order to be bequeathed to future generations. But lifestyle, customs, traditions and rituals also constitute fundamental components of the 'common good', and these too have to be transmitted. The practices of conserving the past thus involve multiple layers of actors and institutions that all struggle to impose their point of view, their narrative and their practices related to heritage (Bondaz, Isnart, & Leblon 2012; Graham, Ashworth & Tunbridge 2000). These can be expressed either through the presentation of cultural heritage sites, exhibitions of cultural heritage items in a museum or through academic research. They involve acknowledged experts from legitimate institutions who aim to produce an 'authorised heritage discourse' (Smith 2006). However, they can also be articulated in the repetition of traditions and everyday practices in communi-ties, which relies on the skills and local authorities that generate another type of discourse, most of the time perceived as dissonant, subaltern, alternative, ordinary or 'from below' (Robertson 2012, Zhu 2015). Each discourse implies a selection of events that will be included in their narrative, to the exclusion of others. As Connerton (1989) notes, acts of commemoration, such as the staging of exemplary events or an ordinary ritual, function as a marker for legitimising choices made by emphasising a unique sense of history, as sanctification of shared values that maintain the group's cohesion and transmits values to the next generation. This neutralises dissonant voices and insists on the continuity between the past, present, and future (Gillis 1994). As memory can lead to the empowerment of social groups,[3] the control of memory plays a crucial role in the construction of narrative and directly impacts multiple identity claims through heritage staging at local and national levels.

The anthropology of heritage-making looks at both built (tangible) and living (intangible) heritage. It scrutinises institutions and their mechanism of legitimacy towards heritage in the process of constructing identity at the local, community, national and international levels. A similar dynamic will be raised when studying heritage within different scales; an institution that mobilises cultural heritage with authority and expertise to define the community's territory and, ultimately, its identity. In the domestic

3   This memory can be 'full' or 'empty' (lapse of memory, blackout, forgetfulness) as it can be expressed through the memorialisation of September 11, the destruction of Bamiyan Buddhas in 2001 or of the sacred Mausoleum of Timbuktu in 2012.

sphere – familial legacy, community goods – political, emotional and legal authorised experts – the father, the wise man, the leader of the community, the notary, etc. – define what has to be transmitted to whom, usually according to patrilineal and private local customs.

A semantic change appeared when cultural heritage became public and designated a territorial and national history, such as the historic monuments (Choay 2001). These were not interpreted simply as objects, but as cultural and social process reflecting specificities of a population and a territory (Smith 2006; Poulot 2006) that has to be protected and safeguarded from destruction and societal amnesia (Tunbridge & Ashworth 1996). A set of devices and apparatuses that regulates social practices emerged for reproducing norms and values within society (Foucault 2008). State institutions within ministries, museums, academies, scientific schools and learned societies involving cultural, legal and scientific experts sought to compare cultural heritages based on new norms and standards about the 'good, true, beautiful, appropriate, authentic' (Zhu 2018) of the authorised heritage discourse (Smith 2006). They were selected according to a 'global hierarchy of values' (Herzfeld 2004) that reflects a political dominance and cultural superiority. Despite its ethnocentrism, the notion of heritage gradually enlarges the scope of its definition by multiplying its extensions. Nathalie Heinich (2009) describes them as chronological, buildings from antiquity until post-industrial heritage; topographic, cultural, natural, mixed sites, landscapes, etc.; categorical, from prestigious to ordinary heritage; and conceptual, from an *unicum* to a *typicum*, or a series.

An international narrative based on 'outstanding universal value' also came into action with the 1972 UNESCO Convention (UNESCO 1972) that imposes a new typology of sites (natural, cultural and mixed) composing the World Heritage List. To ensure the 'right' classification of these 'treasures' of humanity, a complex structure of expertise – UNESCO committee, regional centres, ICOMOS, ICCROM, etc. – produced documentation (such as conventions, charts, and recommendations) for establishing inventories that are used worldwide as tools (Berliner & Bortolotto 2013; Meskell & Brumann 2015). Acknowledging the importance of better linking of monumental and aesthetics sites with living cultures took more than a decade and was expressed in several documents and programmes[4] until its official

---

4   Among them, we find the 1992 adoption of the category of Cultural Landscapes by the World Heritage Committee, 1989 UNESCO Recommendation on the Safeguarding of Traditional Cultural and Folklore, the 1993 UNESCO Living Human Treasures Programme and the 1997-1998 Proclamation of Masterpieces of the Oral and Intangible Heritage of Humanity.

recognition through the 2003 UNESCO Convention for Safeguarding ICH (UNESCO 2003). This includes expressions and traditions (oral, artistic, ritual and festive, environmental and craft-related) and translates a sense of identity and continuity between generations for the communities involved through historical depth and territorial anchoring.

Anthropology Enters the Scene

The recognition of tangible heritage as a universal was first linked to the social sciences and humanities that relate to history, archaeology, art and geography. Not until UNESCO developed the concept of intangible cultural heritage in 2003, did scholars and experts in the fields of anthropology, ethnology or sociology take a more active interest in this process. Seen as a mechanism for equality between nations in the name of the 'cultural diversity' promoted by UNESCO and formulated in the 2005 Convention on the Protection and Promotion of the Diversity of Cultural Expressions (UNESCO 2005) – intangible cultural heritage became a matter of additional distinction (North/South, West/East, developed countries/emerging countries) looking for their 'capital heritage' to appear on the representative list of humanity.

When it comes to heritage, the path from tangible to intangible has not been smooth. Rejecting the paradigm of 'Outstanding Universal Value' that underpinned the 1972 Convention, the new policy for promoting intangible cultural heritage was based on 'exemplarity' and 'representativeness', putting the 'repositories' or 'holders/bearers' of heritage at the heart of the process. As scholars noted, there is a transition from a universal position toward heritage to a relativist one that pays more attention to particularities reflecting local cultures than exemplar sites representing/embodying/ generalising an entire civilisation. Many anthropological studies highlighted to what extent the intangible cultural definition is problematic (Hafstein 2009; Bortolotto 2011; Adell-Gombert et al. 2015). Indeed, there is a constitutive tension between the inscription of this definition in the regime of the past, a kind of inertia linked with the practice of safeguarding and the logic of performativity, its ephemeral dimension and its process of never-ending transformation. Simply put, critical approaches have pinpointed the need of overcoming this distinction between the tangible and the intangible culture, because in some sense *all* heritage is intangible (Herzfeld 2014). Based on contestable assumptions of a clear separation between the symbolic and the material, this distinction still reproduces the authorised heritage discourse (Smith 2006) by selecting what is acceptable to be reified, the official heritage of nation-states, and rejecting the less comfortable, the cultural intimacy of daily life. Anthropology has also taken an interest in the role of intangible heritage, its identification and associated processes in the building and destruction of local practice in relation to national identity, real or 'disneyfied.' As Zhu (2015) has demonstrated with two different categories of heritage-making (the Xingjiao Temple in Xian and the Dongba wedding ritual performances in Lijiang), this is a dynamic process where the view of one affects the view and practice of the other, upon which I will expand presently.

Heritage-making: State Regimes

Heritage-making and nation building

Each member state that ratifies UNESCO Conventions must make a national inventory of items from which candidates or dossiers can be submitted for UNESCO lists. States differ in how they go about this. There are strong, long-observed practices of identifying and listing cultural traditions that have been clearly linked with the nation-building process since the nineteenth century. Cultural, historical, or political studies on surveys of folklore and popular culture demonstrated how important these processes were for the legitimacy of authorities' power and the feeling of belonging to a community, in the West as well as the East (Anderson 1983; Hobsbawm & Ranger 1983; Hung 1985).

China in the twentieth century represents a good example of such practices. It has experienced the transition from multiple uses of popular culture for ideological purposes to the production of a national inventory. The example of the evolution of the *yangge* dance through the various changes of Chinese national identity in the twentieth century presents and summarises the relationship between practice, politics and national identity. After the May 4 movement in 1919, prominent scholars in China such as Gu Jiegang, Zhou Zuoren and Liu Fu led a movement of folklore collection (Graezer Bideau 2012c). Nationalists and communists eventually undertook surveys in order to better understand and fill the gap between elites and commoners, as well as to get closer to masses whom they wanted to convert to their respective political causes. Such results – a national campaign against illiteracy between 1929 and 1933 in the cultural district of Dingxiang in Hebei Province, in collaboration with Sydney Gamble (1953), for example – showed how popular culture was rich, polysemic and performative enough to use as political tools aimed at rural populations.

In the Red capital, Yan'an, Mao Zedong also undertook several surveys among rural artists in order to grasp the 'essence' of popular culture, transform it according to the new norms and values of the revolution, and build a cultural policy. These findings were used in his famous *Yanan Talks* in 1942, which still form the basis of Chinese cultural policy (Mao 1967). This is illustrated by the example of the vast *yangge* movement, a traditional dance practiced mostly during the traditional Chinese New Year in villages by local associations of artists – launched during the 1930s and 1940s in the area (Holm 1991).

Ritual, religious, shamanic, erotic *yangge* were all transformed into a revolutionary dance reflecting topics of propaganda – civil war, land reform, movement of production, Great Leap Forward, marriage law, etc. – with highly simplified choreography and implementation of political meanings. During the 1950s and 1960s, *yangge* dance became part of the official repertoire for national celebrations in Tiananmen Square (Hung 2005). At this time, many national surveys were again undertaken by cultural cadres in charge of identifying and describing the diversity of cultural practices in the entire territory. *Yangge* was eventually forbidden during the Cultural Revolution because it referenced past tradition and religion (*Destroy the Four Olds* – customs, culture, habits and ideas – *and Cultivate the Four News*). It reappeared in the mid 1980s when residents started to occupy public spaces in cities to exercise their body, strengthen social ties among local communities and take part in the consumption revolution that occurred after the opening up reforms (Graezer 1999; Graezer Bideau 2008). Traditions of pilgrimage and local customs celebrating the Chinese New Year became popular and gave new life to cultural practices in many public spaces in cities and villages. Since 2006, *Yangge* dances have been part of the national inventory[5] that will perhaps be submitted once more to the UNESCO list of ICH.

Inventory: the storytelling of a nation

This case study from 20 years ago represents a good example of the ongoing process of making an inventory following political injunctions by

5   China designated this dance as an 'intangible cultural heritage' in 2006 (Chen 2010, 28): it appears in its various forms (types of expression, localities, communities, practitioners). See the measures to ensure protection taken by the central government to integrate the Safeguarding of Intangible Cultural Heritage in the Eleventh Five Year Development Plan of China (2006-2010), which has since been renewed (2011-2015).

Figure 1.1   Chinese New Year procession led by local associations, Beicun Village, Huangling district, Shaanxi province, 2000

Source: Florence Graezer Bideau

the Chinese Communist Party. Even before its ratification of the UNESCO 1972 Conventions in 1985 and of the 2003 Convention in 2004, China had numerous institutions involved in the process of identifying national cultural heritage at the national, provincial and local level. Political authorities, cultural cadres, and scientific experts from many academic disciplines, along with local historians and artists, and heritage fans were part of the mechanism that illustrated Chinese cultural heritage. For example, the national project of inventorying cultural practices was launched in 2005 for a period of four years. The 2011 Chinese periodic report presented at UNESCO Headquarters in Paris cited more than 870,000 items identified in the census. The methodology was based on 'Operational Guidelines for ICH National Inventory' and followed a very top-down approach; from the centre, to provinces, to districts and so on. The content of this process is not made public, but lists of items are circulated for scientific committees composed by cultural cadres, scholars – mostly ethnologists and museum curators at the provincial and local level who are responsible for selecting representative items of the 10 categories: popular literature; traditional music; traditional dance; traditional opera; lyric stories; traditional sports; traditional acrobatics; traditional arts; traditional crafts; and popular customs on the basis of six selection criteria[6] for the Chinese national list of intangible cultural heritage.

In this process we are faced with a hegemonic institution that functions as a chain of administration aimed at diffusing power and symbolic values as a 'tool of governance' including new norms for the construction of identity, experiences and social standings (Smith 2006; Zhu 2015, 2018). In addition, these sources of authority or power embodied in political and administrative entities are entangled with a sphere of expertise. This expertise is not homogeneous but rather is composed of technicians and scholars from several fields, mainly legal and academic, who together produce a strong narrative diffusing and legitimising knowledge related to cultural heritage issues: definitions; norms; values; orthodox practices; authorised agents; project of development; etc. Although tangible and intangible cultural heritage – historical buildings and human experiences – constitute two separate domains of expertise that are perhaps naturalised or objectified by specific institutions or research academies, documents, or industries, they share a 'logic of selection' that involves both political and administrative bodies.

This logic of selection is a universal practice that can be observed in many national heritage-making processes. The approaches reflect state political culture. They can be either top-down, as is usual in China, or bottom-up, as in some parts of Switzerland. In most countries it comes from officials who are directed by the state, which is a top-down approach largely because too many issues – political, symbolic, economic, cultural, etc. – have to be carefully managed. In some federalist countries, such as Switzerland, approaches have to take into account the political mechanism, which involves the principle of subsidiarity. In such cases, the logic of selection is more usually a mix of top-down and bottom-up procedures.

Means of selection were observed in a project on Swiss cultural bureaucracy that aimed to implement the 2003 Convention for Safeguarding Intangible Cultural Heritage from 2009 to 2014. The construction of intangible cultural heritage-making at the federal, cantonal and local levels

6   '1. Have remarkable value as a representative of the creativity of Chinese civilisation; 2. Be rooted in the cultural tradition of a community and being passed from one generation to another, with distinct local characteristics; 3. Play a role as important links for cultural exchange, promotion of national cultural identity of China, in strengthening national cohesion, national solidarity and social stability; 4. Indicate a high level of know-how and traditional skills application; 5. Present an exceptional value as an illustration of national living cultural traditions in China; 6. Be important for the transmission of Chinese national culture while being seriously threatened with extinction because of social changes or the lack of safeguards' (translated from Bureau des relations culturelles extérieures, Ministère de la Culture, 2011, p. 3-4).

was studied as fieldwork and then analysed anthropologically. Observation was mostly of the steering committee and bureaucratic institutions, which were responsible for selecting items for the national inventory that Switzerland was obliged to create for UNESCO. This 'bureaugraphy' – a merger of bureaucracy and ethnography – presented an opportunity to better understand the construction of a national representation or showcase – the inventory – from scratch and observe the negotiations and frictions that occurred in the federalist system, in which the 26 cantons are responsible for the management of culture in their own territory, while following strict operational guidelines produced by the Federal Office for Culture. For this chapter, it is only necessary to highlight two principal findings that perhaps shed some light on the logic of selection processes.

The Swiss inventory is seen as one of the original models for cultural heritage-making (Graezer Bideau 2014). The strict regulation of the division of competencies between the state, the 26 cantons and other institutions in charge of heritage and culture issues implies an entanglement of mechanisms between top-down and bottom-up approaches that regularly come into conflict when debating and managing cultural issues. The implementation framework formulated by the Federal Office for Culture is negotiated intensely with many stakeholders: administration, civil society, bearers of ICH, scholars, journalists, politicians, etc. The 'participative principle', which lies at the heart of the Swiss federal constitution, is applied to each level of territory (federal, cantonal, local) and any topic of public life, with Swiss citizens launching many initiatives and referenda each year. When the participative principle is applied to heritage making, it becomes even more meaningful because of the historical, political and social norms and values that cultural heritage embodies and with which citizens can identify. The Swiss example also highlighted the need for the national production of knowledge that takes into account sensitive realities and historical tensions that are inherent in modern Switzerland. It is here that the Swiss and Chinese cases are similar; within their respective, stated political systems, they both respect the identity of the local people who inhabit the territory.

Of the 387 ICH items selected by the cantons in the Swiss case, 167 were entered on the 'representative lists of ICH in Switzerland' that were established at the federal level, with representatives of the major administrative and cultural institutions of the four Swiss linguistic and cultural areas. A year later, another steering committee extracted only eight propositions that came to constitute Swiss candidatures for submission to UNESCO's Representative list of ICH for Humanity. In each phase of inventory-making the permanent overlap between the technical and political tasks for selection – those responsible for cultural heritage were obliged to enter into a fine-tuning process. This ensured that cantonal propositions were included and reflected, in each phase, the major divisions that are part of Swiss national history (urban/rural, protestant/catholic, alpine/plains, industrial/artisanal, German/French/Italian/Romanschspeaking areas, elite/popular masses and so on) (Graezer Bideau 2012b). Those who were not telling the 'authentic', 'true' story of the nation – indigenous/exogenous populations, contested cultural traditions [cabaret Voltaire, Dada movement 100th Anniversary in 2016], international issues [bank secrecy] – were excluded (Graezer Bideau 2013). This heritage inventory-making highlights the sensitive place of culture in a Federal state. It also questions the role played by experts in this process and the limits of their commitments. By analysing the production of heritage narratives based on different levels of expertise – such as the numerous academic disciplines involved, professionals or amateurs, various degrees of interpretative criteria, and the mechanisms of selection that result, two fundamental questions are notable for their persistence: To whom does culture/cultural heritage belong? And who defines it? (Graezer Bideau 2012a; Hertz, Graezer Bideau, Leimgruber & Munz 2018).

Heritage: The Global Perspective Challenging the Western Model

These questions can be applied on a global scale where the same process of selection can be seen between the national and the international. But it is more interesting to 'zoom in' to the regional scales and study how Asian perspectives challenge the Western hegemony of the 'Authorised Heritage Discourse' (Daly & Winter 2011; Smith 2006; Smith & Akagawa 2009; Winter 2014). Tim Winter (2014), for example, shows how Japanese, Korean and Chinese programmes, among others, tried to redress current asymmetries and, in doing so, created new polarities. Many have argued that the 1994 Nara Document on Authenticity should be considered the turning point reflection on the polarities between tangible and intangible cultural, fixed and dynamic heritage (Akagawa 2015). It reviews the use of authenticity and integrity as conditions for 'outstanding universal value' and for an inscription on the World Heritage List. Consequently, it addressed the need for a broader understanding of cultural diversity and cultural heritage in relation to conservation and safeguarding practices (Munjeri 2004).

East Asia's strong presence is also expressed in the implementation of regional centres for training, educating and knowledge exchange between communities and outside experts. This network of new centres of ICH declarations based in the East (Beijing, Shanghai, Suzhou) has had the effect of what Dipesh Chakrabarty would call 'provincialising Europe' (2000). It helps question the dominant heritage discourse and produce heterodox knowledge that goes beyond Western/Eurocentric classical polarities such as nature/culture tangible/intangible, art/craft or concrete/abstract realities.[7] Thus, Tim Winter concludes, these Asian perspectives can be perceived and analysed as 'products of resistance and interpretation at local/national level in Asia toward the infrastructures of global heritage governance' (2014: 12). The same ideas were also expressed in a much more straightforward way in the *Manifesto* produced by the Association of Critical Heritage Studies:

> Heritage is, as much as anything, a political act and we need to ask serious questions about the power relations that 'heritage' has all too often been invoked to sustain. Nationalism imperialism, colonialism, cultural elitism, Western triumphalism, social exclusion based on class and ethnicity, and the fetishizing of expert knowledge have all exerted strong influences on how heritage is used defined and managed (Association of Critical Heritage Studies 2012).

Cultural Representations and Frictions

What differentiates anthropological approaches from other disciplines when we come to understand heritage-making is definitively its grounded ethnographic methodology. This method looks at the logic of local actors involved in the heritage process in order to better define meanings of heritage. As Harvey (2011) outlines, it is important to understand how heritage acts, as a verb and not as a noun, in other words as a passive object or an essence. While not excluding other disciplines, in anthropology heritage-making is understood as a social and historical construction and not a given fact. Studying heritage as an active verb also clarifies and enhances its agency, highlighting how it engages with its social environment. It includes stakeholders' engagement with the administration, politics at different scales (national, international and local), economic players (tourist industry, real estate, etc.) and the local community.

'Heritage democracy' is a term coined by a few scholars to describe the heritage craze and the extension of its definition worldwide. Indeed, as was

---

7   In the East, object and technique are untangled operations on material and representations. It is a 'fabric without sewing' between material and immaterial culture (Bromberger 2014). For an analysis of the concept of authenticity in the Chinese context, see Zhu 2018.

mentioned earlier, its scope has broadened from tangible to intangible and stakeholders have recently been increasing to include not only legitimised experts but also ordinary bearers of traditions who take an active part in the process of defining and managing them. The principal idea behind this term is to express how heritage works; how it is modified through individual or group practices with the frictions that this almost inevitably entails.

The Case of Miaofengshan

The transformation of Miaofengshan (Marvellous Peak Mountain, referred to below as MFS), a sacred place close to Beijing, is not only an excellent illustration of such frictions about heritage, it is also a case that merges perfectly tangible heritage in a heritage site with intangible cultural heritage. Indeed, within the Buddhist, Taoist and above all popular religious traditions, it is a site famous for its spiritual power. It continues to draw crowds of pilgrims, as it has since the seventeenth century (Naquin 1992). In the late 1990s, Miaofengshan (MFS) became a model for a national folk festival and a showcase for heritage-making policy. The historic study of multiple worshipping practices by local religious and civil associations entangled with Chinese authorities illustrates controversies in the cultural meaning of pilgrimage traditions among practitioners. These frictions were ongoing during fieldwork in 2000.

To illustrate this entanglement, I will outline interactions between the skilled artists who use the space and ordinary citizens and how these have been used. The skilled artists perform dances and martial arts and comprise the well-known traditional societies. Despite regular competition for leadership among their leaders, a cohesive network unifies these imperial or old/venerable associations. As noted by Chinese and Western folklorists (Goodrich 1998; Gu 1988; Li 1925), the artists have reflected lively and historical popular folk culture for more than a century. Their members strongly identify themselves with social norms and religious values, such as exchange of rituals, pure devotion and total respect of the Holy Mother power they worship, which become particularly significant during the fifteen days of the MFS pilgrimage (Graezer 2003).

Ordinary citizens also practice recreational activities in their neighbourhood and form the contemporary associations. They look like 'mass organisations', structured around cultural and social commitments such as everyday physical exercise, musical play, sociability through healthy and amusing practices, mutual aid, participation to political campaign activities, etc. They have been regularly involved in popular culture competitions

Figure 1.2   View on Miaofengshan, near Beijing, May 1999

Source: Florence Graezer Bideau

**Figure 1.3   Traditional association performance at Miaofengshan pilgrimage,
May 2000**

Source: Florence Graezer Bideau

**Figure 1.4   Contemporary *Yangge* association performance at Miaofengshan,
May 2000**

Source: Florence Graezer Bideau

and folk festivals in and around Beijing for a decade. At MFS, they enjoy the tourist tour with their neighbours and family and generally greatly appreciate performing contemporary *yangge* dance before a large audience, their performance being well covered by local media.

Frictions and competition between these two kinds of associations for the cultural meanings of the heritage site surfaced when the Promotion of the Landscape of West Beijing Tourism Company Limited (*Beixi Fengguang Lüyou Kaifa Youxian Gongsi*) took control of the MFS pilgrimage and transformed it into a folk culture festival. Taking MFS as a showcase where tradition and modernity can be easily displayed, those responsible attempted to orchestrate the participation of both kinds of practices by inviting a balanced number of their representatives (Friedman 2004; Nyíri 2006). Traditional associations, which perpetuate the centuries-old rules and the very strict order of the religious procession, consider this new State management a threat to their 'authentic' pilgrimage tradition. In their view, only a generational transmission of orthodox practices can preserve the symbolic significance of MFS. Amateur folklore associations, however, breathe new life into the festival. By enacting new norms and values such as mass art characterised by recreational activities, amateurism and improvisation – and contemporary lifestyles – highlighting consumption, immediate pleasure, tourism (*cf.* Chen 1995; Farquhar & Zhang 2005; Wang 2001) – they innovate, or, in the words of Michel de Certeau (1984), practise *bricolage*, re-inventing the pilgrimage tradition in the framework of the Spiritual and Material Civilisations ideology promoted at that time by the Chinese authorities.

In the eyes of the authorities, this secular interpretation of MFS by contemporary associations practising popular activities,[8] which are also part of preserving Chinese cultural heritage, is most welcome since it makes reference to the heritage site more complex. It blurs the various religious meanings advanced by the traditional associations, and it reinforces the historic and political dimension of the site legitimated by scientific and ideological institutions. The grand narrative supports MFS as an important place for the origin of Chinese folklore, which was institutionalised by a large academic event organised by Peking University in 1995, the first congress of popular culture

8   Popular activities that also embody healthy activities the State encourages for many reasons (Farquhar & Zhang 2005). Associated with the Communist tradition of collective activities, they correspond to a habitus (in Bourdieu's words) shaped by the tools of propaganda to be revived when faced with potential conflicts. Performing an uncontentious dance practice in open spaces, and therefore visible and easy to control, they are part of the 'social docile body' analysed by Ann Anagnost (1997).

in which eminent folklorists such as Sun Fuyuan or Rong Zhaozu participated (Liu 1996). It is also reinforced as an important landmark of 'national treasures', largely promoted by historical and cultural tourism development (David 2007). For example, MFS hosted the Eighth Red Army in the 1930s and 1940s, a time when a large part of the temple complex was bombed, and there is currently a desire to officially commemorate this as a significant civil war site and reinforce its place in the historical memory of this period.

These additional cultural meanings of MFS enforce an official memory of the heritage site that contrasts with the memories of local communities. In the name of the Spiritual and the Material Civilisations this grand narrative neutralises the controversies between the different kinds of pilgrims organised in associations and their claims to the dominant interpretation of this cultural heritage location.[9] In a similar way, Zhu also demonstrated how 'the Chinese Government imposes a certain concept of authenticity on local heritage practices' (2015: 595) and how local individuals or institutions act through embodied practices (participation and engagement in heritage-related activities) and produce new values and meanings that challenge the official interpretation of authenticity. The issue of official memory is one that pervades many of the Chinese case studies, though in many different ways. The following conservation case in Beijing further illustrates this.

Urban Memories in a Historic Urban Landscape: Beijing, Gulou

The issue of an official memory is also at the heart of urban heritage when it is subject to conservation policies involving the Recommendation of Historic Urban Landscape (UNESCO 2011) that tries to integrate the dynamics of urban transformation and the participation of local communities facing change in the everyday life of their neighbourhoods (Bandarin & van Oers 2012). The earlier examples were outlined; here, however, the case will be explored in greater detail to illustrate in some depth the relationship between stakeholders and official policy in respect of tensions around, and ownership of, cultural memory. The international project of which this case study is part specifically discusses challenges of the notion of HUL, which

---

9   Will this new era of cultural heritage recognition meet the challenge of reinventing and legitimating cultural traditions for both the Chinese authorities and local communities? The project to create a large federation of contemporary *yangge* groups, based on the Yuanjungong Federation model, held by the Beijing Bureau for Culture in order to promote a specific type 'controlled' tradition (Graezer Bideau 2012c, 438-439) could provide some answers to this question, but that's not counting the resistance agency of social actors invested in popular culture for generations around the MFS.

consistently triggers scholarly debate in different contexts (specifically Mexico City, Rome and Beijing).[10] Within the context of this project, we have observed that the notion of HUL also plays a role in supporting the inhabitants' identity, because the elements and features of landscapes work as memory coordinates (Jodelet 2010) or mnemonic devices (Osborne 2001).

The term 'memory' is conventionally applied to those 'oral, visual, ritual and bodily practices through which a community's collective remembrance of the past is produced or sustained' (Connerton 1989, quoted by Linke 2001: 2219). At the beginning of the 20th century, the French sociologist Maurice Halbwachs defined the multiple dimensions of what he called collective memory (1950). Using three principal arguments, he shows the role played by spatial frameworks in the remembering process: groups recover their memories within the shape they have given to their environment; there is an isomorphism between the social structure and the material configuration of a city; spatial context delivers a feeling of stability and continuity to the groups (Jodelet 2013).

A seminal work is the typological analysis *Les Lieux de mémoire*, which considers a range of heritage places as supporters of identity (Nora 1997). However, this perspective leaves little room for the popular practice of space appropriation. Since Nora's work, several authors suggest that social memory practices are not only connected to sites of domination, aiming to legitimise a social order (Andris & Graezer Bideau 2014; Confino 1997), or simply limited to authorised heritage sites (Smith 2006; Di Giovine 2009; Yan 2015), but that they also incorporate the physical traces associated with everyday life experience (Bondaz et al. 2014; Hebbert 2005) as well as the unofficial heritage places characterised by struggle and transformation (Pedrazzini 2005). Maurice Halbwachs (1950) suggested that people's attachment to their built environment allows a social group to resist changes such as demolition, destruction, displacement or eviction. This resistance can be expressed through ordinary practices, which challenge demonstrations of power, the transformation of space or struggles for the recognition of popular heritage (de Certeau 1984; Graezer Bideau 2004; Robinson 2006; Scott 1985).

The city of Beijing is generally accepted as the palimpsest of more than a thousand years of Chinese history. However, over time and especially since the Olympic games of 2008, economic forces that are overly reliant on real estate development have become the main drivers for the demolition of

---

10   The Beijing research was conducted in collaboration with Dr. Haiming Yan, Chinese Academy of Cultural Heritage, mainly between 2015 and 2016.

Figure 1.5   Renovation around the Drum Tower, September 2014

Source: Florence Graezer Bideau

the city's historical fabric (Abramson 2007; Zhang 2013). The consequent housing need has resulted in the acquisition of new land for relocation sites and new accommodation areas, which mainly serve as dormitories for Beijing workers. Beijing residents, mainly from the inner city, have been relocated by local authorities because their houses were situated in areas containing land suitable for urban transformation. They were moved to new compounds, or to new towns outside the city. Inhabitants have to go from the 'traditional village structure to an elevator culture' (Shepard 2015), importing their behaviours and habits (Pagani 2015).

Anthropologically this raises interesting questions about their everyday life, enacted into intangible cultural heritage. It is this that makes collective memory for the culture and residents, but what happens to this when there is such a fundamental and transformative change to an embedded way of life? How do these residents go about adapting to their new environment and the changes it forces upon them? Can elements of their past, inherited culture survive? And if so, which elements? These are important questions. Some will be answered using this case study, but others remain as general important points that always arise in the tensions between cultural memory and policy.

The Bell and Drum Towers (*Zhonglou and Gulou*) are located at the north end of the central axis of Beijing's Old City. The two towers served as both a physical and a cultural marker for the capital city (as an icon for the central axis for the northern part of the city and as time-keeping buildings announcing the Beijing resident's rhythm of life). Thus they are fundamental markers for memories of both time and space. From as early as the Yuan Dynasty, the area has been a bustling commercial and residential neighbourhood. It is a multi-layered representation of the city's cultural memory: spatial icon, temporal marker, and social and commercial livelihood. To some extent, as the spatial and temporal functions have gradually ebbed, the commercial and social fabrics have become more integral to the area's cultural connotation. In 2002, the area was designated as one of Beijing's historical and cultural protection zones (Graezer Bideau & Yan 2018).

In 2010, the 'Beijing Time Cultural City' development project was proposed by the local municipal government to improve the residents' quality of life, but in reality it aimed to create a historic-centred place of time-telling celebration, which includes a museum, an underground shopping mall and parking lots. Because of wide ranging criticism from many groups – local inhabitants, NGOs engaged in historic preservation (Beijing Cultural Heritage Protection Centre and the Gulou Preservation team), local cultural activities associations, heritage activists, journalists, etc., denouncing massive relocations and demolition of cultural properties inherent in the realisation of the project, it was ultimately abandoned.

In 2012, the government proposed a less ambitious plan entitled 'Restoration and Renovation Project' where only *hutongs* 'with no historic value' around the Drum and Bell towers would be demolished to clear out recently renovated historical buildings (Rabinovitch 2013). This *hutong* area is one of the last neighbourhoods that still incorporates traditional residents in poor living conditions. No real measures for the renovation and improvement of habitation have been taken or encouraged by local government for decades and this has led to degeneration, with the notable exception of the renewal of public toilets for the Beijing 2008 Olympic games! This failure to upgrade living standards preserves the old fabric of such an area, but the local population complains about a bad and chaotic living environment, problems with electricity, running water and sanitation, and the traffic congestion.

The Gulou area has become a battlefield, in which three major groups of stakeholders are involved with very different claims. The government discourse primarily revolves around terms such as 'restoration', 'authenticity', 'environment improvement', 'cultural', 'art zone', etc., though these are as

Figure 1.6   Renovated Drum and Bell Towers Public Square, January 2017

Source: Florence Graezer Bideau

blurred as they are key. These terms are used as a means to preserve sensitive zones presenting traditional spatial organic structure with a mixed social organisation. Yet they also effectively hide the money-making purpose of the schemes applied in areas such as sensitive zones close to the Beijing central axis. In these areas, the residents' extreme poverty contrasts starkly with the very high land prices, but the focus of the projects may damage an eventual candidature for the UNESCO World Heritage List. Preservationists insist on the necessity of civic participation and question each government statement. They provide counter-statements concerning the historical value of the area and on the necessity to link the physical environment with intangible factors of the neighbourhood's life as mnemonic patterns.

Local inhabitants, both within and outside the eviction area, are the most complex group. There just seems to be too great a distance between the concept of cultural heritage or historic urban landscape and their discourses. Their voices and claims arise from their experience of living in the area. They tend to focus on practical issues such as living conditions, traffic, and environment, all of which re-enforces the clear opposition between 'natives' (*bendiren*) and 'foreigners' (*waidiren*). Our project looks at this very problem: How should we understand the discourses of the three groups?

And to what extent are the narrative claims of local inhabitants a reflection of the social fabric of historic urban landscape in China? Will the recent guidelines on urban planning (21 February 2016) released by the Chinese government influence policymakers to 'differentiate cities with special urban landscapes based on local characteristics' (Cheng 2016) that will provide their residents with 'a sense of pride and identity'? Although struggling to get from words to deeds, the need for Chinese inhabitants to identify with the space, or 'make themselves at home' (Friedmann 2007) is becoming a familiar topic. Indeed, when the city is thought of as the carrier of memory, the architectural fabric needs to define specific communities according to local models which, in turn shape the models through the representations with which they engage.

Conclusion

In conclusion, it can be said that what is at stake in heritage-making is, by definition, the transmission of a common good to the next generation. The examples detailed in the chapter have illustrated the idea with which it began; that in social life circles of selection and competition are entered into in which, according to practices associated with it, living heritage is embedded in both time and place. This is particularly true for the selected showcases that connect the visual atmosphere (*fengmao*), including intangible heritage, with the surrounding environment referencing a past they want to glorify for ideological and economic reasons (Broudehoux 2004). The reference to memory, along with the actions in which they have engaged through a plethora of regulations aimed at the protection of Beijing's traditional areas plays an important role in the picture that the government wants to paint and present on the world stage (Bodolec 2014). The preservation of 'historic districts' and their past traditions is encouraged currently, but there is clearly a greater insistence on valuable cultural heritage than on the intangible heritage. This is especially true in the urban setting, where policies are negotiated with experts in architecture and urban planning, which brings the authorities into fewer conflicts and meets less resistance than with the experts concerned with the participation and preservation of local communities. Nevertheless, friction occurs in the overlapping of cultural values and social norms that are carried as part of cultural heritage. Its function within land use is practical, even pragmatic, and it is central to planning, the development of local economies and to the general interest of the community concerned. Without cultural heritage we are left only with bricks and mortar and the choices of the powerful to represent us. But with it, we have cultural life; living, breathing populations within their environment remembering their past, enacting their present and building their future.

References

Abramson, D. (2007), 'The Aesthetics of City-Scale Preservation Policy in Beijing', *Planning Perspectives* 22 (2):129-166.

Adell-Gombert, N. et al., (eds.) (2015), *Between Imagined Communities and Communities of Practice: Participation, Territory and the Making of Heritage*. Göttingen: Universitätsverlag Göttingen.

Akagawa, N. (2015), *Heritage Conservation in Japan's Cultural Diplomacy. Heritage, National Identity and National Interest*. London: Routledge.

Anagnost, A. (1997), 'The Politicized Body', in *National Past-times: Narrative, Representation, and Power in Modern China*, 98-116. Durham: Duke University Press.

Anderson, B. (1983), *Imagined Communities: Reflections on the Origin and Spread of Nationalism*. London: Verso.

Andris, S. & F. Graezer Bideau (2014), 'Challenging the Notion of Heritage? Introduction', *Tsantsa* 19: 8-18.

Appadurai, A. (ed.) (1986), *The Social Life of Things: Commodities in Cultural Perspective*. Cambridge: Cambridge University Press.

Association of Critical Heritage Studies (2012), 'Association of Critical Heritage Studies'. [Online]. Available from: www.criticalheritagestudies.org (accessed 12 February 2016).

Bandarin, F & R. van Oers (2012), *The Historic Urban Landscape: Managing Heritage in an Urban Century*. Chichester: Wiley Blackwell.

Berliner, D. & C. Bortolotto (2013), 'Le monde selon l'Unesco', *Gradhiva* 18: 4-21,

Bodolec, C. (2014), 'Etre une grande nation culturelle : Les enjeux du patrimoine culturel immatériel pour la Chine', *Tsansta* 19: 19-30.

Bondaz, J., F. Graezer Bideau, C. Isnart & A. Leblon, (eds.) (2014), *Les vocabulaires locaux du 'patrimoine': traductions, négociations et transformations*. Münster/Berlin: Lit Verlag.

Bondaz, J., C. Isnart & A. Leblon (2012), 'Au-delà du consensus patrimonial. Résistances et usages contestataires du patrimoine', *Civilisations* 6 (1): 9-22.

Bortolotto, C. (ed.) (2011), *Le patrimoine culturel immatériel: enjeux d'une nouvelle catégorie*. Paris: Ed. de la Maison des sciences de l'homme.

Bromberger, C. (2014), '"Le patrimoine immatériel" entre ambiguïtés et overdose', *L'Homme* 209: 143-151.

Certeau, M. de (1984), *The Practice of Everyday Life*. Berkeley: University of California Press.

Chakrabarty, D. (2000), *Provincializing Europe: Postcolonial Thought and Historical Difference*. Princeton: Princeton University Press.

Chen, C. (2010), 'Dancing in the Streets of Beijing: Improvised Uses Within the Urban System', in J. Hou (ed.), *Insurgent Public Space. Guerrilla Urbanism and the Remaking of the Contemporary Cities*, 21-35. London: Routledge.

Chen, N. (1995), 'Urban Spaces and Experience of Qigong', in D. Davis et al (eds.), *Urban Spaces in Contemporary China. The Potential for Autonomy and Community in Post-Mao China*, 247-361. Cambridge: Cambridge University Press.

Cheng, X. (2016), 'China Releases Guidelines to Build Better Cities', China Radio International (CRI) English.

Choay, F. (2001), *The Invention of the Historic Monument*. Cambridge: Cambridge University Press.

Confino, A. (1997), 'Collective Memory and Cultural History: Problems of Method', *The American Historical Review* 102 (5): 1386-1403.

Connerton, P. (1989), *How Societies Remember*. Cambridge: Cambridge University Press.

Daly, P. & T. Winter (eds.) (2011), *Routledge Handbook of Heritage in Asia*. London: Routledge.

David, B. (2007), 'Tourisme et politique: la sacralisation touristique de la nation en Chine', *Hérodote* 125 (2): 143-156.

Di Giovine, M. (2009), *The Heritage-Scape: UNESCO, World Heritage, and Tourism*. Lanham: Lexington Books.

Farquhar, J. & Q. Zhang (2005), 'Biopolitical Beijing. Pleasure, Sovereignty, and Self-Cultivation in China's Capital', *Cultural Anthropology* 20 (3): 303-327.

Foucault, M. (2008), *The Birth of Biopolitics: Lectures at the Collège de France, 1978-1979*. New York: Palgrave Macmillan.

Friedman, S. (2004), 'Embodying Civility: Civilizing Processes and Symbolic Citizenship in Southeastern China', *The Journal of Asian Studies* 63 (3): 687-718.

Friedmann, J. (2007), 'Reflections on Place and Place-making in the Cities of China', *Journal of Urban and Regional Research* 31 (2): 257-279.

Gamble, S. (1953), *Ting Hsien. A North China Rural Community*. Stanford: Stanford University Press.

Gillis, J. (1994), *Commemorations: the Politics of National Identity*. Princeton: Princeton University Press.

Goodrich, A. (1998), 'Miaofeng Shan', *Asian Folklore Studies* 57 (1): 87-97.

Graezer, F. (1999), 'The *Yangge* in Contemporary China: Popular Daily Activity and Neighbourhood Community Life', *China Perspectives* 24: 31-42.

Graezer, F. (2003), 'Le festival de Miaofeng shan: culture populaire et politique culturelle', *Etudes chinoises* XXII: 283-295.

Graezer Bideau, F. (2004), 'Breathing New Life into Beijing Culture: New 'Traditional' Public Spaces and the Chaoyang Neighbourhood Yangge Associations', in S. Feuchtwang (ed.). *Making Place: State Projects, Globalisation and Local Responses in China*, 61-78. London: University College Press.

Graezer Bideau, F. (2008), 'L'instrumentalisation de la culture populaire. Le cas de la danse du yangge en Chine', *Tsantsa* 13: 52-60.

Graezer Bideau, F. (2012a), 'Identifying 'Living Traditions' in Switzerland: Re-enacting Federalism Through the Application of the UNESCO Convention', in R. Bendix et al (eds.), *Heritage Regimes and the State*, 303-325. Göttingen: Universitätsverlag Göttingen.

Graezer Bideau, F. (2012b), 'Inventorier les 'traditions vivantes'. Approches du patrimoine culturel immatériel dans le système fédéral suisse', *Ethnographiques. org* 24. [Online]. Available from: http://www.ethnographiques.org/2012/ Graezer-Bideau (accessed 15 February 2016).

Graezer Bideau, F. (2012c), *La danse du yangge: culture et politique dans la Chine du XXe siècle*. Paris: La Découverte.

Graezer Bideau, F. (2013), 'Travelling sur les processus d'exclusion dans l'inventaire des traditions vivantes en Suisse: enjeux et raison d'un (out)casting', in M.-O. Gonseth et al. (eds.), *Hors-champs: éclats du patrimoine culturel immatériel*, 112-118. Neuchâtel: Musée d'ethnographie de Neuchâtel.

Graezer Bideau, F. (2014), '"Traditions vivantes", une catégorie bonne à penser? : le cas de la Suisse', in J. Bondaz et al (eds.), *Les vocabulaires locaux du 'patrimoine': traductions, négociations et transformations*, 123-144. Münster/Berlin: LIT Verlag.

Graezer Bideau, F. & H. Yan (2018), 'Historic Urban Landscape in Beijing: The Gulou Project and its Contested Memories', in M. Svensson & C. Maags (eds.), *Chinese Cultural Heritage in the Making: Experiences, Negotiations and Contestations*, 93-118. Amsterdam: Amsterdam University Press.

Graham, B., G. Ashworth & J. Tunbridge (2000), *A Geography of Heritage : Power, Culture and Economy*. London: Arnold.

Gu, J. (1988) [1925], *Miaofeng Shan*. Shanghai: Shanghai wenyi chubanshe.

Hafstein, V. (2009), 'Intangible Heritage as a List. From Masterpieces to Representation', in L. Smith & N. Akagawa (eds.), *Intangible Heritage*, 93-111. London: Taylor and Francis.

Halbwachs, M. (1950), *La mémoire collective*. Paris: Albin Michel.

Harvey, D. (2011), 'Heritage Pasts and Heritage Present: Temporality, Meaning and the Scope of Heritage Studies', *International Journal of Heritage Studies* 7 (4): 319-338.

Hebbert, M. (2005), 'The Street as Locus of Collective Memory', *Environment and Planning D: Society and Space* 23: 581-596.

Heinich, N. (2009), *La fabrique du patrimoine: de la cathédrale à la petite cuillère.* Paris: Ed. de la Maison des sciences de l'homme.

Hertz, E., F. Graezer Bideau, W. Leimgruber & H. Munz (2018), *Politiques de la tradition: Le patrimoine culturel immatériel.* Lausanne: Presses polytechniques universitaires romandes.

Herzfeld, M. (2004), *The Body Impolitic: Artisans and Artifice in the Global Hierarchy of Value.* Chicago: University of Chicago Press.

Herzfeld, M. (2014), 'Intangible Delicacies: Production and Embarrassment in International Settings', *Ethnologies* 36 (1-2): 47-62.

Hobsbawm, E. & T. Ranger (eds.) (1983), *The Invention of Tradition.* Cambridge: Cambridge University Press.

Holm, D. (1991), *Art and Ideology in Revolutionary China.* Oxford: Clarendon Press.

Hung, C.-T. (1985), *Going to the People: Chinese Intellectuals and Folk Literature, 1918-1937.* Cambridge, MA: Harvard University Press.

Hung, C.-T. (2005), 'The Dance of Revolution: Yangge in Beijing in the Early 1950s', *The China Quarterly* 181: 82-99.

Jodelet, D. (2010), 'La memoria de los lugares urbanos', *Alteridades* 20 (39): 81-89.

Jodelet, D. (2013), 'Les inscriptions spatiales des conflits de mémoire', *Psicologia E Saber Social* 2 (1): 5-16.

Li, J. (1925), 'Miaofeng shan chaoding jinxiangdi diaocha (Survey on Miaofeng Shan Pilgrimage)', *Shehuixue zazhi* 2 (5-6): 1-42.

Linke, U. (2001), 'Anthropology of Collective Memory', in J. Wright (ed.), *International Encyclopedia of the Social & Behavioral Sciences*, 2219-2223. Oxford: Elsevier.

Liu, X. (1996), *Miaofeng shan – Shiji zhijiao de Zhongguo minsu liubian (Miaofeng Shan – Change in Chinese Folklore at the Turn of the Century).* Beijing: Zhongguo chengshi chubanshe.

Mao, Z. (1967), *On New Democracy. Talks at the Yenan Forum on Literature and Art.* Peking: Foreign Languages Press.

Meskell, L. & C. Brumann (2015), 'UNESCO and New World Orders', in L. Meskell (ed.), *Global Heritage: A Reader*, 22-42. Chichester: John Wiley & Sons.

Munjeri, D. (2004), 'Tangible and Intangible Heritage: From Difference to Convergence', *Museum International* 56 (1-2): 12-20.

Naquin, S. (1992), 'The Peking Pilgrimage to Miaofeng Shan: Religious Organizations and Sacred Sites', in S. Naquin & C.-F. Yü (eds.), *Pilgrims and Sacred Sites in China*, 333-377. Berkeley: University of California Press.

Nora, P. (ed.) (1997), *Les lieux de mémoire.* Paris: Gallimard.

Nyíri, P. (2006), *Scenic Spots: Chinese Tourism, the State, and Cultural Authority.* Seattle: University of Washington Press.

Osborne, B. (2001), 'Landscapes, Memory, Monuments, and Commemoration: Putting Identity in Its Place', *Canadian Ethnic Studies* 33 (3): 39-77.

Pagani, A. (2015), *Hutongs-Transformation: A Battle Between Memories*, Master's thesis, Department of Architecture and Design, Politecnico di Torino.

Pedrazzini, Y. (2005). *La violence des villes*. Paris: Ed. de l'Atelier.

Poulot, D. (2006), *Une histoire du patrimoine en Occident, XVIIIe-XXIe siècle: du monument aux valeurs*. Paris: Presses universitaires de France.

Rabinovitch, S. (2013), 'Structural Revolution', 26 April, *Financial Times*. [Online]. Available from: http://www.ft.com/intl/cms/s/2/eb0384c0-a812-11e2-b031-00144feabdc0.html#slide010.4000/gc.1427 (accessed 12 Feb 2016).

Robertson, I. (2012), *Heritage from Below*. Farnham, Surrey: Ashgate.

Robinson, J. (2006), *Ordinary Cities: Between Modernity and Development, Questioning Cities*. London: Routledge.

Scott, J. (1985), *Weapons of the Weak: Everyday Forms of Peasant Resistance*. New Haven: Yale University Press.

Shepard, W. (2015), *Ghost Cities of China: the Story of Cities Without People in the World's Most Populated Country*. London: Zed Books.

Smith, L. (2006), *Uses of Heritage*. London: Routledge.

Smith, L. & N. Akagawa, (eds.) (2009), *Intangible Heritage*. London: Routledge.

Tunbridge, J. & G. Ashworth (1996), *Dissonant Heritage: The Management of the Past as a Resource in Conflict*. Chichester: John Wiley and Sons.

UNESCO (1972), 'Convention concerning the Protection of the World Cultural, Natural Heritage'. [Online]. Available from: http://unesdoc.unesco.org/images/0011/001140/114044f.pdf (accessed 2 February 2016).

UNESCO (2003), 'Convention for the Safeguarding of the Intangible Cultural Heritage'. [Online]. Available from: http://unesdoc.unesco.org/images/0015/001543/154391eo.pdf (accessed 2 February 2016).

UNESCO (2005), 'Convention on the Protection and Promotion of the Diversity of Cultural Expressions'. Available from: http://unesdoc.unesco.org/images/0014/001429/142919e.pdf (accessed 7 February 2016).

UNESCO (2011), 'Recommendation on the Historic Urban Landscape'. [Online]. Available from: http://unesdoc.unesco.org/images/0021/002110/211094e.pdf (accessed 11 February 2016).

Wang, J. (2001), 'Culture as Leisure and Culture as Capital', *Positions* 9 (1): 69-104.

Winter, T. (2014), 'Beyond Eurocentrism? Heritage Conservation and the Politics of Difference', *International Journal of Heritage Studies* 20 (2): 123-137.

Winter, T. (2015), 'Heritage Diplomacy', *International Journal of Heritage Studies* 21 (10): 997-1015.

Yan, H. (2015), 'World Heritage as Discourse: Knowledge, Discipline and Dissonance in Fujian Tulou Sites', *International Journal of Heritage Studies* 21 (1): 65-80.

Zhang, Y. (2013), *The Fragmented Politics of Urban Preservation: Beijing, Chicago, and Paris*. Minneapolis: University of Minneapolis Press.

Zhu, Y. (2015), 'Cultural Effects of Authenticity: Contested Heritage Practices in China', *International Journal of Heritage Studies* 21 (6): 594-608.

Zhu, Y. (2018), *Heritage and Romantic Consumption in China*. Amsterdam: Amsterdam University Press.

About the Author

FLORENCE GRAEZER BIDEAU is a Senior Lecturer and Senior Scientist in Anthropology at the College of Humanities, Swiss Federal Institute for Technology (EPFL). Her work engages with culture and power, cultural policies and heritage processes as well as urban studies in China, Malaysia and Switzerland.

2 Confucian Academies and the Materialisation of Cultural Heritage

Linda Walton

Abstract

The past two decades have witnessed a 'boom' in the restoration and reconstruction of traditional Confucian academies (*shuyuan* 书院) as cultural heritage sites. This phenomenon is related to the promotion of Confucianism since the 1990s as both a value system of global relevance and a distinctive marker of Chinese cultural – and national – identity. The renovation of academies is also motivated by economic development strategies undertaken by local and regional governments. However, I will argue that public pedagogy, more than commercial profit, motivates the investment of state resources in academies as sites of cultural heritage tourism. The transformation of academies into cultural heritage sites can be seen as the materialisation of a classless, ahistorical Confucian past in the service of a socialist *and* nationalist present. It also signifies the appropriation of a historically elite institution as a medium of mass education.

Keywords: academies, Confucianism, cultural heritage, tourism, national identity

Introduction

Beginning around 2000, many Confucian academies (*shuyuan* 书院) – some dating to as early as the tenth century – have been renovated, and even completely rebuilt, by local governments across China as cultural heritage sites. Investment in the restoration of historic academies by municipal or county governments can be seen as a development strategy designed to boost the local economy by attracting domestic tourism (Sofield & Li 1998; Wu,

Ludwig, Carol, Linda Walton, and Yi-Wen Wang (eds), *The Heritage Turn in China: The Reinvention, Dissemination and Consumption of Heritage*. Amsterdam: Amsterdam University Press 2020

DOI: 10.5117/9789462985667_CH02

Zhu & Xu 2000; Shepherd 2017:566). Along with potential economic benefits, restoring academies is also a means for political leaders to add cultural capital to their communities by promoting local places as sites of historic importance, regionally and even nationally. As tourist destinations, newly restored academies testify to the cultural and historic importance of the city, the county, or the region.[1] Restored academies are seen as materialisations of the cultural efflorescence of the region in earlier times, as well as important historical resources (Hu 2005: 21). Whether sponsored by municipal, county, or provincial authorities, restored academies help to create a sense of common historic and cultural identity among residents, and foster bonds of national identity among visitors – tourists who come from all over China.

I will argue that dramatic growth in domestic tourism, the post-1989 National Studies (*guoxue* 国学) movement, and renewed interest in Confucianism combined to spur the recent academy revival. I will also suggest that the restoration of academies should be regarded as an important example of the materialisation of Confucian cultural heritage in the service of the nation. Through the development of tourism at these sites, Confucianism has been distilled into moral and ethical teachings embodied in sages and teachers of the past to reach a mass audience. Academies thus represent a sanitised Confucian past used to cultivate a contemporary form of cultural nationalism. Viewing the surge in academy restorations through the lens of broader historical themes (such as the revival of Confucianism and the National Studies movement) that characterise China in the first decade of the twenty-first century, the analytical approach adopted here focuses on the use of cultural heritage as a political tool to advance the interests of the state in promoting its own authority (Smith 2006).

Based in part on fieldwork at four major recently restored academies located in three different provinces, north and south, this chapter describes the modern transformation of these academies into important cultural heritage sites. It contextualises the revival of these academies as part of broader cultural and political developments in the era of *kaifang gaige* 开放改革 ('openness and reform') beginning in the 1980s, arguing that restored academies are materialisations of a homogenised and ahistorical

---

1   Lavishly illustrated popular publications with evocative titles have appeared, such as *The Great School of Confucians: Ancient Academies in the Yangzi River Valley,* which posits a kind of cultural unity to Yangzi Valley civilisation symbolised by academies such as Yuelu and White Deer Grotto (Jin and Zhou 2005). Even more scholarly publications, such as *Academies in the Yangzi River Valley* (Zhu, et al. 2004), part of a series on Yangzi River Cultural Studies, declares in the introduction that the ancient culture of the Yangzi River Valley is comparable to that of the Yellow River Valley, the traditional heartland of Chinese civilisation.

Confucianism that serves the interests of the state at local, regional, and national levels. The restoration of Confucian academies as cultural heritage sites signifies the appropriation of a historically elite institution as a medium of mass education. Visitors are prompted by brochures and posted informational signs to 'read' the academies as materialisations of a distinctive Chinese cultural heritage and national patrimony. They may also regard visiting such sites as evidence of direct participation in that cultural heritage, and thus lay claim to a Confucian past that belongs to them as well as to the state.

Originating as scholars' retreats in the eighth and ninth centuries, during the early Northern Song (960-1126), academies received name plaques and bequests of books from the imperial court, in turn for which they provided education geared toward government service. The establishment of a system of state schools rendered them effectively obsolete. In the following Southern Song (1127-1279), academies once again became important as places where scholars studied and taught the new philosophy of Neo-Confucianism. During the twelfth and thirteenth centuries, academies flourished through their association with this new ideology, and both eventually gained state recognition and approval. Thus, academies became increasingly tied to the state, and during the Mongol rule of China in the thirteenth and fourteenth centuries, many continued to thrive as largely state-supported places for lecturing and teaching. Academies remained important institutions throughout the Ming (1368-1644) and Qing (1644-1911) dynasties, and during the early twentieth century, under Western influence, many of them became public schools, colleges, and universities. Academies thus largely disappeared into Westernised educational institutions until the late twentieth century post-Cultural Revolution reforms opened up new – and positive – perspectives on the Confucian past, including National Studies and New Confucianism.

National Studies, New Confucianism, and Patriotic Education

National Studies as an intellectual and cultural movement can be traced at least to the early part of the twentieth century. The term *guoxue* was imported from Japan then and used to refer to the historical and cultural foundations of what was Chinese, in contrast to imported foreign ideas and culture (notwithstanding the fact that the term itself was a foreign import) (Dirlik 2011: 7). After 1949, it was not until the 'culture fever' (*wenhua re* 文化热) of the 1980s that National Studies once again became an important focus of intellectual debate. Scholars and public intellectuals debated such topics as the role of traditional culture (*chuantong wenhua* 传统文化) in National Studies, and the relationship between Marxism and National Studies (Makeham 2008: 67-72). National Studies reached a broader, more popular audience in the aftermath of Tian'anmen, facilitated by both media and the market (Makeham 2011: 14), although clearly also promoted by official policies.

The ambiguity of meaning that surrounded *guoxue* was equally true of 'New Confucianism' (*xinruxue* 新儒学). After the founding of the PRC, as early as 1958 there was an effort to recognise Confucianism as part of the 'cultural DNA' of Chinese society, and therefore 'national essence' (*guocui* 国粹), but subject to state oversight in its interpretation and propagation (Dirlik 2011: 10). Following the 'opening and reform' of the 1980s, new interest was awakened in Confucianism (Song 2003; Bell 2008; Chen 2012; Kang 2012). A number of new Confucian-oriented organisations appeared, such as the Academy of Confucian Culture and the China Confucius Foundation (Makeham 2008: 49). International conferences sponsored by these and other organisations brought global attention to Confucianism among scholars worldwide. Since the 1990s, Confucianism has been embraced as part of National Studies, although not without continuing debates about its appropriate place, especially in relation to both Marxism and modernity (Chen 2011; Xie 2011; Liu 2011).

The Patriotic Education Campaign was a related development in the 1990s. Like the revival of National Studies, it was also in part a response to the spectre of disaffection and resistance raised by Tian'anmen. Launched in 1991 to educate the public – especially students – about both the recent and remote past, the Patriotic Education Campaign was designed to instill patriotism by cultivating national identity. The key document that made this campaign official highlighted 'cultural relics' as a tool of patriotic education (Wang 2008: 794). The campaign focused attention on revolutionary artifacts and sites that were testimonials either to national humiliation (and therefore designed to fire up feelings of national pride and patriotism) or to heroic struggles against enemies within and without. The term 'cultural relics' also encompassed prerevolutionary artifacts and sites such as the Great Wall (Waldron 1995). The full-scale implementation of the campaign came in 1994 and required local governments at all levels to establish 'patriotic education bases' as one of the most important aspects of the campaign (Wang 2008: 794). Tourist sites of all kinds (including museums, historical and scenic sites, memorials, etc.) were ordered to highlight their patriotic identities (Zhao 1998: 295). The resumption of this campaign a decade later in 2004 was aimed at 'strengthening and improving the work of patriotic education bases' (Wang 2008: 796). 'Red Tourism', connected to revolutionary history, was the focus of patriotic education, but it also included cultural relics of the prerevolutionary past, such as academies (Wang 2012).

The Transformation of Academies into Cultural Heritage Sites

Beginning with the 1982 *Law on the Protection of Cultural Heritage of the People's Republic of China*, the CCP leadership began to pay more attention to the idea of cultural heritage, creating a new term for material culture by replacing 'cultural relic' (*wenwu* 文物) with the neologism 'heritage' (*yichan* 遗产) (Hu 2005; Shepherd 2016: 46.). This law also explicitly linked heritage preservation with the goals of nationalism and revolutionary socialism (Sofield & Li 1998: 370-371). The Cultural Revolution disrupted the initial PRC (and Maoist) policy of claiming the legacy of the past, rather than destroying it, so the 1990s and later support of cultural heritage was actually to some degree a return to pre-Cultural Revolution attitudes and policies toward the past (Ai 2008). 'Cultural heritage' (*wenhua yichan* 文化遗产), however, was described in very broad terms, often equated with 'Chinese civilisation' or 'Chinese tradition,' both of which incorporated Confucianism (Ai 2012).

As quintessentially Confucian institutions, the restoration of academies is one important example of increased official attention paid to both cultural heritage and Confucianism in the 1990s (Chen 2012; Kang 2012). The revival of Confucianism in the public sphere, however, began in the first decade of the twenty-first century (Billioud 2010). While not directly orchestrated by state campaigns, popular engagement in Confucian-based activities was encouraged through state affirmation of local practices and institutions; these were deemed to be useful in cultivating social order and improving social mores (Billioud & Thoraval 2015). Heightened public awareness and knowledge of Confucianism dovetailed with the dramatic expansion of domestic tourism, one aspect of which was 'culture tourism' (Wu, et al. 2000). Local governments, and even educational institutions, now sponsor the restoration of these ancient Confucian schools as cultural heritage sites, but in the initial stages academies were officially designated by state agencies at the national and provincial levels as places of cultural importance.

White Deer Grotto Academy

Located on the slopes of Jiangxi province's Mount Lu in what is still one of the most scenic landscapes in China – and undergoing rapid development for outdoor recreational activities – White Deer Grotto (Bailudong 白鹿洞) is the most famous of the Song era academies. It was later known as one of the 'Four great academies' of the Northern Song, along with Yuelu 岳麓 (Hunan), Suiyang 睢阳(Henan), and Songyang 嵩阳(Henan), and in the Southern Song, it was closely associated with the major Neo-Confucian philosopher, Zhu Xi 朱熹 (1130-1200).

Immediately after the revolution in 1949 the Mount Lu Botanical Research Institute was set up, and White Deer Grotto was placed under its administration (Li & Gao 2007: 275). A decade later, the Jiangxi Provincial Government named White Deer Grotto a 'Provincial Cultural Relic Unit' (*sheng wenwu danwei* 省文物单位) but it was not until 1979 that a dedicated cultural administrative office for White Deer Grotto began its work (Li & Gao 2007: 276). Finally, in 1988 the central government's State Council declared White Deer Grotto a 'National Key Cultural Conservation Unit' (*quanguo zhongdian wenwu baohu danwei* 全国重点文物保护单位), a category that had been created in 1961 by the State Council with provision for funding restoration and preservation (Shepherd & Yu 2013:45). Beginning in the early 1990s, along with other administrative changes, several agencies were set up there to deal with various aspects of tourism (Li & Gao 2007: 302-304). These included a Cultural Tourism Service Company, the White Deer Travel Bureau, a handicraft and arts factory, and a business office divided between oversight of the handicrafts and arts factory and the guest hostel.

According to one account, the flourishing of the tourism enterprise at White Deer Grotto in the 1990s was in line with the deepening of the policies of 'openness and reform' because it promoted a valuable cultural legacy, advanced cultural exchange, and contributed to the fostering of 'patriotic education' (*aiguo zhuyi jiaoyu* 爱国主义教育) (Li & Gao 2007: 302). Among the attractions listed here for the development of tourism are the beauty of the environment and the richness of the thousand-year-old cultural heritage. Tourists can both enjoy the natural setting of mountains and water and gain spiritual sustenance from the cultural education offered by the history of the academy.

The nearest city, Jiujiang, is the site of Jiujiang College, which boasts a Mount Lu Cultural Research Centre, including everything from architecture and religion to poetry and philosophy related to the area, as well as studies on White Deer Grotto Academy. Its stated mission is to promote the traditional culture of the people. One publication in a series issued by the Research Centre for Mount Lu Culture is a collection of inscriptions, poems, and other writings on White Deer Grotto Academy primarily from the Song, Yuan,

Ming, and Qing dynasties (roughly tenth through the nineteenth centuries), and it includes a history of the academy since the founding of the People's Republic (Li & Gao 2007). This history of White Deer Grotto's development in the modern era also stresses its role in environmental preservation of the forested mountain landscape, even in pre-revolutionary times, dating back to as early as the beginning of the twentieth century (Li & Gao 2007: 278-281). It details the complicated decisions made in 1982 by various levels of government and the administration of White Deer Grotto regarding the establishment of boundaries for farming, tax assessments and regulations for the usage of mountain lands surrounding the academy (Li & Gao 2007: 279). It is difficult to determine the extent to which this process may have been an exercise in state control of land allotments in which private farmers were forced to accept whatever the authorities dictated; but in light of more recent conflicts between government officials and villagers whose property has been forcibly taken for highways, factories, and other enterprises, it would not be surprising to discover that something similar went on in the decisions regarding lands on Mount Lu.

Beginning in the late 1980s and continuing to expand in the 1990s and 2000s attention was paid to reviving the original scholarly role of the academy by convening academic conferences and issuing related publications (Li & Gao 2007: 285-302). White Deer Grotto also played a role in the National Studies movement during the first decade of the twenty-first century. In 2007 for the purpose of 'promoting National Studies', Jiujiang College and White Deer Grotto Academy jointly founded the White Deer Grotto Cultural Research Institute, which joined the Mount Lu Cultural Research Centre at the college (Li & Gao 2007: 291). In the same year, People's University in Beijing sent more than 40 students and faculty from their National Studies Institute to White Deer Grotto to 'advance National Studies.' Hosted and paid for by the Mount Lu Administrative Agency, the People's University faculty and students 'energetically studied "White Deer National Learning"' and worked on editing related materials for publication (Li & Gao 2007: 296). National Studies initiatives at White Deer Grotto also engaged scholars from Taiwan. In 2007 a Taiwan educational foundation joined together with the Beijing University Resources Centre, Jiujiang College, and White Deer Grotto Academy in the 'White Deer Grotto National Learning Research Camp.' Scholars and graduate students from 14 higher education institutions in Taiwan, including Tsinghua University, came to the academy to transmit and promote National Learning, 'to enable Taiwan scholars to recognize the beauty of Chinese traditional culture' (Li & Gao 2007: 296).

Yuelu Academy

Like White Deer Grotto, Yuelu Academy was named a 'National Key Cultural Conservation Unit' in 1988. Founded in 976, Yuelu Academy had been transformed in 1926 into Hunan University, and it is still located within the University in the provincial capital of Changsha. It was damaged in the Cultural Revolution, but in 1979 the decision was made by the provincial (Hunan) and municipal (Changsha) governments to completely restore it (Yang 2003: 254-261). In 1981, the responsibility for Yuelu Academy's restoration and administration was turned over to Hunan University, and with the establishment of the Yuelu Academy Cultural Research Centre in 1984, the academic mission of the academy was revived along with its physical structure. Although in 1986 there had been a commemoration of the 1010th year anniversary of Yuelu Academy, along with the 60th anniversary of Hunan University, it was not until 1996 that an international conference on Confucian educational thought and human civilisation was held to commemorate the 1020th anniversary of the founding of the academy.[2] In 1999, Yuelu Academy collaborated with Hunan Television to produce the 'Forum on the Thousand-Year-Old College', a television documentary that featured presentations by prominent educators. These developments in the 1990s were clearly aligned with the National Studies movement, and in 2001 the Ministry of Education and the Office of National Culture approved the establishment of a Chinese Academy Museum in Hunan, which opened in 2012 on the grounds of Yuelu Academy. Today, in addition to a research institute and graduate student education, Yuelu Academy is a major tourist destination. According to statistics provided by Hunan University, annual visitors to Yuelu Academy in 2014 numbered approximately 650,000, with an average 2,000 per day, and have continued to increase.

Stone Drum Academy

Located on a spit of land along Hunan's Xiang River, Stone Drum Academy was first recognised by the Song court in 1035. Although not typically included among the 'four great' Northern Song academies, it was traditionally regarded as one of the most important because of its association with prominent Neo-Confucian thinkers in the Southern Song. It now lies within the municipal boundaries of Hengyang, the second largest city in

---

2   In late October 2016, the 1,040[th] anniversary of the academy was commemorated with a conference on "The Historical Spread and Transmission of Confucianism."

the province of Hunan. Like many other academies in the later imperial period, as the weakening Qing monarchy tried to modernise, in 1902 Stone Drum Academy became a public school for elementary, middle, and high school students (Guo & Guo 2014: 165). In 1944, along with much of the city, the academy was destroyed in a Japanese bombing raid (Guo & Guo 2014: 170). After the revolution, it became a public park in 1965 (Guo & Guo 2014: 172). Over the next three decades, efforts were made to preserve the former site of Stone Drum Academy. The dilatory process, however, took a toll: when stamps were issued in 1988 commemorating the 'Four Great Academies' of the Song, Stone Drum was replaced with Songyang (Guo & Guo 2014: 175). Finally, in 2000 the Hengyang municipal government, together with the Hunan Provincial Government put forward a proposal to restore the academy. In 2005 the Hengyang municipal Communist Party committee, together with the Hengyang municipal government, issued a joint statement declaring their intention to complete the restoration (Guo & Guo 2014: 174-175). According to one account, public contributions toward the rebuilding totaled more than ten million RMB (Guo & Guo 2014: 175).

A collection of annotated historical poetry about Stone Drum Mountain (the original landscape attraction) and Stone Drum Academy from as early as the fourth century was published in 2007, the year the reconstructed academy opened to the public (Dai 2007).[3] This is the first volume in the planned *Stone Drum Academy Cultural Tourism Series* (*Shigu shuyuan wenhua lüyou congshu* 石鼓书院文化旅游丛书). Annotated poetry clearly aims at a more educated and sophisticated audience than generalisations about ancient cultural heritage and descriptions of academy architecture and landscape. Academy publicity also places emphasis on Stone Drum as a representation of regional culture: *Huxiang wenhua* 湖湘文化 (Qiu & Wen 2010). In previous eras, and even in the parlance of modern Chinese scholarship, Huxiang is a geographic marker for a school of thought, unified presumably by its association with key thinkers who came from the watershed of the Xiang River, south of the lake (Poyang Lake) or who taught there.

More than 20 years after the initial humiliation of not having been included in the 1988 commemorative Four Great Academy stamps series, stamps celebrating Stone Drum Academy were issued in 2009 by the Chinese Postal Service in the second 'Ancient Academy' stamp series, and subsequently, a series was devoted specifically to Stone Drum Academy.[4]

---

3   When I visited the academy in 2012, construction was ongoing, even though it had been opened to the public several years earlier.

4   See http://www.baike.com/wiki/《古代书院（二）特种邮票》

In 2010, Stone Drum Academy was named a 'Provincial Patriotic Education Site' (*sheng aiguo zhuyi jiaoyu jidi* 省爱国主义教育基地), and in 2011 the provincial government declared it a 'Provincial Cultural Conservation Unit' (*sheng wenwu baohu danwei* 省文物保护单位) (Guo & Guo 2014: 174). The latter placed it in the category of national AAA-class 'Cultural Tourism Site' (*renwen lüyou jingqu* 人文旅游景区). In 2015 Stone Drum Academy achieved one step higher recognition as a national 4A category site, a status that was officially celebrated in the local press when a banner was hung in front of the academy announcing it (*Hengyang ribao* 2015-12-23). The path to recognition of Stone Drum Academy as an important cultural heritage site was slow and uneven, until the realisation of potential economic benefits from tourism apparently overrode fiscal concerns. Stone Drum Academy, however, is not even mentioned as a cultural resource in a recent publication on tourism development in Hengyang (Liu & Jian 2014).

Songyang Academy

Songyang Academy, built in 1035 (the same year that Stone Drum was recognised by the Song court) on an ancient Buddhist site below Mount Song, one of the five sacred mountains, is located about 80 kilometres southwest of Henan's provincial capital, Zhengzhou, in Dengfeng County. Like the other Song academies that became important cultural heritage sites, Songyang was first named a 'First Class Provincial Level Key Cultural Conservation Unit' (*diyipi shengji zhongdian wenwu baohu danwei* 第一批省级重点文物保护单位) in 1963, on the cusp of the Cultural Revolution (Gong 2001: 11; Zhang 2012: 25). It was not, however, until almost 20 years later that the renovation of the main buildings of the academy began, and over the next five years (1982-1987) the academy and its surroundings were completely restored. One of the most popular features – and tourist attractions – of Songyang Academy is the pair of ancient cypresses standing in the courtyard, named the 'Great General' and the 'Assistant General' and reported to be more than 4500 years old. There is also a large Tang era stone stele (about eight metres tall) in front of the academy.

In 1989 the Henan provincial government proclaimed Songyang Academy a 'key conservation domain' (*zhongdian baohu fanwei* 重点保护范围), expanding the perimetre of restricted access to the academy grounds. Ten years later, in 1999, it was named a 'Provincial Level Patriotic Education Site' (*shengji aiguozhuyi jiaoyu jidi* 省级爱国主义教育基地) (Zhang 2012: 25; Gong 2001: 12), together with both White Deer Grotto and Yuelu Academies. Finally, in 2001, Songyang received the designation of 'National Cultural

Relic Conservation Unit' (*guojia wenwu baohu danwei*国家文物保护单位). In recent years the Dengfeng County Cultural Office has assembled over one hundred Confucian steles and has begun building an exhibition hall to house them, along with other artifacts, maps, and so on. According to the director of Songyang Academy, Gong Songtao 宫嵩焘, these represent a very rich repository, making Songyang Academy not only a famous scenic spot for tourism in the Central Plain area but also an important cultural resource. In 2010 Songyang Academy achieved World Heritage Site status as one of 11 'Historic Monuments of Dengfeng in the Centre of Heaven and Earth' approved by UNESCO ('Historic Monuments of Dengfeng in "The 'Centre of Heaven and Earth"'). The only other one of the four great academies of the Northern Song – or of any similar academies – to attain this standing is White Deer Grotto, which is part of Lushan National Park, designated as a World Heritage Site in 1996 ('Lushan National Park'). Affiliation with World Heritage Site status signifies the globalisation of these domestic cultural heritage sites, as academies are moved into the realm of representing Chinese culture on a world stage.

Although both Yuelu and White Deer Grotto Academies have close relationships with institutions of higher education, Songyang Academy is distinguished by being directly attached to Zhengzhou University. In fact, the main gates of the university include the name of Songyang Academy along with Zhengzhou University, suggesting to the observer that they are one and the same. The connection between Songyang Academy and Zhengzhou University was formally initiated in 1999 when the university established a cultural education site for its students at the academy, in line with the official promotion of patriotic education sites. Although Dengfeng county administers Songyang Academy, Zhengzhou University supplied the funds to restore it in 2007, and the academy provides a kind of Confucian campus for the university. One manifestation of this is the opening convocation for the academic year, regularly held for freshmen students at the academy.

In 2012, for example, approximately 135 students from the History College were bussed from the main campus to Songyang Academy, where they listened to a series of formal speeches, presented by university officials (including the chief Party official attached to the university) and professors, exhorting them to follow Confucian principles and study hard. After the opening speeches, a traditional scholar's desk was brought out and a professor from the College lectured on Confucianism. This was designed to replicate for the students an experience of the past when scholars lectured on Confucian texts at the academy, and to instill in them a sense of their own cultural identity both as heirs of a Confucian historical tradition and as citizens of the nation as the bearer of that tradition. Following the lecture, the students had a short time to explore the academy, taking lots of photos, before being bussed off to lunch and then another local historic site: a Mongol era observatory that was damaged by Japanese bombs during the Sino-Japanese War.[5] This added another layer of – in this case modern – history to the academic excursion, precisely in the way that the framers of the patriotic education campaign intended. For Zhengzhou University educators, having students visit the academy is a form of experiential learning designed to inculcate values that is as powerful as – or perhaps more powerful than – attending university classes or simply reading texts.

A more concrete expression of the experiential learning embodied in the academy is displayed in a collection of writings by Zhengzhou University faculty and students entitled *Encountering Songyang* (Song & Jiang 2010). The preface to this collection, written by a history professor, Zheng Yongfu 郑永福, expounds on the importance of the university's mission to foster in their students both an appreciation of the 'brilliance' of Chinese civilisation and a sense of their responsibility as its heirs (Song & Jiang 2010: 1). This mission is part of the National Studies movement, and the university's role was recognised initially by the provincial party secretary, Xu Guangchun 徐光春, when he visited the campus in early 2006 and praised the enthusiasm among Zhengzhou University students for National Studies. The book's preface repeatedly emphasises the connection between Zhengzhou's location in the Central Plain, the cultural heartland of China, and the university's mission to cultivate and promote the ancient civilisation that flourished there. Given the concerns that he and others had about children in the 1980s and 1990s growing up without a sense of duty and not studying hard enough, he acknowledges being gratified to see that these concerns were unfounded. He says that 'the vitality and longevity of [Chinese traditional civilisation] is now in the hands of the young generation of students' (Song & Jiang 2010: 1). He further links Songyang Academy to this enterprise, describing the role of the academy in the education of students as like 'planting a seed in their hearts' (Song & Jiang 2010: 2).

The subsequent editorial foreward uses the term 'academy spirit' (*shuyuan jingshen*书院精神) in reference to a series of campaigns conducted by Zhengzhou University in 2008 under the slogan 'Songyang Academy, Central Plain Culture, Zhengda Spirit' (Song & Jiang 2010: 1). One of the main

5   This description is based on the author's observations and participation, but see also 'Gaishu you gen, qi mao can yun – Lishi xueyuan 2012 xinsheng kaisue dianli ji Songyang shuyuan guoxue huijiang'.

activities associated with these campaigns was a competition for writings on the tripartite theme. From about two hundred entries submitted by faculty and students over a period of three months, sixty were selected for inclusion in this collection, consisting of essays, poetry, and other literary reflections. The term 'spirit' in the campaign slogan is used along with Zhengda (Zhengzhou University), but 'academy spirit' appears throughout the collection, along with variations using 'spirit', including university (*daxue*), humanism (*renwen*), culture (*wenhua*), and people (*minzu*). 'Academy spirit', however, is the most frequently used term, reflecting current trends in academic scholarship as well as in the writings of the contributors to the collection.[6] Like other uses of 'spirit' in modern Chinese public and official discourse, the term is vague and malleable enough to enable its use to refer to a vast range of different things, including those that are virtually opposite from each other.

Academies serve well as materialisations of an idealised Confucian humanistic pedagogy, but this can be a two-edged sword, as some of the essays in *Encountering Songyang* suggest. One essay describes Confucian ideals of learning as including not only self-cultivation and ethical training, but also freedom of academic research (Song & Jiang 2010: 57-59). The author argues that an 'atmosphere of liberation, freedom, and truth-seeking is a precondition for the development of science', and therefore academic freedom should be a basic standard for the modern university (Song & Jiang: 61). Others similarly emphasise 'academy spirit' as open debating among proponents of different ideas, harmonious interactions between teachers and students, and learning that comprises both moral conduct and intellectual development (Song & Jiang 2010: 146-166). These could be dangerous ideas in the context of the contemporary Chinese university. Some authors in the collection also portray Songyang Academy as the transmitter of 'Central Plain Culture' because of the scholars who taught there and compiled books that embody 'the soul of the Chinese people' (Song & Jiang 2010: 71). Zhengzhou University then is the modern counterpart of Songyang Academy, and it has a central role to play in the transmission of 'Central Plain Culture'.

---

6   Testimony to the ubiquity of this term, a recent book by Zhu Hanmin 朱汉民 , director of Hunan University's Yuelu Academy, is entitled *Shuyuan jingshen yu Rujia jiaoyu* 书院精神与儒家教育 (2013). Professor Zhu also currently offers a related MOOC entitled 'Shuyuan jingshen yu shuyuan zhidu 书院精神与书院制度' (http://mooc.chaoxing.com/course/154504.html). A title search of this term in the CNKI database for the past 15 years shows a fairly steady increase from one or two articles to between 10 and 15 in the past couple of years. A search by subject peaked at 152 in 2014, showing a steady increase since the early 2000s. Searching all text results in a peak of 10,766 in 2014.

Following up on this theme, an essay by a professor of history and vice director of Zhengzhou University-Songyang Academy, entitled 'Songyang Academy from the Perspective of Cultural Heritage', provides an appropriately historical discussion of the place of Songyang Academy in Central Plain culture. It identifies four main characteristics of Central Plain culture and then of Songyang Academy's position in it. The historic role of Songyang Academy as a place that fostered the development of Neo-Confucianism and also a site that represented the interaction among Buddhism, Daoism, and Confucianism is related in the present day to the revival of National Studies research (Song & Jiang 2010: 230). Continuing this theme, the development and use of Songyang Academy as a cultural heritage site is connected to the goal of utilising Henan's cultural resources as a means to strengthen the place of the province in national cultural production, with accompanying economic and social benefits (Song & Jiang 2010:237). The essay concludes with a proposal for Zhengzhou University-Songyang Academy to create a National Studies Institute that would promote scientific research, training of both undergraduate and graduate students, and develop cultural resources in the region (Song & Jiang 2010: 238). In this way cultural heritage embodied in the academy helps to legitimise the university's role in modern education for National Studies at the same time that it brings recognition to the region as the heartland of national culture.

Conclusions

Beyond the examples discussed here, there are hundreds of academies across China that have been restored or are in the process of being restored, and most of this activity has taken place since 2000. A recent commentary published in a local newspaper in Pingxiang, Jiangxi entitled 'In Praise of Restoring and Rebuilding Aozhou Academy' expresses a popular view of academies and the purpose of their restoration:

Today [10 July 2015] the municipal committee and the municipal government decided to restore Aozhou [Sea Turtle Islet] Academy [...] Rebuilding the academy can embellish the city's culture. Ancient academies are regional and even national cultural landmarks; they are a cultural 'front' where everyone discusses and ideas contend [...] We are now in an era of transformation, people's hearts and minds are restless, morality is declining, integrity is scarce, but what the academy can spread is humaneness, uprightness, propriety, wisdom, and sincerity [...] It is exactly what people need urgently to nourish the repair of culture and to nurture humanism. After the restoration and rebuilding of Aozhou Academy beginning with National Studies [...] it will help to purify and strengthen the spirit of the citizens, washing away social ills and evils. The rebuilding of the academy can strengthen the functioning of the city. Our nation's ancient four academies – Yingtian, White Deer, Yuelu, Songyang – all are cultural landmarks and cultural highlands. And they are also municipal landmarks and famous landscapes. Pingxiang's Aozhou Academy is one of Jiangxi's four great academies, and it is also one of Ping[xiang] city's 10 ancient sceneries [...] It is to be hoped that the process of restoration and rebuilding will be absorbed into the city's development [...] and will blend into the elements of modernization [...] On the banks of the Ping River, Aozhou Academy, together with the Confucian Temple and the Pingxiang Museum, the Anyuan Theater, reflecting past and present, will become our city's distinctive cultural landscape. (Wenyi, 'Shiping: Wei huifu chongjian Aozhou shuyuan diancan')

Rebuilding the academy is seen by this writer as a means to enhance the life of people in the city by drawing on the cultural tradition associated with the academy. The academy is one of several landmarks that represent local cultural heritage, and its distinctive role is to promote municipal harmony simply by being brought back to life as a model of moral education.

Academies have been appropriated in a multiplicity of ways as cultural heritage sites. They were historically institutions that represented elite scholarly culture. Their transformation into Western-style schools in the early twentieth century, coupled with the rejection of Confucianism in the May 4th Movement of 1919, the 1949 Revolution, and even more virulently, the Cultural Revolution of the 1960s-1970s, temporarily relegated academies to the dustbin of history. But, like ancestral halls and religious institutions, academies have enjoyed a resurgence in the climate of 'openness and reform' that began in the 1980s. Unlike clan ancestral halls or community temples, however, the restoration of academies has been primarily a state-sponsored initiative (Svensson 2006). Local governments seeking to develop tourism invest resources in restoring academies, but, I would argue, even more important than prospects of economic gain or promotion of cultural capital is the public pedagogical role of academies.[7] While the partnership between Songyang Academy

---

7   Shepherd & Yu 2013 discuss what they call the 'moral pedagogy' of the revolution, in the context of broader analysis of the relationship among tourism promotion, heritage preservation, and national moral campaigns (pp.55-59). He also traces the evolution of 'spiritual civilization' campaigns under Deng (1982) and Jiang (1996) [pp.59-63].

and Zhengzhou University has a specialised pedagogical purpose within the realm of higher education, the majority of restored academies might better be understood in relation to the concept of 'public pedagogy'. This term refers to the ways in which sites of domestic cultural heritage tourism provide didactic experiences for visitors. As materialisations of a Confucian past claimed by the nation, academies inspire patriotic pride among public audiences and serve the interests of the state in cultivating a strong national identity. Academies can also represent regional identity, as in the case of Huxiang culture at Stone Drum or, even more vividly, Central Plain culture at Songyang. National claims to Confucianism do not necessarily collide with regional claims to distinct schools of thought that can be collapsed under the general rubric of Confucianism. Reinforcing regional identities can equally well serve the purpose of fostering social harmony amid the strains of social (and even political) conflict fostered by economic development.

Visiting an academy may serve the state's interests in fostering patriotism, but the experience can also be seen by the visitors themselves as a marker of education and social status. They seek both to educate themselves and to display their cultural awareness as Chinese. In becoming sites of cultural heritage tourism, academies have been transformed from historically elite institutions into modern public ones, appropriated by the state but also potentially by the people who visit them (Smith 2006: 67). Considering agency on the part of visitors, future research should systematically assess audience reception through surveys of academy visitors, documenting attitudes, assumptions, and knowledge, both pre- and post-visit. Complicating the assessment of reception, foreign tourists will likely be an increasingly significant portion of the audience because at least two academies discussed here belong to World Heritage Sites (White Deer and Songyang) that attract foreign tourism, and there will surely be more (Shepherd & Yu 2013: 46-47).[8] The materialisation of cultural heritage displayed at academies has become a feature of China's soft power on the global stage as well as a domestic political strategy to promote cultural nationalism among Chinese citizens.[9] The revival of academies thus presents a compelling arena for exploring

---

[8]   The majority of foreign tourists through the first decade of the twenty-first century continued to be either ethnic Chinese from Taiwan, Hong Kong, or Macao, or from the region (Japan, Korea, Russia, Southeast Asia). See Shepherd & Yu 2013: 44.

[9]   The most obvious international example of China's soft power is that of the Confucius Institutes, which have expanded globally since 2004 to promote understanding of Chinese culture and language. Adopting the name of Confucius as the iconic representation of Chinese civilisation, the Chinese government has invested substantial resources to fund these institutes. Among the many critical studies of these institutions, see Hartig 2012, Lo and Pan 2014, Lahtinen 2015.

both how the Chinese state presents itself internationally and how Chinese people are groomed to see themselves as proud heirs of a common and culturally valued past in a modern national present.[10]

References

Ai, J. (2008), 'Refunctioning Confucianism: The Mainland Chinese Intellectual Response to Confucianism since the 1980s', *Issues and Studies* 44 (2): 29-78.

Ai, J. (2012), '"Selecting the Refined and Discarding the Dross": The Post-1990 Chinese Leadership's Attitude Towards Cultural Tradition', in P. Daly & T. Winter (eds.), *Routledge Handbook of Heritage in Asia*, 129-138. London: Routledge.

Ai, J. (2015), *Politics and Traditional Culture: The Political Uses of Traditions in Contemporary China.* Singapore: World Scientific Publishing.

Bell, D. (2008), *China's New Confucianism: Politics and Everyday Life in a Changing Society.* Princeton, NJ and Oxford: Princeton University Press.

Billioud, S. (2010), 'Carrying the Confucian Torch to the Masses: The Challenge of Structuring the Confucian Revival in the People's Republic of China', *Oriens extremus* 49: 201-224.

Billioud, S. & J. Thoraval (2015), *The Sage and The People.* New York: Oxford University Press.

Blumenfield, T. & H. Silverman (eds.) (2014), *Cultural Heritage Politics in China.* New York: Springer.

Chen, J. (2011), 'The National Studies Craze: The Phenomena, the Controversies, and Some Reflections', *China Perspectives* (French Centre for Research on Contemporary China) 2011/1: 22-30.

Chen, Y. (2012), 'Renewing Confucianism as a Living Tradition in 21st Century China: Reciting Classics, Reviving Academies, and Restoring Rituals', in G. Giordan & E. Pace (eds.), *Mapping Religion and Spirituality in a Postsecular World,* 63-83. Leiden: Brill.

Dai, S. 戴述秋 (ed.) (2007), *Shigu shuyuan shici xuan* 石鼓书院诗词选. Changsha: Hunan ditu chubanshe.

Dirlik, A. (2011), 'Guoxue/National Learning in the Age of Global Modernity', *China Perspectives* (French Centre for Research on Contemporary China), 2011/1: 4-13.

'Gaishu you gen, qi mao can yun – Lishi xueyuan 2012 xinsheng kaixue dianli ji Songyang shuyuan guoxue huijiang 盖树有根，其茂参云 – 历史学院新生开

学典礼嵩阳书院国学会讲'. [Online]. Available from: http://www5.zzu.edu.cn/lsxy/info/1019/1305.htm (accessed 12 February 2016).

Gong, S.宫嵩涛 (2001), *Songyang shuyuan*嵩阳书院. Beijing: Dangdai shijie chubanshe.

Gong, S. 宫嵩涛 (2014), *Songyang shuyuan* 嵩阳书院. Zhongguo shuyuan wenhua congshu. Changsha: Hunan daxue chubanshe.

Guo, J. 郭建衡and X. Guo 郭幸君 (2014), *Shigu shuyuan*石鼓书院. Changsha: Hunan renmin chubanshe.

Guo, Y. (2004), *Cultural Nationalism in Contemporary China: The Search for National Identity under Reform.* London: RoutledgeCurzon.

Hartig, F. (2012), 'Confucius Institutes and the Rise of China', *Journal of Chinese Political Science* 17: 53-76.

Hengyang ribao 衡阳日报 (2015), 'Shigu shuyuan da guojia 4A jingqu biaozhun 石鼓书院达国家队4A 景区标准,' 23 December 2015. [Online]. Available from: http://epaper.hyqss.cn/hyrb/html/2015-12/23/content_1_6.htm (accessed 7 February 2016).

'Historic Monuments of Dengfeng at "The Centre of Heaven and Earth"'. [Online]. Available from: http://unesco.org/en/list/1305 (accessed 7 July 2014).

Hu, B. 胡彬彬 (2005), '"Shuyuan wenwu" dingyi jieding chutan "书院文物"定义界定初探"', *Hunan daxue xuebao (Shehui kexue ban)* 19.3, pp.19-21.

Jin, M. 金敏 & Zhou Z. 周祖文 (2005), *Rujia da xuetang: Changjiang liuyude gudai shuyuan* 儒家大学堂: 长江流域的古代书院. Hangzhou: Zhejiang daxue chubanshe.

Kang, X. (2012), 'A Study of the Renaissance of Traditional Confucian Culture in Contemporary China', in F. Yang & J. Tamney (eds.), *Confucianism and Spiritual Traditions in Modern China and Beyond*, 33-73. Leiden: Brill.

Lahtinen, A. (2015), 'China's Soft Power: Challenges of Confucianism and Confucius Institutes', *Journal of Comparative Asian Development* 14 (2): 200-226.

Li, N. 李宁宁and F. Gao 高峰 (eds.) (2007), *Bailudong shuyuan yiwen xinzhi* 白鹿洞书院艺文新志. Nanchang: Jiangxi renmin chubanshe.

Liu, D. (2011), 'National Learning (Guoxue): Six Perspectives and Six Definitions', *China Perspectives* (French Centre for Research on Contemporary China) 2011/1: 46-54.

Liu, X. & X. Jian (2014), 'Development Strategy of Regional Tourism: A Case Study of Hengyang', *Cross-Cultural Communication* 10 (1): 110-113.

Lo, J. & S. Pan (2014), 'Confucius Institutes and China's Soft Power: Practices and Paradoxes', *Compare: A Journal of Comparative and International Education* 46 (4): 512-532.

'Lushan National Park'. [Online]. Available from: http://whc.unesco.org/en/list/778 (accessed 7 July 2014).

Makeham, J. (ed.) (2003), *New Confucianism.* New York: Palgrave Macmillan.

Makeham, J. (2008), *Lost Soul: 'Confucianism' in Contemporary Chinese Academic Discourse*. Cambridge, MA & London: Harvard University Asia Centre; Harvard University Press.

Makeham, J. (2011), 'The Revival of Guoxue: Historical Antecedents and Contemporary Aspirations', *China Perspectives* (French Centre for Research on Contemporary China) 2011/1: 14-21.

Qiu L. 邱凌 & L. Wen 文莉 (2010), 'Cong Shigu shuyuan shici wenhua jiexu Huxiang wenhua jingshen 从石鼓书院诗词文化解读湖湘文化精神', *Nanhua daxue xuebao (Shehui kexue ban)* 11 (4): 5-7.

Shepherd, R. (2016), *Faith in Heritage: Displacement, Development, and Religious Tourism in Contemporary China*. London: Routledge.

Shepherd, R. (2017), 'UNESCO's Tangled Web of Preservation: Community, Heritage and Development in China', *Journal of Contemporary Asia* 47 (4): 557-574.

Shepherd, R. & L. Yu (2013), *Heritage Management, Tourism, and Governance in China: Managing the Past to Serve the Present*. Springer Briefs in Archaeology 2. New York: Springer.

Smith, L. (2006), *Uses of Heritage*. London: Routledge.

Sofield, T. & F. Li (1998), 'Tourism Development and Cultural Policies in China', *Annals of Tourism Research* 25 (2): 362-392.

Song M. 宋毛平 & J. Jiang 姜建设 (eds.) (2010), *Songyang: Weile yu ni xiangyu* 嵩阳: 为了与你想遇. Zhengzhou: Zhengzhou daxue chubanshe.

Song, X. (2003), 'Reconstructing the Confucian Ideal in 1980s China: The "Culture Craze" and New Confucianism', in J. Makeham (ed.), *New Confucianism*, 81-104. New York: Palgrave Macmillan.

Svensson, M. (2006), *In the Ancestors' Shadow: Cultural Heritage Contestations in Chinese Villages*. Working Papers in Contemporary Asian Studies, No.17, ed. Roger Greatrex. Lund University Centre for East and South-East Asian Studies.

Tong, Q. (2011), 'National Learning, National Literature, and National Language', *China Perspectives* (French Centre for Research in Contemporary China) 2011/1: 32-38.

Waldron, A. (1995), 'Scholarship and Patriotic Education: The Great Wall Conference, 1994', *The China Quarterly* 143: 844-850.

Wang, H. (2012), 'War and Revolution as National Heritage: "Red Tourism" in China', in P. Daly & T. Winter (eds.), *Routledge Handbook of Heritage in Asia,* 218-233. London: Routledge.

Wang, Z. (2008), 'National Humiliation, History Education, and the Politics of Historical Memory: Patriotic Education Campaign in China', *International Studies Quarterly* 52 (4): 783-806.

Wenyi 文怡, (2015) 'Shiping: Wei huifu chongjian Aozhou shuyuan dianzan 时评: 为恢复重建鳌洲书院点赞'. [Online]. Available from: http://px.jxnews.com.cn/system/2015/07/10/014032558.shtml (accessed 21 January 2016).

Wu, B., H. Zhu, & X. Xu (2000), 'Trends in China's Domestic Tourism Development at the Turn of the Century', *International Journal of Contemporary Hospitality Management* 12(5): 296-299.

Wu, Z. (2014), 'Let Fragments Speak for Themselves: Vernacular Heritage, Emptiness, and Confucian Discourses of Narrating the Past', *International Journal of Heritage Studies* 20 (7-8): 851-865.

Xie S. (2011), 'Guoxue Re and the Ambiguity of Chinese Modernity', *China Perspectives* (French Centre for Research on Contemporary China) 2011/1: 39-45.

Yan H. & B. Bramwell (2008), 'Cultural Tourism, Ceremony and the State in China', *Annals of Tourism Research* 35 (4): 969-989.

Yang, S. 杨慎初 (ed.) (2003), *Yuelu shuyuan jianzhu yu wenhua* 岳麓书院建筑与文化. Changsha: Hunan kexue jishu chubanshe.

Zhang, H. 张慧 (2012), 'Songyang shuyuan lüyou ziyuan kaifa yanjiu嵩阳书院旅游资源开发研究', *Journal of Sanmenxia Polytechnic* 11 (2): 23-26.

Zhao, S. (1998), 'A State-led Nationalism: The Patriotic Education Campaign in Post-Tiananmen China', *Communist and Post-Communist Studies* 31 (3): 287-302.

Zhu, H. 朱汉民 (2013), *Shuyuan jingshen yu Rujia jiaoyu* 书院精神与儒家教育. Shanghai: Huadong shifan daxue chubanshe.

Zhu, H. 朱汉民, H. Deng 邓洪波, & F. Gao 高峰煜 (2004), *Changjiang liuyude shuyuan* 长江流域的书院. Wuhan: Hubei jiaoyu chubanshe.

About the Author

Linda Walton is Professor Emerita of History at Portland State University and Visiting Professor at Hunan University Yuelu Academy Research Institute. A historian of Song and Yuan China, especially academies, she has recently been studying the revival of Song-era academies in contemporary China and their role as sites of cultural heritage tourism.

3   From Destruction to Reconstruction

China's Confucian Heritage, Nationalism, and National Identity

Yingjie Guo

Abstract

The preservation and expansion of the 'Three Confucian Sites' at Qufu are no doubt driven by tourism, but a more important reason is the Chinese Communist Party's change of heart about China's cultural heritage and national identity since 1989. In 2013, President Xi Jinping unequivocally abandoned the Party's decades-long tradition of iconoclasm and confirmed its return to Chinese cultural roots. Governments at various levels have now set about promoting Confucian values and fostering a Confucian identity. While the effects of the state's nation-building remain to be seen, there is no denying that China's disremembered Confucian heritage is being re-materialised, re-interpreted and re-invented as never before in the People's Republic of China or during the past century.

Keywords: cultural heritage, Confucianism, Qufu, national identity, nationalism

Introduction

The 'Three Confucian Sites' (*san Kong*) in Qufu, birthplace of Confucius (551-479 BCE) in East China's Shandong Province, are the centrepiece of the country's tangible Confucian heritage and rank among the best known complexes of ancient Chinese architecture, alongside the Forbidden City and the Chengde Summer Resort. Their past and present glory can only be attributed to the remarkable stature and resilience of Confucius (551-479 BC). For the better part of the past two millennia, Confucianism was China's state religion (*guojiao*), while Confucius was commonly known in the country

Ludwig, Carol, Linda Walton, and Yi-Wen Wang (eds), *The Heritage Turn in China: The Reinvention, Dissemination and Consumption of Heritage*. Amsterdam: Amsterdam University Press 2020
DOI: 10.5117/9789462985667_CH03

as 'Master Kong' (*Kongzi*), 'Grand Master Kong (*Kong Fuzi*), 'Great Sage' (*Zhisheng*), 'First Teacher' (*Xianshi*), and 'Model Teacher for Ten Thousand Ages' (*Wanshi Shibiao*). However, the Sage was knocked off his pedestal as iconoclastic intellectuals set about 'smashing the Confucius shop' during the New Culture and May Fourth Movements that swept across China in the first two decades of the twentieth century. The Confucian sites suffered unprecedented damage during the Cultural Revolution (1966-1976) as Red Guards went on their own rampage against Confucius and his ideas.

Yet, in a dramatic twist of events towards the end of the 1980s, the Chinese Party-state not only began to rehabilitate Confucius and Confucianism but also to revive China's largely disremembered Confucian past and to re-create Confucian rituals in Qufu and Confucius Temples across the country. At the same time, the city of Qufu has been reconstructed and expanded to restore it to its former glory and turn it into a 'Confucian Mecca', 'China's Jerusalem' or the 'Holy City of the Orient'. The conservation-restoration and expansion of the Confucian sites are no doubt driven by tourism and imperatives of economic development but would have been inconceivable had it not been for the Chinese Communist Party's (CCP) change of heart about Confucianism and its political choices with respect to heritage conservation.

The Party-state's unprecedented dedication to heritage conservation-restoration was no doubt aimed in part at a global audience, as indicated by the successful inscription of the Confucian sites in Qufu as a World Heritage site in 1994. However, this chapter will focus instead on domestic cultural politics surrounding the development of Qufu's Confucian sites. I argue here that the significance of the Chinese government's heritage conservation-restoration project is primarily twofold. It illustrates the close linkage between conservation and nationalism as well as the primacy of identity politics in deciding the fortune of the Confucian sites. Its significance also lies in the fact that it is both a result and manifestation of the systemic transformation of the Party and the state. It represents a fundamental paradigm shift in the CCP's decades-long tradition of iconoclasm, its official ideology of state socialism, its self-identity and raison-d'être, as well as its vision about the Chinese nation-state and its place in the world. Furthermore, the CCP's endorsement and promotion of Confucianism and renewed interest in China's Confucian heritage among the populace are clear signs of a sea change in China that finds no parallel since the New Culture and May Fourth Movements. As has never happened since then, two strands of nationalism that were at loggerheads for most of the twentieth century, namely iconoclastic political nationalism and conservative cultural nationalism, have begun to merge. Their convergence is a major trend in cultural and political change in contemporary China that is not just altering China's political and cultural identities today but also shaping its future. The country's rejected and largely disremembered Confucian heritage has thus gained a new lease on life and is being re-created and re-materialised to reclaim, express and symbolise China's Confucian identity.

That does not mean, however, that the Party-state is merely interested in conservation for conservation's sake or only intends to re-materialise the disremembered Confucian past. The government's heritage conservation policy consists of four principles: to concentrate on protection, rescue endangered relics as a top priority, rationally utilise heritage, and strengthen management (Article 4, Law on the Protection of Cultural Relics, 1982). So far as the central government is concerned, while the intrinsic values of the Confucians sites in Qufu are increasingly recognised, the political use of Confucian heritage appears to be more important than anything else. For local authorities, 'rational utilisation' of heritage has meant, first and foremost, large-scale tourism and urban development. In other words, different goals are pursued in the protection and expansion of the Confucian sites and yet all are embedded in a unitary and unifying discourse on heritage conservation and cultural renaissance so that they can be legitimised and justified. The varying goals are both contradictory and complementary, and the political and economic uses of China's Confucian and other cultural heritage appear to be driving the current resurgence of cultural restoration-conservation.

Chinese Nationalism and China's Confucian Heritage

Approaches to heritage conservation in modern and contemporary China have been intricately tied to nationalism and the politics of national identity. On the one hand, nationalism dictates political choices as to whether China's cultural heritage is to be protected or destroyed and what elements of that heritage are to be preserved or forgotten; it also generates much pressure for upholding the perceived integrity and authenticity of the endorsed heritage. However, nationalists are not always in a position to ensure 'authenticity' as they see it because they have to compete with other social actors including local officials, tourist operators and urban planners who might be more interested in economic benefits than cultural 'authenticity' (Zhu 2015). Despite differing motives of key actors, re-invented heritage has a vital role to play in articulating the ideology, mythology, symbolism and consciousness of nationalism and in expressing, substantiating and reinforcing the identity of the nation through appropriate images, myths, symbols, cultural sites, and historic places.

While nationalism can be understood, following Anthony Smith (1993), as an ideological movement that seeks to retain or maintain national autonomy, unity and identity, it must be added that what is often referred to as 'Chinese nationalism' in academia and the mass media is not a homogeneous movement committed to retaining or maintaining the same national identity. In fact, until recently 'Chinese nationalism' has split down the middle into two strands opposed to each other in a broad range of areas. There is a cultural nationalism that aims to retain and maintain national autonomy, unity and identity in cultural terms by defending 'a distinctive and historically-rooted way of life' and identifying the nation to itself by returning to its 'creative life-principle' (Hutchinson 1987: 122-123, 1999: 392). Central to this strand of nationalism is the creation of a mode of cultural communication and socialisation, in which ethnic values, myths and memories become the basis of the national community. The goal is to substantiate and crystalise the idea of the nation in the minds of the members of the community by creating a widespread awareness of the myths, history, and traditions of the community (Smith 1993: 12 and 129). There is also a political nationalism that aims to reconstruct the political authority of the state at the expense of China's cultural heritage and to replace the old culture with one that would go with such a state and serve nation-building, state-building and China's modernisation. This latter strand prevailed over its much weaker opponent during the New Culture and May Fourth Movements and the greater part of the Mao era.

The political nationalists of May Fourth did not just reject Confucianism as feudalistic, they included much of China's cultural heritage in their notion of feudalism and renounced it as well. Like the cultural nationalists, they continued to see Confucianism as the 'mainstream', the 'backbone', the 'central pillar' or the 'mainstay' of Chinese culture, but they condemned it as a 'sterile orthodoxy', a 'relic of feudalism', a 'dead weight from the past', an 'obsolete but immovable fixture of the old order', or a 'stumbling block to modernity'. In their modernisation discourse, Confucianism, more than any other elements of 'feudalism', stood for all that was backward and benighted in China and it was pitted against the new, modern, progressive and enlightened culture they wanted to bring into China from advanced civilisations. Their anti-traditionalist ideology and frontal assault on Chinese traditions were comprehensive, as they assumed that 'a change in the system of symbols, values, and beliefs could best be achieved by changing ideas concerning the individual's conception of, and relationship to, both cosmic and human reality', that the social-cultural-political order of the past must be treated as a whole and rejected as a whole (Lin 1979: 26-28).

In other words, unless China rid itself of its cultural Chineseness, it would be unable to achieve the goals of economic prosperity, military strength and national salvation or become an equal member of the modern world of nation-states. The CCP, born of the May Fourth ethos of iconoclasm, carried on the tradition of May Fourth iconoclasm in the People's Republic of China (PRC) with varying degrees of commitment until the 1989 Tiananmen Incident, except that they opted for modernisation by the route of state socialism, and political nationalism came to be institutionalised through the Party-state.

The persistence of anti-traditionalism made it undesirable and difficult for China to tap its traditional spiritual resources for over seven decades and created what Anthony Smith (1993: 96) calls 'the crisis of dual legitimation'. The crisis is understood 'in terms of received religion and tradition versus legitimation by appeal to reason and observation'; this is a situation of 'assault on authority, on identity, on belief; a decline in solidarity; a denigration of established status' (Smith 1971: 133, 1993: 96). In the PRC, the crisis did not appear acute under the hegemony of Marxism-Maoism, which offered the Chinese the prospect of a socialist utopia and provided a basis for a socialist national identity, but with the increasing decay and irrelevance of Marxism-Maoism in the reform era, it has been more apparent than ever since 1949. A corollary of the debunking of the CCP's official ideology is the disintegration of the socialist identity constructed on that basis. Thus, the collective identity of the nation can no longer be taken for granted now that both the Confucian identity and the socialist identity have become delegitimised and debilitated.

A convenient solution to 'the crisis of dual legitimation', as Smith notes (1993: 97), is nationalism, which 'sinks or "realizes" individual identity within the new collective cultural identity of the nation', so that 'we' are who 'we' are because of 'our' national heritage and historic culture. As the identity of China, the nation is undergoing drastic reconstruction in the post-Mao era, China's Confucian heritage, together with its cultural traditions in general, is re-evaluated, re-interpreted and re-created accordingly. The prevailing trend in the re-evaluation and re-interpretation dictates political choices regarding heritage conservation-restoration and expansion, whilst the conserved, restored and expanded heritage must exhibit, institutionalise and reinforce the dominant national identity emerging through contestation.

Smith is right to stress that intellectuals undergoing an identity crisis as a result of the 'crisis of dual legitimation' are a central link in the rise of nationalism and play a vital part in the renaissance of ethnic cultures. However, the dynamics and trajectory of nationalism in post-Mao China do not fully support Smith's proposition that the nationalist resolution is the primary function of nationalism in general (Guo 2004). Intellectuals, including Confucians, have been able to promote Confucianism and Chinese cultural heritage since the late 1980s only after the CCP relaxed its political control over expression and retreated from its entrenched iconoclastic position. In the Patriotic Education Campaign that was launched in response to the Tiananmen Incident of 1989, the Party-state included love for Chinese cultural traditions as an essential component of patriotism and instructed Chinese schools and universities to instil a patriotic spirit in young Chinese. Before long large numbers of books about traditional Chinese culture, ranging from classical literature and philosophy to divination and *fengshui,* appeared in bookstores and at newsstands, and renewed interest in China's cultural heritage began to spread across the country.

As the CCP has abandoned its decades-long tradition of iconoclasm and decided to return to Chinese cultural roots, the Party has thus embraced elements of cultural nationalism. It finds itself in a new united front with cultural nationalists who are dedicated to the conservation-restoration of China's cultural heritage and value its role in keeping cultural traditions alive, fostering national identity and reconstructing a sense of community through a shared past and common culture. From the point of view of the new integrated nationalism, the conserved, restored and expanded heritage has a vital role to play as nationalism is a form of culture, a language, mythology, symbolism and consciousness while the nation is a type of identity whose meaning and priority is presupposed by this form of culture and must be conveyed in appropriate images, myths and symbols. It is true that the Party continues to pay lip service to Marxism and state socialism, but its words are not followed by action aimed at accomplishing China's transition from capitalism to communism and transforming the Chinese into a new species of socialist men and women. In fact, the CCP's historical mission has shifted from continuous revolution to economic development, 'harmonious society' and the 'China Dream'. The shift entails the transformation of the Party from a class organisation, as it was defined for over eight decades, to a 'national party' that upholds and is attuned to traditional Chinese values.

Ups and Downs of China's Confucian Heritage

The ups and downs of China Confucian heritage have been invariably related to ideological vagaries and the political choices of the powers that be since the very beginning. Confucius's house in Qufu was consecrated as a temple in 478 BCE by the Prince of Lu, within two years after Confucius's death. The temple gradually expanded into what became known as the 'Three Confucian Sites'. It is devoted to the memory of Confucius and the Confucian sages and was continuously in use for around 2,400 years since it was established. The existing structures of the mansion date back to the Ming (1368-1644) and Qing (1636-1912) dynasties and occupy an area of 12,470 square metres. The 200-hectare cemetery contains Confucius's tomb and the remains of his descendants. Before the Cultural Revolution (1966-1976), more than 100,000 historic artefacts and 300,000 files were kept in the 300 buildings, and there were approximately 100,000 tombs and 17,000 ancient trees in the cemetery.

However, in an event commonly known as 'the burning of books and burying of scholars', which took place during the reign of the First Emperor of the short-lived Qin Dynasty (221-206 BCE), most copies of the Confucian classics kept at the Confucian sites in Qufu, as well as elsewhere in the empire, were destroyed. The event ensued from the controversy between the emperor and his Legalist Prime Minister Li Si on the one hand, and Confucian scholars on the other, who called for a return to the old feudal order. Legalism prevailed under the auspices of the state whereas Confucian and other competing schools of thought were suppressed. The succeeding Han Dynasty (206 BCE-AD 220) favoured Confucianism over Legalism such that the former became the state religion. The pro-Confucian Emperor Gaozu of Han (r.206-195 BCE) launched an intensive campaign to replace and reproduce the classics and was the first emperor to offer sacrifices to the memory of Confucius in Qufu. Numerous successive emperors and high officials followed his example: between then and the twentieth century, 12 emperors paid 19 personal visits to Qufu to worship Confucius while 100 others sent their deputies for 196 official visits (Kong 2009: 6). At the same time, Qufu's Confucian sites were protected and restored after fires and kept expanding from time to time until the early years of the Qing Dynasty regardless of the change of dynasties and frequent wars.

Despite their ferocious assaults on Confucianism, there were few deliberate attempts during the New Culture and May Fourth Movements and the Communist Revolution to damage or destroy historic places. From 1949 to 1965, the Chinese government's policy towards tangible heritage shifted between protection and neglect as the pendulum of the CCP's ideology swung left and right, between continuous revolution and economic development, between ideologically-driven class struggle on the one hand and, on the other, firm commitment to heritage protection and pragmatic efforts to build overarching united fronts designed to garner as much support as possible for the Party. In 1957, before the onset of the ultra-leftist campaign of the Great Leap Forward, the Shandong provincial government designated the Temple of Confucius as a protected site. In 1961, when moderates within the Party gained the upper hand, the State Council included the Confucian sites in the first batch of 'cultural sites under national priority protection'. Still, cultural heritage was largely fossilised and exhibited in the museum, while much was done to ensure that the masses were insulated from the ideas, beliefs, values and practices embodied in the heritage, which were mostly deemed to be negative, reactionary and opposed to the revolutionary or socialist value system and national identity that the CCP wished to construct.

The Chinese government's protection of cultural heritage was brought to an end during the Cultural Revolution. An editorial in the *People's Daily* (1966) on 1 June 1966 called on the masses to smash the 'four olds' (old thinking, old cultures, old customs and old habits). The CCP's 'Resolution Regarding the Great Cultural Revolution' (1966) stated explicitly that 'smashing the four olds' was a major goal of the Cultural Revolution. Leading Maoists in Beijing specifically allowed and encouraged Red Guards to destroy the Confucian sites in Qufu. On 9 November 1966, Tan Houlan – one of the five top Red Guard leaders in Beijing – and some 200 Red Guards from Beijing Normal University arrived at Qufu and soon managed to overcome resistance by local officials. The Red Guards went on the rampage between 15 November and 6 December, breaking statues of Confucius and his disciples, smashing steles, monuments and ornamental columns, tearing up paintings and calligraphy, and digging up the graves of Confucius and those of selected generations of his descendants. Local residents and peasants in and near Qufu joined in the rampage, and mass looting began after the Red Guards found gold, silver and jewelry in one of the graves. In all, 6,618 relics were destroyed; 2,700 rare books were burnt; nearly 2,000 graves were dug up; about 1,000 tomb stones were knocked down; and over 10,000 trees were cut down. The rampage was the only recorded act of massive destruction of the Confucian sites in Qufu and led to unprecedented and irreparable damage to the sites, marking the apex of the long tradition of iconoclasm in China (Zhang 2013). Later on, local schools and other work units turned parts of the Kong Family Cemetery into farmland.

The wanton destruction of Qufu's Confucian sites stopped on 7 December 1966, when Tan Houlan and her fellow Red Guards felt they had accomplished their mission of 'smashing the Confucius shop'. But the nationwide assault on Confucius and Confucianism was sustained throughout the Cultural Revolution and escalated to new levels during the 'Criticise Lin Biao and Criticise Confucius' Campaign of 1974. The Campaign and the radical rhetoric against Confucianism during the Cultural Revolution made it impossible to speak positively of the Confucian heritage or give much thought to the conservation-restoration of Confucian sites. It was only after 'reform and opening-up' began that the government moved again to prevent further damage to the Confucian sites and to protect cultural heritage across the country.[1]

Two government initiatives in 1982 were milestones in the development of historical conservation in China. One was the Law of the People's Republic of China on the Protection of Cultural Relics, which re-established a legal framework for historical protection. The other was the creation of a List of Famous Chinese Historic Cities and the introduction of associated management regulations to preserve ancient cities and towns. Qufu was included in China's twenty-four 'famous historical and cultural cities'. The regulations for the implementation of the law were issued in 1992 to provide for its technical support. The law was revised in 1991, 2002, 2007, 2013 and 2015 and has become the basis for conservation policymaking at national and local levels. The law and the list of famous historical and cultural cities are clear manifestations of the Party-state's ideological shift and its recent political choices with respect to cultural heritage. Government policy has moved from destruction and neglect to protection and reconstruction and further to promotion.

Given the continued assault in China on Confucius and Confucianism over more than seven decades and the unresolvable tension between Confucianism and Marxism, it is surprising that Confucianism should 'advance toward the twenty-first century with a smile on its lips' (*People's Daily* 8 September 1994: 1). Clear indications of the Confucian revival include the emergence of colossal statues of Confucius at the new Shanghai Library and the People's University in Beijing and Tiananmen Square,[2] the establishment of Confucius Institutes and Confucius Classrooms in over a hundred countries, and the officially sponsored celebrations since 1994 of the anniversaries of Confucius's birth. The celebration in 1994 was of particular political significance not just because for the first time a high-ranking Party-state official, former vice-premier Gu Mu, chaired the conference as

---

1   During his visit to Qufu in May 1978, Li Xiannian, Deputy Chairman of the CCP and Vice-Premier of the State Council, reiterated angrily that those who damage the Confucian sites should be severely punished.

2   The statue of Confucius only stayed in front of the Chinese National Museum on the eastern side of the Square for a hundred days. Its appearance and disappearance seem to suggest the lack of consensus amongst the top leadership about the status of Confucius and Confucianism in the Party-state's official ideology and iconography.

Chairman of the China Confucius Foundation, but also because President Jiang Zemin graced the event and spent two hours talking about his own Confucian upbringing. Gu Mu's keynote speech on the occasion left no doubt at all that, instead of condemning Confucianism as 'feudalistic' and 'reactionary', as the CCP had done previously, he reclaimed Chinese culture as quintessentially Confucian and presented Confucianism as enlightened and progressive (Gu 2009: 12).

The Party-state has warmed further to Confucius and Confucianism since President Xi Jinping came to power. Cultural nationalists welcomed the president's visit to Qufu on 26 November 2013 and have taken advantage of it in promoting Confucianism and cultural traditions. Xu Jialu (Xu 2014), former Deputy Chairman of the National People's Congress and an articulate cultural nationalist, has compared the visit to Deng Xiaoping's 'southern tour' because, he believes, it has settled ideological disputes over the place of Confucian values and cultural traditions in contemporary Chinese society and in the Party-state's revamped 'core value system'. Consistent with Xi's new cultural conservatism, governments at various levels now have no ideological qualms about promoting Confucian values, fostering a Confucian national identity and enhancing China's soft power on the back of the Confucian revival.

Qufu's heritage conservation has been boosted by generous financial aid and technical assistance from upper-level governments and domestic institutions including Tsinghua University and Tongji University, and international organisations such as the World Bank and the European Commission's Asia URBS Programme. The French cities of Rennes and St-Jacques-de-Compostelle collaborated with Qufu in 2005-2007 on a joint urban planning project. The World Bank provided Qufu with a loan of $50 million in June 2011 for cultural heritage conservation in the city. Ever greater amounts of funding have flown to Qufu from the central and local governments. Between 2013 and 2015 alone the central and provincial governments injected 1.1 billion yuan into heritage projects in Qufu (You 2015). Both national and international players work in unison to facilitate Qufu's endeavour, even though the central Party-state's political use of cultural heritage and local operators' economic focus may not be acceptable to all international supporters.

The Conservation-Restoration of the Confucian Sites

The objectives of the central Party-state's and the local government's approaches to heritage conservation and utilisation are by no means uniform or consistent. The vision of the central leadership is most explicitly articulated in President Xi Jinping's speech in Qufu, where he made four points of critical importance for the promotion of Confucianism and cultural traditions (Xi Jinping, 26 Nov 2013). First, it is imperative to make clear that, since every country and every nation has its own historical traditions and deep-rooted cultures, the basic national conditions differ, and so do their models of development. Second, it must be clearly understood that the spiritual pursuit of the Chinese nation is rooted in Chinese culture and the latter gives the nation rich nourishment and enables it to survive and thrive generation after generation. Third, it is important to realise that Chinese culture is the Chinese nation's unique advantage and its richest source of soft power. And fourth, it must be explained clearly that socialism with Chinese characteristics is deeply rooted in the fertile soil of Chinese culture.

It is clear that President Xi's approach to cultural heritage focuses on both its extrinsic and its intrinsic values. On the one hand, he points to the connection between the national spirit and traditional culture, underscoring the importance of maintaining cultural continuity and national identity. On the other hand, an overriding purpose of his promotion of heritage conservation is to legitimise and justify China's current political system and state socialism by representing them both as historically and culturally determined and as a natural outgrowth of cultural traditions and history.

Whilst echoing the central leaders' heritage discourse, local officials in Qufu focus even more on the extrinsic values of the city's Confucian sites, especially tourism and urban development. One of the roles that Qufu's Confucian sites have is to leverage economic development with the Confucian sites. The other two roles, which take precedence in the local authorities' heritage conservation narrative, if not in practice, include exhibiting (*zhanshi*) and disseminating (*chuanbo*) Confucian culture and the cultural spirit of Confucius – 'the hallmark and essence of Qufu' (People's Government of Qufu 2009). In order to exhibit Qufu's Confucian heritage and disseminate Confucian culture, the local authorities moved quickly to take over the Confucian sites as a top priority. They had already asked all the work units based in the Confucian Mansion to move out as early as 1978, years before the central Party-state openly endorsed Confucianism. The local government went on to gradually close Confucius Mansion Road (west) to traffic starting from 2007 and embarked on the conservation-restoration of historic buildings on this road a couple of years later. Shopping stalls are no longer allowed within the secondary gate of the Cemetery, and all vehicles except electric-driven sightseeing buses are prohibited from entering the sites. Additionally, the Qufu city wall, which was built during the Ming Dynasty to protect the Mansion and the Temple, has been repaired and restored.

The local government's general conservation-restoration strategy and specific protective procedures are spelt out in the 'Measures of Qufu City for the Protection and Management of Cultural Relics' (People's Government of Qufu, 1995). The Measures stipulate that, within the protection domain of the sites of cultural relics:

- the ancient buildings and their auxiliary buildings may not be damaged, demolished or rebuilt;
- no new buildings or other construction projects may be built or conducted;
- no inflammable, explosive or other dangerous materials may be stored in or beside the buildings;
- repairs and restoration projects should be carefully planned and reported to government departments with the technical know-how for handling cultural conservation-restoration;
- when maintaining or restoring memorial buildings, ancient buildings and stone carvings (including their adjuncts, such as frescos, statues and stele inscriptions), efforts should be made to observe the principle of preserving the original status and strictly abide by the technical standards of restoration so that the original format, structure, materials and technique of the ancient buildings will be maintained.

A principal protective measure of the Qufu government is the demarcation of the protection domain (51.4 hectares) and the management of the construction control zones in accordance with the law. The zones are divided into four categories. The Grade 1 Zone (G1Z) is an 'absolute protection area' where no individual or organisation may change the original status, look and environment without government approval and where no buildings or structures of any description may be built. Only greening projects, fire routes and necessary utility projects are allowed in G1Z. The measures have identified existing modern buildings that must be relocated and dangerous houses overhauled, although no action has been taken so far. In order that no government departments or developers could take advantage of the project needs in G1Z, every restoration project must be approved by the Qufu City Cultural Relics Administration Committee and the Department of Urban Planning.

The Grade 2 Zone (G2Z) is a 'strictly controlled area' where single-story buildings are to be retained and may not be rebuilt or expanded. Only

dangerous houses can be overhauled, although they must be rebuilt into
courtyard-style buildings, and only buildings with eave heights less than 7.92
metres are allowed in the Grade 3 Zone (G3Z). The Grade 3 Zone (G3Z) is a
'special control area around cultural sites with special protection require-
ments'. The height of building eaves allowed in the G3Z is 9 metres. While
more flexibility is allowed in G3Z, projects that may change the terrain
and topography, plantation, road and water system are strictly forbidden.
In both G2Z and G3Z, it is required that the courtyard-style buildings
and new buildings be harmonised with the Confucian Sites and the sites
of other cultural relics in shape, size, colour, general look and so on, and
their architectural design be endorsed by the Qufu City Cultural Relics
Administration Committee and approved by the Department of Urban
Planning. Finally, the Grade 4 Zone (G4Z) is an 'environmental coordination
area'. Construction is allowed in the zone so long as it is geared towards
meeting the needs of heritage protection.

The demarcated areas surrounding the Temple and the Mansion fall
within the protection scope and the bulk of them are situated in G1Zs and
G2Zs. The protection scope of the Cemetery begins from ten metres within
the southern wall of the Cemetery and five metres within the western,
northern and eastern walls. The bulk of the Cemetery is included in the
G1Z. The conservation-restoration of the Confucian Sites has focused on the
protection and care of artworks, architecture, and museum collections with
a view to reducing the rate of deterioration. It includes numerous activities
ranging from preventive conservation and examination of architecture,
stabilisation of architectural structure, consolidation and surface cleaning to the treatment and documentation of artefacts, collection care and
management through tracking, examination, documentation, exhibition,
storage, preventative conservation, and research, and education.

A major conservation-restoration project was the repairing of the Dacheng
Gate to the Temple, the Apricot Altar, the Bedroom Hall of the Mansion, the
northern part of the eastern walls of the Temple, the repainting of the doors
and window frames of the buildings on the axial line of the Temple and the
Cemetery, and the restoration of the niches in the eastern and western wings
of the Temple. The local authorities also rebuilt the Western Warehouse in
the Mansion and established a new Exhibition Hall of Han and Wei Steles
in the Warehouse. Similar interventive methodologies were used to set up a
new archives office in the Mansion. Much has also been done to restore the
original look of the Temple and the Sacred Way (*Shengdao*) and to protect
ancient trees in the Cemetery. The asphalt road (the Sacred Way) which was
built during the Cultural Revolution has been reconstructed using stone

pavers. The sandstone roads around the Cemetery have been resurfaced with stone, too. Another major conservation-restoration project, costing over three hundred million yuan, is currently underway. The project involves surface cleaning, consolidation through repairing flaking paint and the painting of an area of around 140,000 square metres. Nothing on this scale has taken place at Qufu's Confucian Sites since the Qing Dynasty. This is indisputable evidence that the Party-state is attaching greater importance to the Confucian heritage than at any other time since the last dynasty.

There is now a computerised management system that monitors the cultural properties around the clock, including the ancient trees and the monuments at the sites. The existing lighting facilities in the ancient buildings of the Temple and the Mansion have been replaced with new lighting systems while the electricity wiring has been placed underground for safety and aesthetic reasons. The local authorities have also installed a system of safety and fire prevention that cost more than thirteen million yuan. No security incident has taken place at the Confucian Sites since they were inscribed in 1994. In addition, qualified and trained professionals are engaged in comprehensive collection care and management through tracking, examination, documentation, exhibition, storage, and restoration, while scholars and professionals have created files detailing the ancient trees in the Cemetery and the steles on the sites, and compiled a large series of books, including the critically acclaimed *A Complete Collection of Qufu Steles*. Researchers affiliated with the Confucian sites and other local institutions have published numerous works on aspects of Confucius, Confucianism and the sites. Others have been involved as consultants and advisors in the making of documentaries and TV drama, such as the six-episode *Archives of the Confucius Mansion* and *Confucius*, both of which have been broadcast on China Central Television. A digitised 'Confucius-Mencius Information System' was launched in October 2015 to enable tourists and netizens to view 3-D images of the Confucian and Mencian sites and to access detailed information about every aspect of the sites as well as the life and philosophy of Confucius and Mencius. The digitisation of the more than 9,000 volumes of files kept in the Mansion was completed in December 2016, and the local government has promised to make digitised files available to the public.

Admittedly, a question remains as to whether the local government's conservation regulations are strictly implemented or effectively policed and to what extent conservation principles are followed. Only qualified professionals will be able to assess the quality and effects of Qufu's conservation-restoration work. Still, despite indisputable evidence of non-compliance in practice,[3] the Qufu government's policies and regulations appear to demonstrate ethical stewardship and are designed to protect the Confucian heritage using methods effective in keeping the sites as close to their original condition as possible for as long as possible. The local authorities claim in a report accepted by UNESCO that the maintenance of the Confucian Sites has been successful in preserving their authenticity and integrity (Qufu City Cultural Relics Administration Committee 2004). If official accolades are to be believed, Qufu's achievements in conservation are certainly recognised by national authorities. The city received an award in 1998 as one of the 'advanced units in the protection of world heritage in China' from the State Administration of Cultural Heritage, the Ministry of Construction, and the Chinese National Commission for UNESCO. The Confucian Sites in Qufu became one of China's 'most valuable tourist destinations of cultural heritage' in 2014. The state Bureau of Tourism designated the sites as a 'Demonstrative Base for Educational Tourism' (*yanxue lüyou jidi*) in January 2016.

Utilisation of the Confucian Sites

Governments at various levels and local entrepreneurs have proven to be quite adept at 'playing the Confucius card' and creative in their 'rational utilisation' of Qufu's Confucian Sites and intangible Confucian heritage, and there can be no doubt that they are vigorously leveraging economic development in and around Qufu with its rich cultural heritage. The utility of Qufu's Confucian Sites and cultural heritage is most noticeable in three areas: urban development in the city and beyond, tourism, and education. As the central and local governments capitalise on the sites, Qufu's tangible Confucian heritage has been increasingly expanded and incorporated into national and international networks of cultural heritage and cultural transmission. Over the past decade, new Confucian sites have been constructed in Qufu, the most publicised sites being the Confucius Museum, the Confucius Research Institute, the Confucius Gallery of Calligraphy and Paintings, and the Analects Steles Garden. There is also the Six-Arts City (*Liuyi Cheng*), a Confucius theme park where visiting students and tourists learn or watch demonstrations of the six arts that formed the basis of education in ancient Chinese culture, including rites, music, archery,

---

3   For example, when Qufu's Cultural Relics and Tourist Service Division cleaned the Confucian Sites between 6 and 13 December 2000, staff washed, brushed and wiped the relics and damaged parts of ancient buildings in the Mansion and Temple.

charioteering, calligraphy, and mathematics. Parks and galleries in Qufu display images and statues of Confucius and his disciples as well as brief descriptions and explanations of essential Confucian classics and Confucian values. The city is now collaborating with newly established Confucius Halls in China and a large number of the two thousand or so Confucius Temples in the country and overseas on the promotion of Confucius and Confucian values. It is thus no exaggeration to say that Qufu has become a national and international stronghold of Confucianism.

The local government is hard at work on the integration of Qufu with Zouping, a neighbouring city with rich cultural heritage, together with the numerous cultural sites between the two cities, including the Temple of Confucius on Nishan, the Temple of Mencius, the Cemetery of Mencius's Mother, the Temple of Yan Hui, the supposed birthplace of the Yellow Emperor, the tomb of Shaohao (the Yellow Emperor's son), the Temple of the Duke of Zhou, and so on. Trying to emulate the success of the 'special economic zones' such as Shenzhen but innovating the development model, the Shandong provincial government decided in January 2013 to make Qufu a 'special cultural-economic zone' (Liu and Wang 2015). The vision of a great many local officials, scholars, urban planners and developers, as can be gleaned from local newspapers, posters and billboards, is to create a 'heritage zone', a 'Chinese cultural symbolic city', the 'spiritual sanctuary of the Chinese nation', the 'Holy City of the Orient', a 'Confucian Mecca', or 'China's Jerusalem'. Actually, the city already calls itself the 'Holy City of the Orient'.[4]

Meanwhile, the central government and national organisations have set up demonstrative bases for educational and training purposes as well for transmitting Confucian values and fostering a common cultural identity between the PRC and Taiwan. Those who visit Qufu can see signs of the Hanban's Experience Centre at the Confucius Institute Headquarters and Base for Training International Volunteers, the China Confucius Foundation's Demonstrative Base for the Transmission of Excellent Traditional Culture, the State Council's Base for Cross-Strait Exchange. In March 2016 the central government designated Qufu as a national base for the 'transmission of excellent traditional culture' in its thirteenth Five-Year Plan (Xinhua 2016). The Hanban's initiative is designed to add more substance to the name of Confucius Institutes by bringing students and volunteers who are selected to teach Chinese at the Institutes to Qufu, where they will learn about Confucian beliefs, ideas, values and practices (Li and Huang 2014). Selected Party-state cadres come to Qufu to study Confucian virtues as a bulwark

4   This name appears on the front wall of the magnificent Tourist Centre of Qufu.

against corruption. School principals, teachers and students from all over the country relive the Confucian past by discussing the Sage's teachings at the Apricot Altar, where he used to talk with his students (Uqufu Net 2016a).

Even more important to Qufu's local economy is tourism, which has been combined in recent years with educational activities designed to involve both visitors and locals. The number of tourists to Qufu has now exceeded 4.5 million a year (Uqufu Net 2016b). That is no small feat, given that Qufu is only a county-level city. If every tourist enters the Confucian Sites and a quarter of them go to the Confucius Museum, the Confucius Research Institute, Confucius Gallery of Calligraphy and Paintings, and the Six Arts City, the annual admission fees alone will be over a billion yuan. What the tourists spend on travelling, accommodation, food and souvenirs would easily add another two to three billion yuan to the local economy. This is the reason why the local authorities can afford to offer 50 per cent concession tickets to students and people over sixty and to stop charging an increasing number of locals, teachers and descendants of Confucius for entry to the Confucian Sites. Since 2013, they have responded to President Xi's call for promoting traditional culture by making more free passes available to locals and involving more ordinary citizens in the annual commemoration of Confucius. In the past, only a few thousand scholars, overseas Chinese, representatives of Confucius Institutes descendants of Confucius and other selected individuals were allowed to attend the official commemorations taking place during the 'Confucius Festival' in late September, which are co-sponsored by the Ministry of Education, the Ministry of Culture, the Bureau of Tourism, the government of Shandong Province, and the Confucius Wine Company. Now additional commemorations are conducted every Monday and Friday between 26 October and 25 November to enable and encourage ordinary citizens to participate (Uqufu Net 2016b). Nearly 300,000 locals attended the commemorations in 2015. Consequently, the commemorations have become popular rather than elitist events with a much larger number of attendees.

Mass tourism and increasing redevelopment in Qufu have caused concerns about their negative effects on the city's Confucian heritage (Liu 2010; Chu 2014). Perhaps more pertinent to socialisation and cultural identification than the perceived authenticity of Qufu's tangible Confucian heritage are the living history presentations or historical re-enactments, since such events have a more pivotal role to play in demonstrating and transmitting Confucius's moral and spiritual values (Zhu 2012). Criticisms of the Disneyfication and commodification of the Confucian heritage are certainly justified in the case of the Six-Arts City. One example is the re-enactment of everyday life of Confucius's time in an area of the City named 'Confucius's Hometown', where employees wearing period costumes pretend to be working as weavers, carpenters, blacksmiths, paper-makers, and so on. Some of them take their job seriously, but others look bored and kill time wandering around, smoking cigarettes, making calls on their mobile phones, or talking to each other in pairs or groups. It is clearly off-putting to the many tourists who walk away quickly or complain to their families or fellow travellers about the re-enactment, which they obviously do not find 'authentic' or even entertaining.

Another example is the musical and dancing performances in the Hall of Music, which are ostensibly designed to show the audience how music and dance were performed in Confucius's time and to demonstrate the importance of music in the Sage's thinking about rites, social harmony and personality cultivation, but which is really meant to attract tourists to a large restaurant in the Hall with a seating capacity of three hundred customers. The music is drowned out by the noise as a large number of customers try to gather with their families or fellow travellers, find a table, order their food and drinks, talk to each other and call out to the waiters and waitresses over the noise. Few are likely to walk away from 'Confucius's Hometown' or the Hall with a better idea about the Sage's life or his ideas about music or to become more inclined towards the moral and spiritual values of Confucianism.

These examples illustrate not only negative responses to the poor quality of the living history presentations or historical re-enactments but also the obvious impossibility of recreating the past. Though more earnestness, professionalism and technical expertise on the part of local operators and employees may improve the tourist experience of Qufu's Confucian heritage, even the most skilled presentations and re-enactments might not succeed in demonstrating and transmitting Confucius's moral and spiritual values. In other words, the promotion of the Confucian heritage is one thing and the identification with, or internalisation of, these values is quite another, although there is little dispute that the promotion of heritage has a positive effect on identification and socialisation in comparison with its rejection and destruction.

Conclusion

The scale and depth of the changes in cultural restoration-conservation in China are easily gauged from the contrasts between millions of tourists visiting Qufu and Red Guards going on the rampage at the Confucian Sites; and between the official promotion of Confucian values and renewed interest in Confucianism in Chinese society on the one hand, and the frontal assault on Confucianism sustained over the better part of the twentieth century, on the other. Gone is the iconoclastic ethos permeating Chinese society from May Fourth 1919 to June Fourth 1989 and the anti-traditionalist, political nationalism that sought to rid China of its Chineseness for the sake of modernisation and national salvation. It has now given way to an integrated nationalism that aims to retain and maintain national identity, autonomy and unity in both political and cultural senses. Moreover, the political autonomy and unity of China the nation has come to be regarded as dependent upon a Chinese cultural identity, and China's rejected and destroyed Confucian heritage must be protected, reconstructed and utilised to foster, express and symbolise that identity.

Perhaps the convergence of political and cultural nationalism in recent years is a sign of a nation that is recovering from the 'century of humiliation', overcoming doubts about its own civilisation, resolving its identity crisis, and coming to terms with itself. The emergent national confidence is by no means related to the CCP's official ideology or the PRC's political system, as the Party claims, but stems from China's 'economic miracle' and the resultant, rising purchasing power among the populace, which some trace to Confucian values. Eminent Confucian scholar Tu Wei-ming, for example, notes that 'the Confucian ethic is not compatible with the capitalist spirit but may actually have helped East Asia to develop a different form of modern industrial capitalism' (Tu 1996, 10). There is consequently no need for critical introspection, condemnation of Chinese civilisation or 'self-hate'. To the contrary, Chinese must show confidence in line with the nation's status as a rising superpower. Confidence rests, among other things, on pride in Chinese cultural heritage, and a superpower needs cultural soft power to match its economic, political and military hard power. The Party-state's soft power surely stands to benefit more from Confucianism and traditional Chinese values than from Marxism, Sinicised or not: a Confucian China will be more stable, cohesive, confident and respectable than a socialist China with or without Chinese characteristics. Thus, China's Confucian past has been revived and utilised as a source of soft power and as part of the state's cultural repertoire in the construction of a new narrative of belonging, common destiny and national identity.

Further research is needed to investigate the extent to which the Party-state is actually able to derive coveted soft power from Confucian and other cultural heritage and to which ordinary Chinese citizens subscribe to the narrative and identify with the Confucian nation under construction. Nevertheless, there is no denying that the CCP and China are both undergoing fundamental transformation. The former is no longer an anti-Confucian and anti-traditionalist party but promotes Confucianism and traditional Chinese culture, while Chinese identity is increasingly expressed and symbolised through Confucian language, images and myths, and reinforced through the restoration of Confucian cultural and historic sites such as those at Qufu.

References

Chu, M. (2014), 'A Study of the Protection and Development of Historical and Cultural City of Qufu [Shandong Qufu lishi wenhua mingcheng baohu yu kaifa wenti yanjiu]'. MA thesis, Shaanxi Normal University.

Kong, D. (2009), 'Qufu san Kong [Qufu san Kong]', *Duiwai chuanbo* 9: 5-7.

Gu, M. (2009), 'Wo dui Kongzi de renshi [My views about Confucius]', *Guangming ribao*, 23 March. [Online]. Available from: http://www.gmw.cn/ (accessed 25 May 2017).

Guo, Y. (2004), *Cultural Nationalism in Contemporary China: The Search for National Identity under Reform*. London: Routledge.

Hutchinson, J. (1987), *The Dynamics of Cultural Nationalism: The Gaelic Revival and the Creation of the Irish Nation State*. London: Allen & Unwin.

Hutchinson, J. (1999), 'Reinterpreting cultural nationalism', *The Australian Journal of Politics and History* 45 (3): 392-409.

Li, X. & P. Huang (2014), 'Konzi xueyuan zongbu tiyan jidi luohu Kongzi guli Shandong Qufu [The experiential base of the headquarters of Confucius Institutes is based in Qufu, Confucius's hometown]', China News, 28 September. [Online]. Available from: http://www.chinanews.com/cul/2014/09-28/6639554.shtml (accessed 11 May 2017).

Lin, Y. (1979), *The Crisis of Chinese Consciousness: Radical Antitraditionalism in the May Fourth Era*. Madison: University of Wisconsin Press.

Liu, B. & H. Wang (2015), 'Qufu, Shandong: Kongzi guli yu chuangjan "jingji wenhua tequ" [Qufu Shandong: Confucius's Hometown Plans to Establish an 'Economic-Cultural Special Zone]', Xinhua Net, 25 January. [Online]. Available from: http://news.xinhuanet.com/local/2013-01/25/c_114505320.htm (accessed 11 May 2017).

Liu, L. (2010), 'Qufu lishi wenhua mingcheng baohu shijian huigu ji sisuo [A Reflection on the Practice of the Protection of the Historical and Cultural City of Qufu]'. MA thesis, Shandong Architectural University.

People's Daily (1966), 'Hengsao yiqie niu gui she shen' [Eliminate all bad elements], 1 June.

People's Government of Qufu (1995), 'Qufu shi wenwu baohu guanli banfa [The Measures of Qufu City for the Protection and Management of Cultural Relics]'. [Online]. Available from: http://www.chinaac.net/mcyj-view.asp?id=13041&lbid=376 (accessed 12 February 2016).

People's Government of Qufu (2009), 'Zhunque dingwei, youxu fanzhan – guanyu lishi wenhua mingcheng Qufu jianshe de jidian yijian [Accurate Conceptualisation and Orderly Development – Several Views on the Construction of the Famous Historical and Cultural City of Qufu]'. *China Ancient City*, 26 February. [Online]. Available from: http://www.chinaac.net/mcyj-view.asp?id=13041&lbid=376 (accessed 12 February 2016).

Qufu City Cultural Relics Administration Committee (2004), *A Regular Report on the Implementation of the Convention Concerning the Protection of World Cultural and Natural Heritage.*

Smith, A. (1971), *Theories of Nationalism*. New York: Harper & Row.

Smith, A. (1993), *National Identity*. Reno: University Nevada Press.

Tu, W. (ed.) (1996), *Confucian Traditions in East Asian Moernity*, Cambridge, MA: Harvard University Press.

Uqufu Net (2016a), 'Dengtan lundao qianshou mingqi Qufu Kongzi yanxueyou zai qihang [Speak on the Apricot Altar, Connect with Famous Companies and Conduct a Study Tour in Qufu]', 10 October. [Online]. Available from: http://www.uqufu.com/html/2016/1110/2669.html (accessed 11 May 2017).

Uqufu Net (2016b), '2016 nian ji Kong dadian 9 yue 28 ri Qufu juxing [The 2016b Commemoration of Confucius Takes Place in Qufu on 28 September]', 27 September. [Online]. Available from: http://www.uqufu.com/html/2016/1110/2669.html (accessed 11 May 2017).

Xi, Jinping, 'Speech at the Confucius Research Institute in Qufu', 26 November 2013. [Online]. Available from: http://www.chinakongzi.org/xwzx/201511/t20151126_13397538.htm (accessed 20 February 2016).

Xinhua (2016), 'Zhonghua renmingongheguo guomin jingji he shehui fazhan shisan ge wunian guiha gangyao [The Thirteenth Five-year Plan for Economic and Social Development of the People's Republic of China]', Xinhua Net, 17 March. [Online]. Available from: http://news.xinhuanet.com/politics/2016lh/2016-03/17/c_1118366322.htm (accessed 11 May 2017).

Xu, J. (2014), 'Xu Jialu chuxi Shandong renwen sheke yanjiu xiezuoti nianhui [Xu Jialu Attends the Annual Conference of the Consortium of the Humanities and Social Sciences in Shandong]', Advanced Institute of Confucian Studies, Shandong University. [Online]. Available from: http://www.rxgdyjy.sdu.edu.cn/showarticle.php?articleid=2618 (accessed 26 January 2014).

You, S. (2015), 'Shandong shishi rujia wenhua yichan baohu gongcheng guojia he
    sheng touru 11 yi [The Central and Provincial Governments inject 1.1 Billion Yuan
    into Confucian Heritage Projects in Shandong]', *Dazhong ribao*, 9 January 2015.
    [Online]. Available from: http://dzrb.dzwww.com/ (accessed 25 May 2017).
Zhang, H. (2013), '"Wenge" chuqi Qufu "San Kong" zaoyu kongqian jienan shimo' [The
    Sabotage of the 'San Kong' at Qufu at the Beginning of the Cultural Revolution],
    Duzhe wenzhai (9): 55-59.
Zhu, Y. (2012), 'Performing Heritage: Rethinking Authenticity in Tourism', *Annals
    of Tourism Research* 39 (3): 1495-1513.
Zhu, Y. (2015), 'Cultural Effects of Authenticity: Contested Heritage Practices in
    China', *International Journal of Heritage Studies* 21 (6): 594-608.

About the Author

YINGJIE GUO is Professor of Chinese Studies at the University of Sydney.
Author of *Cultural Nationalism in Contemporary China* (2004), his research
interests include China's cultural heritage, collective memories and nationalism in contemporary China.

4   Set in Stone

Continuity and Omission in Possessive Representations of the Great Wall

Kristin Bayer

Abstract
The Great Wall(s) of China have been imagined, re-imagined, analysed and re-visited through a variety of media, including written records, visual materials, and literature. The various myths and cultural attachments to the Wall have even coalesced in an interest-based field referred to as Great Wall studies (Waldron 1995, Luo Zhewen 2006, Cheng Dalin 2006, Barmé 2005, Lindesay 2008). A backward-looking gaze at the history of the wall has compelled historians, writers, architects, geographers, and photographers to take on the construction, deterioration, and preservation of it to create a definition of China that serves both Chinese national and foreign interests. The recently recovered archive of the American Great Wall enthusiast William Edgar Geil (1865-1924), housed in a local historical society in Doylestown, Pennsylvania, USA, contains many photographs that add to our understanding of the role of the Wall as artefact, image, and even fetish. Geil's archive captures contemporary Great Wall tensions among amateur/ scholar, photographer/preservationist, and national/international identities.

Keywords: conservation, preservation, Great Wall of China, rephotography, William Edgar Geil, William Lindesay

> 'Here is one relic [The Great Wall] still standing in its original position –
> not transferred to the British Museum.'
> – *Geil 1908: np*

By 1908 many explorers and travellers could think that most of the great relics of the world had indeed been placed under glass in museums around

Ludwig, Carol, Linda Walton, and Yi-Wen Wang (eds), *The Heritage Turn in China: The Reinvention, Dissemination and Consumption of Heritage*. Amsterdam: Amsterdam University Press 2020
DOI: 10.5117/9789462985667_CH04

the world. Notorious archaeologists, tomb robbers and even botanists had collected artefacts from China and other parts of the world and removed them to museum collections in their home countries. Here we take the very familiar, solid, and permanent-seeming Great Wall to examine how it was not removed, but nonetheless taken possession of, by people who ultimately used it to translate China for their own cultural purposes. Great Wall enthusiasts consumed and reimagined the Great Wall in ways that currently influence contemporary meanings of it. Foreigners seeking to distinguish themselves through their association with the Wall used it as a marker of China, the Chinese population, and their own accomplishments, most prominently through writing about and photographing the Wall. Foreign attention to the Great Wall often also included an erasure or minimisation of the Chinese themselves.

In 1909 the American evangelist and adventurer William Edgar Geil (1865-1924) published one of the earliest English language accounts, entitled *The Great Wall of China,* which included his own text and photography. The book documented Geil's trek along the Wall, his impressions of it and the Chinese people he encountered, and his assessment of Chinese culture in relation to his own American Christian identity. Grounded in archival research and in dialogue with critical historicisation of the Great Wall by historians, photographers, and preservationists, this chapter places Geil's work in the context of how the Great Wall has been imagined, re-imagined, and re-visited through a variety of media, with particular attention to photographic records. The fetishisation of the Great Wall includes various myths and extensive cross-cultural attachments to the Wall which have even coalesced in an interest-based field referred to as 'Great Wall studies' and through which Geil's legacy has been revived. The recently recovered archive of William Edgar Geil, housed in a local historical society in Doylestown, Pennsylvania, USA, contains photographs that add layers of meaning to the Wall as artefact and image. This rich archive captures contemporary Great Wall tensions among amateur/scholar, photographer/preservationist, and national/international identities.

Geil's early photographs of the Great Wall and his corresponding text more fully trace the historic consumption of the Great Wall by those whom we might call early non-Chinese 'China Watchers', and puts them in dialogue with some current photographic uses of the Wall. Compared to that of more famous archaeologists such as Aurel Stein (1862-1943) and missionaries such as W.A.P. Martin (1827-1916), the Geil archive expands our lens to include the seemingly unpoliticised observer, enthusiast, and preserver in the complicated picture of heritage. Although mostly forgotten now, Geil was once globally influential and his work fills in gaps left by the more widely recognised chroniclers of the Great Wall. Situated between the age of high imperialism and political revolution in China, his representations reveal an array of foreign uses of the Wall for independent ends, including what ownership over such heritage means both nationally and internationally. From those who identified the Wall as an indication of China's great past, to a marker of the potential of the Chinese, to a modern criticism of environmental neglect, the Wall continues to operate as a fetish that reveals historic stakes in its representations. A backward-looking gaze at the history of the Wall has compelled historians, writers, architects, geographers, and photographers to disseminate their ideas on the construction, deterioration, and preservation of it to create a meaning of China that serves both foreign and Chinese interests.

The chapter is organised to engage thematically with the twisting physicality of the Wall while also marking how past depictions have influenced current interpretations and uses of the imagined Great Wall. It begins with positioning William Edgar Geil among early twentieth century China enthusiasts and continues to historicise the way the Wall was marked as divider and unifier of land and people by foreigners. This is followed by an analysis of the historic perceptions of the Wall, concluding with comparative interpretations of the role photography has played from Geil to William Lindesay (b.1956), founder of Friends of the Great Wall and advocate of conservation and preservation. The conclusion addresses the complicated relationship between different interventions with the Wall and the merging of history and photographic images as they reveal a nuanced understanding of heritage sites and their value.

Geil's preparatory notes and journals do not explain the quotidian details of his Great Wall China trip. We do not know how he decided to take on the challenge of extensive travel in difficult terrain, how he funded the trip, and who facilitated his ability to travel far with delicate and cumbersome equipment, while entirely lacking any Chinese language ability of his own. However, we do know that as with many other foreigners who travelled to China at the time, his way was eased by foreign missionaries such as the renowned W.A.P. Martin who corresponded with and informed Geil's project. As *The Great Wall of China* was his fifth successful foreign adventure book, Geil was by then popular enough to crowd lecture halls around the world when he gave public talks on his travels. These lectures directly linked his explorer's interests with his commitment to Christian evangelical efforts. In his lifetime Geil was quite famous for both his travelling and his religious zeal. In the quotation that begins this chapter, Geil acknowledges the practice of foreign explorers, archaeologists, botanists, and other scientists and adventurers who targeted geographic regions distinct from their own to analyse and dissect. Many of these enthusiastic outsiders supplemented their literary or scientific chronicling of the territories they encountered by returning home with stolen heritage-identified treasures, or in the words of Aurel Stein, '… antiquarian and artistic spoils' (1915: 405). No one took home the Great Wall. But they photographed it, memorialised it, and fetishised it. To some extent, the co-opting of the Great Wall by foreign China watchers and actors of the early twentieth century mirrored the ownership that many other imperialists claimed over treasures such as the Buddhist scriptures at Mogao and chipped off remnants of frescoes there as well as from other now recognised UNESCO World Heritage sites such as the Longmen grottos.

The Great Wall was not transferred out of China, but its meaning and symbolism was manufactured to fit both non-Chinese and Chinese imaginings. This is to say that those enamoured with the idea of the Great Wall participated in a dialogue of global heritage, including and excluding China and the Chinese across historic moments. The Great Wall could be used to represent and share both positive and negative descriptions of the Chinese to non-Chinese audiences, and it could just as well be used to indicate one's appreciation of China to a Chinese audience. One can find both foreign and Chinese purveyors of such appreciation, some of whom appear in this chapter. The Wall could simultaneously give one fame and recognition for approaching it as a foreign explorer who fashioned himself a discoverer, while also justify one's interest in China because it was so great, so old, and so resilient. For Geil, his trek along the Great Wall emphasised his self-styled role as adventurer. It also shrouded his interest in converting the industrious, and in his mind once great, Chinese to Christianity beneath that dominant explorer image in his Great Wall book and lectures. For Geil, the Wall marked the Chinese as worthy of his conversion efforts. Geil was neither the first nor the last to see the Great Wall in symbiotic terms. Earlier, the British Lord Macartney (1737-1806) on his visit to the Qianlong emperor's court in 1793 saw the Wall as evidence of Chinese wisdom, virtuosity, and 'regard for posterity' (Macartney 1962: 113). How Macartney saw the Chinese of the past worked as a foil to his designs toward gaining greater privilege for the British among other foreign traders at Guangzhou. His recognition of the Chinese past could be seen as a way to soften the critical way he assessed Chinese trade practices of the time. Aurel Stein, Mao Zedong, Deng Xiaoping, and William Lindesay all also imagined the Great Wall as a symbol. They wrote and lectured about the Wall and accepted, re-inscribed, or rejected Chinese lore about the Wall while also creating their own self-referential or national significance. From the Jesuits in the Kangxi emperor's court to current myths, the questions and answers about the Wall continue: was it one continuous wall or many? How was it constructed? By whom? Is folklore about women weeping to the extent that their tears excavated the bones of their husbands who laboured at the Wall evidence of workers dying and being buried within the wall? (Tucker 2007: 8). Various observers and scholars engaged with these ideas as either authorities or naysayers. Verity can be fluid if theories such as the visibility of the Wall from space is repeated enough to seem true. Thus, the Wall was used to mean different and sometimes counter imaginings of China, as shown by Arthur Waldron's thorough documentation of the history of perceptions of the Great Wall (Waldron 1983).

The Great Wall has come to mean many things but in its most popular representations it has been used to strengthen a narrator and his or her intentions. For Aurel Stein, his excavations in Central Asia and into China followed along the Great Wall and put him on the map for marking and identifying ruins; Mao Zedong claimed that one is only great if one travels to the Great Wall; and Deng Xiaoping called upon the Chinese people to 'Love China, Rebuild the Great Wall', claiming that it represents 'The Chinese peoples' extraordinary intelligence and untiring spirit' (Spence 2007: xii). While these Great Wall enthusiasts have gone so far as to fetishise the Wall itself as being important beyond its actual structure, the population living near the Wall – perhaps whom we can conceive of as a Great Wall community – are mostly absent from the above narratives. Perhaps they too could be used to satisfy a particular agenda. For example, some critical analyses of conservation efforts seek to call out privileging animals over humans as in the conflict between endangered owls, tree preservation and logging in the North American Pacific Northwest. One could imagine Great Wall communities being used to counter conservation efforts as pressure upon land for population and agriculture are debated. While Great Wall communities have been important sources and resources for Great Wall enthusiasts, they do not appear as equally significant to the Great Wall image related by Wall devotees such as Geil.

Geil's tone of appreciation of the Great Wall as both a structure and natural environment connects to later conservation and preservation efforts to maintain or publicise heritage sites. In fact, Geil hoped that his book would not only inform future historians of the Wall but also somehow aid the 'unconquerable yellow race' (Geil 1909: 8). Using Geil's book as a positive reference, Harvard historian Albert Bushnell Hart, writing in the early twentieth century, noted:

> It has become the fashion to speak slightingly of the wall as a waste of human energy, as an absurd attempt to keep out armies by the sight of a parapet. Travellers, geographers, and military have jeered at a fortification 2,000 miles long, carried over the summits of inaccessible mountains. A day on the end of Shan-hai-kwan brings doubt upon these criticisms (1910: 438).

Hart's views built on Geil's positive assessment of the Wall but also used its structure as a parallel to modern railways such that, according to Hart, 'Every mile of railroad is a new bond to hold China together' (1910: 438). Hart's awareness and articulation of a trend to disparage the Wall speaks to how the structure became a way to pass judgement on a culture, and how that tendency could engender a variety of perceptions and policies. From the Qin to Ming and from Mao to Deng, official involvement with the Wall has mobilised construction, manned the Wall militarily, and subjugated its structural existence to population and development expansion. Geil and others embarked upon image-making of the Wall for various purposes, but they also did slowly craft an ownership of the Wall while not overtly acquiring it. The recently recovered archive of William Edgar Geil has compelled both private efforts at preservation and state efforts at popularising the Great Wall, once again globalising this heritage site.

The Great Wall as History, Heritage, and Myth

> 'The Great Wall is not a Myth.'
> – *Chinese Recorder and Missionary Journal, 1888: 239*

Geil may have been one of the earliest foreigners to fetishise the Great Wall, but he is now being utilised to tap into the current global imagination of the Wall – for independent and international conservation efforts and national heritage representations – once again as a way to trace a history of the Wall to connect the past and present in a constructed continuity. While Geil conceived his edge of the twentieth century view from the Wall to encompass a vision he described as: 'From the end of the wall I can look along it in 3 directions: along it into the past, along it into the future, along it in the present' (Geil 1908), Arthur Waldron (1983, 1990) and others have critically deconstructed such positioning of foreign and Chinese internalising visions from the Wall.

While the walls that were built from the time of the Qin Dynasty (221-206 BCE) to the much later Ming (1366-1644 CE) previously have been regarded as one Great Wall, it is widely known now that it is in fact a series of walls and wall-like structures of varying materials and connectedness. For the purposes of this chapter, we will refer to the discontinuous wall construction over vast stretches of time as the Great Wall or the Wall to indicate that this current reference is to the imaginings of the Wall, not necessarily to a specific section or origin. This must include a consideration of periodisation since in dynastic times mobilisation of labour to construct and monitor the Wall primarily engaged the local population in the development of the structure. Its meaning was varied as well and Waldron convincingly argues that Ming era 'ruins of ... fortifications ..., when properly interpreted, [are] a record, in earth and stone, of changes in that dynasty's military strength, strategic thinking, and even palace politics' (Waldron 1990: 55). Therefore, the Wall embeds information of varying historical depths. William Lindesay's recently released book, *The Great Wall in 50 Objects*, further attests to the ways in which the Great Wall contains history in and around it.

As an imagined entity, including that of myth, the Great Wall was considered by many foreigners to be an example of Chinese ingenuity, and also proof of a culturally associated tendency for cruelty toward labourers. As a boundary, it provided evidence of what was referred to as Chinese xenophobia and yet also a connector among border peoples. Most recently the deterioration of the Great Wall indicates to both foreign and domestic audiences the Chinese government's lack of responsibility toward the environment. As with global interest in other awe-inspiring sites such as the Egyptian pyramids, questions about the construction of the Wall inspired notoriety. For example, legends concerning the poor treatment of the workers and builders of the Wall represented to foreign observers China's despotic disinterest in the plight of its subjects. Furthermore, the Wall was perceived by foreigners solely as a means to keep others out, providing yet another negative image of China as a despotic and inward-looking empire. Beyond stereotypes of China as being uniquely xenophobic or disparaging toward 'foreigners', the Wall, according to Waldron, symbolises the opposite. '... the Wall ... is the product of particular ideas and circumstances, and that these in no way constitute an exhaustive or even unique definition of Chineseness' (Waldron 1990: 191).

Lately and in direct contrast to previous interpretations, Great Wall researchers mentioned above (Waldron, etc.) argue that the Wall was and is more of a bridge connecting people over geographic space and culture than a mere demarcation. Members of the Wall community consistently interacted with people across the Wall and the settled Chinese populations and nomads from the steppes traded among themselves. People around the Wall appeared more interested in trade and relationships with nomads than with their military service duties at stages along the Wall (Waldron 1990: 150). Currently, the people of either the Great Wall community or those connected to existing Wall remnants through commuting across the Great Wall region are drawn into a parallel discussion of environmental impact on the heritage site. Recent restoration efforts focused on the Great Wall intersect with global criticism of Chinese industrialisation, alluding to an idea of mismanagement such as is argued in global news reports focusing on Chinese pollution and its effects upon the population and structures both. In the arena of modern preservation, William Lindesay and his 'International Friends of the Great Wall' society recreate the bridging element of the Wall by making it a site for people, although not necessarily Great Wall locals, to come together for environmental clean-up (WildWall Experiences 2017).

Perceptions of the Great Wall

Primary source accounts tell us just as much about the person making the record as they do about the topic itself. Interpretations of the Great Wall between the early twentieth century and today reflect the great attention paid to China by the outside world because of epochal events taking place there. William Edgar Geil's Great Wall trip of 1908 was squeezed in between two significant events in Chinese history: the Boxer uprising of 1900 and the end of the Manchu Qing Dynasty in 1911. Geil was thus producing representations of China at a time when most of the world was watching as China experienced drastic change. Geil's focus on the Great Wall followed a long history of interest in the Wall, and his perceptions reflected how the Wall marked both the Chinese and the narrator, in this case, Geil himself. For Geil, the Wall was intimately connected to his ideas about China and the Chinese. Before Geil even had the opportunity to engage directly with any Great Wall community, he did consider 'The one "wonder" of the East still stands but a greater "wonder" is the multitudes of men who live south of the Wall and around the wall', as he recorded in his notes before his trek began (Geil 1908: np). Furthermore, he posited that the Chinese no longer had any practical use for the Wall. According to Geil, the Wall was not the main wonder, but rather the Chinese nation and its potential Christian transformation was the marvel of note (Geil 1908: np). Geil had reimagined the significance of the Great Wall onto Chinese propensity for Christianity.

Geil's own role in relation to the historic Wall included fashioning himself the first 'white' person to walk the length of the Great Wall, a claim difficult to substantiate. The Kangxi emperor (r. 1661-1722) had much earlier instructed Jesuits at his court to map 'the Great Walls' for him in 1708 (Clarke 2006: 227). The extent of their exploration is not documented but as a cartographic assignment it seems the intention was to comprehensively represent the extent of the Wall, necessitating Jesuit travel along the Wall. This is significant because not only does it counter the idea that the Ming era fortifications were at once solely connected to Ming, i.e., ethnic Han Chinese political legitimacy, but also that the Manchu Qing were not interested in the border structure that they overcame in their conquering of Ming China in 1644. In a certain sense, then, the absence of references to past experiences of other religious and scientific predecessors to Geil reminds us that constructed continuities in history have a counterpart in constructed omissions as well. Geil did not seem aware of this earlier Jesuit-Qing enterprise although he and most other foreigners in China understood that much linguistic and cultural knowledge of China arrived in Europe through the writings of the early Jesuits. The Kangxi mapping of the Great Wall did not include mention of Great Wall populations although presumably people living along the Wall served the same purpose as they did for Stein, Geil, and William Lindesay as well: founts of information about and directions for Wall research, workers to support exploration, and the sources of local historical knowledge and memory. While the Jesuits of the seventeenth and eighteenth centuries did identify themselves with both their proselytising efforts and scientific work in China, Geil's approach to China switched the emphasis to targeting the Great Wall for a photographic and book project and therefore emphasised his adventurer/explorer status over his otherwise dominant religious work. One hundred years on, Lindesay connected with Geil's project but again shifted his photographic emphasis to historicise the status of the Wall to promote a more gentle approach to conservation. It should be noted that despite Lindesay's origins he does live in China and work along the Wall – a practice distinct from that of other foreign Wall enthusiasts.

As mentioned above, explorers before Geil considered the Great Wall proof of essentialist Chinese industry in complicated ways, just as people then and now refer to early Chinese inventions and discoveries as part of a static past. The narrative proceeds as thus: how could they build such an impressive Wall but not continue to build things in which foreign observers could see themselves reflected? It is as if the Great Wall went the way of gunpowder and the compass: great ideas with potential not harnessed and utilised in ways that Europeans and Americans considered valuable or modern. Travelers to China claimed people living near the Wall lacked a corresponding appreciation of the structure along the lines of what foreign, mostly western, observers embraced. The above cited volume of the *Chinese Recorder and Missionary Review* included in its section refuting the Wall as myth a comment on Great Wall locals. The Reverend J.A. Roberts wrote, 'Of the Chinese who live close by the Great Wall … there are two classes of people who never know it or see it, namely those who are blind and those who are very busy …' (Roberts 1888: 239). This idea of a lack of appreciation or significant ability to preserve has guided foreign capture of antiquities all over the world, including from China. Furthermore, when the Wall is not referred to with awe matching that of outsiders, it is an example of Chinese suffering going all the way back to the Qin and the forced labour that, it is asserted, left bodies alongside it. Countless sources mention how the construction of the Great Wall cost lives: from Hart to the China scholar Julia Lovell to Lindesay and beyond, the 'human cost' of the Wall is mentioned without reference to any sources that could tell us more. Therefore, the Wall is contaminated with the tyrannical rule of the Qin and anything related to that era having equalled suffering (Tucker 2007: 8). In addition, while soldiers were militarily invested in the Wall and lived near it in either isolation or confrontation, other Great Wall inhabitants arrived as a form of punishment when they were exiled to the borderlands of the Great Wall. These characterisations and mischaracterisations are summed up more recently in a 1996 edition of the Lonely Planet guidebook that proclaimed, 'Oddly, the depiction of the wall as an object of great beauty is a bizarre one. It's really a symbol of tyranny, like the Berlin Wall used to be' (Taylor, Storey & Goncharoff 1996: 226). The Wall, like other heritage sites embraced by global interest, is hence double-edged. It draws attention and admiration while also generating hostility. The Great Wall heritage site has historically been reimagined as a great accomplishment, an emblem of stagnancy, or a protective talisman.

Geil's Uses of the Great Wall

Geil has become a catalyst for both international and Chinese reimaginings of the Great Wall. Geil was originally an evangelist who later presented himself as an adventurer and photographer. His 1908 trek along the Wall established him beyond his religious affiliations. The Wall became a fetish as a signifier through which Geil drew attention to himself as an originator of photographing the extent of the Wall, claiming sole experience trekking its length and thereby establishing his seriousness as an explorer by his attention to the artefact. He claimed this Chinese heritage site. His desire to leave his work for later historians has been realised through current interest in the photography and preservation of the Wall. Geil has been used to link current conservation efforts of recording and preserving the Wall through and among William Lindesay's 'International Friends of the Great Wall', along with Lindesay's rephotography of Geil's work (see below) in *The Great Wall Revisited* and a further parallel text to Geil's theme and images in *The Great Wall of Two Williams* (published only in Chinese to date). Lindesay's use of Geil's book and photographs to establish an independent foreigner interest in the Great Wall is further expanded by CCTV's new mini-series on the Great Wall, which also uses Geil's photography and channels his enthusiasm (Fuchs 2015, CCTV.com English).

Geil's appreciation of the Wall was also an appreciation of the Chinese and their capacity for Christianity, which further links him to the earlier Jesuits. The Jesuits also battled with considering the Chinese a population that was both worthy of saving and in need of saving. Geil, while positive about the Chinese in ways that were unusual among Americans at the time, nonetheless got a lot wrong. For him, the Great Wall fell into the category of ingenuity, and he breathlessly describes the standard early accomplishments of the Chinese (as he praises the first Qin emperor for liberalism, but would like to omit the bloodthirstiness). His tentative steps into the footprints of established China travellers revealed his rather superficial knowledge. His misunderstanding of the Qin Dynasty and Qin Shihuangdi was roundly criticised in reviews of *The Great Wall* (J.T. 1909: 220). Nonetheless, his enthusiasm, approach and photography were indeed lasting and important as a starting point in recording the Wall. In the published book, Geil saw and represented the Wall as very much a marker of separation – of land and races – and he thought of Christianity as a unifier, 'The Wall is the sign of separation, the Cross of union' (Geil 1909: 6).

For Geil, the Great Wall represented the past of Chinese achievement that he felt needed to be tapped into, as something historically modern and indicative of what the Chinese were capable of accomplishing. In some ways he was using the Great Wall to sell the Chinese to an American Christian public. He argued that they were on the verge of a major transformation and their historical achievements were evidence of what great things they would do. This is only slightly unusual for his time period as China at the beginning of the twentieth century was a rapidly changing place, with activists in China and the Chinese diaspora developing new theories of nationalism and independence. It is his passion for documenting through photography and to some extent engaging with history that sets him apart and brings him into the discourse of conservation.

Despite problems with Geil's text, as was determined by reviews of his book at the time, and despite his use of the Great Wall to propel himself into the arena of popular exploration, his photographic record now serves to promote a less invasive form of conservation as compared to judgmental outside critiques of conservation efforts currently underway. Maintaining and preserving historic and heritage sites can be tricky in that it requires an action upon spaces potentially unstable. Considering the diverse environment across the Great Wall, uncontrollable factors such as the sands of the Gobi greatly affect what can and cannot be done to preserve it. Visitors to the Great Wall, whatever their intentions, contribute to its deterioration as well. Heavily visited areas, such as Badaling, have garbage concerns and sections not as consistently maintained suffer from physical use. On the other hand, historic and comparative photography does not necessarily involve chipping away at the Wall, walking all over it, or digging around it. It merely marks the course of time and people along the Wall as a way to show the value of protecting it. This essay began with Geil's remark that the Wall hasn't been taken out of China and put in a museum. Geil did not bring home spoils of exploration like others and while his trek along the Great Wall likely had an impact upon it, his virtual hold on the Wall did less damage. His photographic record has been re-used and distributed by William Lindesay for another photography-based effort at virtual, not physical, control of the Wall.

Rephotography

William Lindesay, founder of the 'International Friends of the Great Wall' uses rephotography to trace the lack of deterioration, and stages of deterioration over time and as a 'powerful conservation-awareness tool' (Lindesay 2008: 89). Rephotography involves researching and following historic photographs as if they were footprints and photographing the same image or site again. It is a way to mark and share historic change along the Wall in a less invasive form of consumption and reinvention. (Lindesay 2008: 48-50). Lindesay has gathered a trove of early photographs of both popular and distant sections of the Wall in which William Geil's photography is significantly represented. Lindesay's work reveals the unsurprising fact that parts of the Wall less visited by anyone, archaeologists, scientists, government representatives, or tourists, is better preserved. As his photographs take us from the western reach of the Han Wall at Yumenguan, east along sections of the Ming Wall toward

Shanhaiguan, we can trace the positive and negative effects of interest and attention to the Wall (Lindesay 2008). While deterioration due to wind and sand has marked the western sections observed even by Stein in 1907, it also appears that government intervention inspired the fencing of parts of the Wall in the farther western and less visited sections where there are few communities or officials to regularly oversee it. Indeed, adherence to the barriers to the sites remains at the discretion of visitors and might be of little effect. Lindesay himself breached a fenced-in section of the Wall to have himself photographed in the same pose as the famous explorer and archaeologist Aurel Stein, who was photographed at the same location in 1907 (Lindesay 2008: 73). More involved preservation has been pursued at the Qilian Gorge through private and governmental investment, which funded a breakwater to stem water deterioration of that section of the Wall as well. Hence Lindesay's work is also documenting conservation progress in addition to the toll taken by both nature and humans on the Wall and its environs (Lindesay 2008: 92). As Lindesay continues to carry us along the Wall, using Geil's photography as a guide, moving eastward toward greater population centres near the Wall, the effects of and contradictions over awareness, conservation, and human change are further exposed. Electricity lines, expressways, and even agricultural development interact with Wall preservation and conservation. Lindesay is careful in his documentation and characterisation of recently established wheat cultivation at one of the better-preserved sites of rammed-earth style sections of the Wall. The possibility of increased agricultural production for the local population and, as Lindesay notes, the potential that such farming could counter sand winds and sand drifts and their corrosive effect, also has contributed to tensions surrounding the Wall. Standing water and increased populations of wildlife such as rodents is negatively impacting the Wall there as well (Lindesay 2008: 110). The Wall is now a tool measuring the effects of change as either progress or regression.

As with previous explorers of the Wall, Lindesay utilises local knowledge for information and lore about it. He mentions, 'as always, [I] started in a village, talking to one elder' but otherwise local communities and their sense of 'their' Wall, is absent (Lindesay 2008: 124). From Aurel Stein and his Uighur guides and translators to Geil's native support workers and those he photographed to indicate the scale of the Wall, to the local knowledge Lindesay seeks, overwhelmingly the engagement with people of the Great Wall is consistently liminal to the productions of Great Wall documenters. This is not to say that the actions of Great Wall explorers did not put them in dialogue with the Chinese population. Geil hired translators and used his experiences in China and elsewhere to bridge his own interests in evangelism with his home and the world. The motivations for Geil's work and explanations for his lack of overt, even-handed, positive engagement with Great Wall communities, is absent from his text. Nonetheless, he documented his exploration of the Great Wall and left a trail for conservationists to follow. Lindesay has spearheaded local, national, and international interest and activism over the cause of Wall conservation. As with the previously mentioned Great Wall enthusiasts, Lindesay involves local populations in his conservation efforts, such as the clean-up event. As to how Great Wall communities are impacted by conservation, there is less attention given as indicated by the tension between agricultural needs for communities around the Wall and preservation concerns. Since much conservation involves the Chinese government, it too intervenes in the way larger efforts fail to consider local needs. In at least some instances officials have sought neither expert advice nor local responses to rebuilding sections of the Wall (Barmé 2005). Again, there is some continuity to the omission of either Great Wall communities or the needs and attitudes of Great Wall dwellers in both explorer and conservation accounts of the Wall. The other side of this continuity is the tone of historical figures such as Geil, indicating across time that populations living near portions of the Great Wall did not appreciate the significance of the structures (Geil 1909: 45).

Preservation, Publicity, and Profit

The funding required for preservation complicates the representation of efforts to maintain the Great Wall and to what end(s). Just as in past eras, leadership across the world is as capable of promoting national heritage as it is to destroying or neglecting it. While Deng Xiaoping might have evoked the Great Wall in order to articulate once again the development of the Chinese nation in relation to its past, actual attention to the Wall in the form of tourism is potentially dangerous.

In the case of the Great Wall, publicising heritage sites for tourism while bringing in revenue also brings wear and tear and abuse. As noted by Lindesay's photographs, the far western reaches of the Wall are better preserved. Rebuilding according to international UNESCO standards helps protect while also drawing attention to sites on the part of tourists, historians, explorers, archaeologists, and so on, who can continue to participate in the documenting of the Wall. But the in between – either chronologically or geographically – leaves room for vulnerable sections to disappear. Geographic proximity to large industrial regions, although not highly attractive tourist areas, seems to mark also the more vulnerable areas of the Wall. It is easy to make claims about policies of destruction; Lindesay argues that both the Great Leap Forward and the Cultural Revolution led to destruction of the Great Wall, but he does not provide photographic evidence or reference any documentation (Lindesay 2008: 46). This is not to say that those events did not involve Great Wall damage, but it does appear that most of the damage to the Wall happened even before Geil took his photographs. The period before the naming of the Wall as a heritage site is another time marker for either simple deterioration or poorly orchestrated attempts at renovation as opposed to restoration. In order to preserve the Wall, it also has to be sold as worthy of the cost and effort.

Considering that rephotography can spread awareness through a medium that we are accustomed to treating as evidence, it can potentially reinforce the different options for preservation and conservation to promote the most responsible efforts available. In that way, Lindesay's book is indeed a gentler type of intervention than previous actions by outsiders on China's history and heritage. But exposing the Wall's changes in this way can also draw the attention of globalisation actors, which further complicates not only maintaining heritage sites but the role of industrial impact.

If expressways and trains have been diverted under or around the Great Wall, we understand the influence of the sort of attention Lindesay and others have exerted. To some degree, it sets a standard for future industrialisation in the region. The 'International Friends of the Great Wall' collaborated on Lindesay's project with the Beijing Administration of Cultural Heritage and could be able to further interact with Great Wall communities affected by both government policies and preservation initiatives. Through Lindesay's work for Shell Companies regarding a West East gas pipeline, he was able to engage with their social and environmental advisor (Lindesay 2008: 279). This has the mark of both environmental preservation and Great Wall conservation while at the same time, considering the track record of the gas industry elsewhere, disastrous. The fact that the Wall covers such a vast distance means that development inevitably affects it and major enterprises such as fuel pipelines are going to both disrupt it and potentially create a stake for companies like Shell to take an interest in re-creating their reputation, however cynical that might sound. As Frynas and numerous others have noted, fuel companies have been wreaking havoc on the environment for decades, but they have also created corporate departments that appear to attend to social impact studies as well. This has increasingly become an issue in major news organs globally. Social impact departments of multinational corporations do not appear to be able to tip the balance from destructiveness to conservation or preservation (Frynas 2005).

Conclusion

> 'All these Wall-centred activities seem quite natural to most participants: the
> cult of the Wall had the authenticity of the dragon dance ...'
>
> – *Waldron 1990: 225*

The image and silhouette of the Great Wall is practically everywhere. As others have shown, the image has come to represent China itself. As a structure it has been used to define Chinese characteristics, as a comparison to its past; and for outsiders the Wall has brought fame and a kind of legitimacy. To those seeking natural resources, the Wall gets in the way of extraction. Preservationists and conservationists have followed the same path of past explorers and not unlike the adventures of Great Wall enthusiasts of history, the process of conservation carries risks. Conservation, like exploration and archaeology, can preserve heritage but it can also displace communities and privilege larger interests over everyday life experiences and needs. Private, international, and non-profit interests can coincide or conflict with governmental goals or the needs of local communities.

The resurrection of the Geil archive has altered Geil's amateur and questionable historical analysis of the Wall and his unconfirmed local configuration as 'The first white man to traverse the Great Wall'. That moniker has fallen away, to focus instead on his usefulness as a relevant marker of historic international appreciation of China and its Wall. Recently, CCTV has begun a mini-series on the Great Wall and will devote an episode to Geil and his photographic record (Fuchs 2015). If interest and appreciation of national heritage sites brought a desire to physically remove artefacts from their origins, the photographic tradition obviates the need for possessive ownership. Geil's materials have set a precedent for individual foreign appreciation linked to the conservation and preservation advocated by the 'International Friends of the Great Wall. Lindesay's efforts at conservation and preservation accomplish more than attempts to fund appreciation through tourism-directed renovation. Yet promotion of heritage sites that seeks to draw attention, even for funding to restore them, can founder on the tendency to fetishise. As population needs increase alongside the desire for increased extraction of natural resources, these heritage sites run the risk of catching the gaze of powerful profit-seekers and their version of consuming the Wall. This is to say that accepting financial support from profit-driven sources will detract from the mission to preserve. It thus runs counter to the non-invasive visual conservation effort revealed through the photographic record and its complementary rephotography; the revelations of the visual changes in the Wall demand redress. It need not attract dangerous attention. Hence, Lindesay's photographic compilation book spreads information about the heritage site but he cannot control the effects of the tourism and industrial interest that could follow.

In the end, so much has been written and said about the Wall. Whether it is rendered as Great Wall, or Great Walls, our sense of it cannot be anything other than saturation. And it is that saturation of image and experience that calls attention to the juxtaposition of awe and absence in historic encounters between foreigners, the Chinese population, and the Wall. Its future, and that of other historic sites might depend on interventions that represent and show the significance of preservation and conservation, rather than those that tell and dictate. In the most universal and perhaps generous analysis of the uses of the Great Wall, China scholar Jonathan Spence, in his introduction to Chen Changfen's photograph collection book, argues for the potential of the Great Wall to give meaning to humanity (2007: x). While the Great Wall itself, as we have seen, has almost universal referential significance, perhaps our view can be widened to encompass not only the structure but also its environs and the populations who engage with it – the Great Wall communities and all the visitors, saviours, and commentators of the Great Wall. This is distinct from China-centred, or China-focused uses of the Wall, and reminds us that heritage sites have a multiplicity of meanings for diverse audiences and stakeholders, both domestic and global.

References

Anonymous (1888), *Chinese Recorder and Missionary Journal* 19 (6): 239.

Barmé, G. (2005), 'The Great Wall of China: Tangible, Intangible and Destructible' *China Heritage Newsletter* 1 (March) [Online]. Available from: http://www.chinaheritagequarterly.org/features.php?searchterm=001_greatwall.inc&issue=001 (accessed 12 August 2017).

CCTV.com English [Online]. Available from: http://english.cntv.cn/program/cultureexpress/20121019/103245.shtml (accessed 18 November 2017).

Cheng, D. (2006), 'The Great Tourist Icon' in C. Roberts and G. Barmé (eds.), *The Great Wall of China*, 26-32. Sydney: Powerhouse Publishing.

Clarke, J. (2006), 'Mapping for the Kingdom', in C. Roberts and G. Barmé (eds.), *The Great Wall of China*, 221-227. Sydney: Powerhouse Publishing.

Frynas, J. (2005), 'The False Developmental Promise of Corporate Social Responsibility: Evidence from Multinational Oil Companies', *International Affairs* 81(3): 1468-2346.

Fuchs, C. (2015), 'Walking the Great Wall: Long Lost Papers Reveal Pennsylvania Man's Place in History', 20 August 2015. [Online]. Available from: The Great Wall Man's Place in History' [Online]. http://www.nbcnews.com/news/asian-america/ was-man-first-walk-great-wall-china-n405421 (accessed 12 August 2017).

Geil, W. (1908), 'Notes on Great Wall'. Unpaginated manuscript. Doylestown Historical Society Archives, Doylestown, Pennsylvania, USA.

Geil, W. (1909), *The Great Wall*. New York: Sturgis and Walton.

Hart, A. (1910), 'The Great Wall of China', *Bulleting of the American Geographical Society* 42(6): 438-441.

Lindesay, W. (2008), *The Great Wall Revisited*. Cambridge, MA: Harvard University Press.

Macartney, G. (1962), *An Embassy to China; Being the journal Kept by Lord Macartney During his Embassy to the Emperor Ch'ien-lung, 1793-1794*. London: Longmans.

Luo, Z. (2006), 'The Great Walls of China' in C. Roberts and G. Barmé (eds.), *The Great Wall of China*, 42-51. Sydney: Powerhouse Publishing.

Spence, J. (2007), 'Introduction', in A. Tucker (ed.), *The Great Wall of China: Photographs by Chen Changfen*, x-xiii. New Haven: Yale University Press.

T, J. (1909),'Great Wall of China', Nature 8 (2095): 220-221.

Taylor, C., Storey R., and Goncharoff, N. (1996), *Lonely Planet China: A Travel Survival Kit*. N.p.: Lonely Planet Books.

Tucker, A. (2007), *The Great Wall of China: Photographs by Chen Changfen*. New Haven: Yale University Press.

Waldron, A. (1983), 'The Problem of the Great Wall of China', *Harvard Journal of Asiatic Studies* 43(2): 643-663.

Waldron, A. (1990), *The Great Wall of China: from History to Myth*. Cambridge: Cambridge University Press.

Waldron, A. (1995), 'Scholarship and Patriotic Education: The Great Wall Conference, 1994', *The China Quarterly* 143 (Sep): 844-850

Wild Wall Experiences (2016), 'Saving the Wall' [Online]. Available from: http:// www.wildwall.com/saving-the-wall (accessed 12 August 2017).

About the Author

KRISTIN BAYER teaches Asian history at Marist College, USA, concentrating on representation and global revolution. Her research interests include representations of China and the Chinese in relation to commodities and consumption. She is currently studying nineteenth-century photography in, and of, China.

Section 2

Creating Identities: Constructing Pasts,

Disseminating Heritage

5 Contemporary Fabrication of Pasts and the Creation of New Identities?

Open-Air Museums and Historical Theme Parks in the UK and China

Carol Ludwig and Yi-Wen Wang

Abstract

This chapter examines the selective usage of history, relics and practice to reconstruct specific versions of the past. The open-air Beamish Museum in Durham, UK and the historical theme parks in Hangzhou and Kaifeng, China are used as comparative case studies to unpack first, how 'heritage' is conceptualised in each context, and second, how particular versions of the past are selected, (re)invented, disseminated and consumed for contemporary purposes. Set within a theoretical framework of 'living heritage' and an analytical framework of the overlapping themes of authenticity, identity and national pride, tourism and education, the chapter examines the different ways in which the appropriation of cultural heritage takes place at each site. In doing so, we draw attention to the disparate interpretations of conservation practice and the idea of 'living heritage' in the UK and China and debate their continued relevance in the contemporary heritage discourse.

Keywords: living heritage, perceived authenticity, open-air museums, historical theme parks

Introduction

The purpose of this chapter is to examine the selective usage of history, relics and practice to reconstruct specific versions of the past. The open-air Beamish Museum in Durham, UK and the Song Dynasty theme parks in

Ludwig, Carol, Linda Walton, and Yi-Wen Wang (eds), *The Heritage Turn in China: The Reinvention, Dissemination and Consumption of Heritage*. Amsterdam: Amsterdam University Press 2020
DOI: 10.5117/9789462985667_CH05

Hangzhou and Kaifeng, China are used as comparative case studies to unpack first, how 'heritage' is conceptualised in each context; and second, how particular versions of the past are selected, (re)invented, disseminated and consumed for contemporary purposes. Using the over-lapping themes of authenticity, the (re)construction of identities, tourism and education as an analytical framework, the different ways in which the appropriation of cultural heritage takes place at each site is critically examined. In do-ing so, we draw attention to the disparate interpretations of conservation practice and the idea of 'living heritage' in the UK and China and debate their continued relevance in the contemporary heritage discourse. The theoretical context within which these interpretations are positioned is briefly introduced below.

Theoretical Framework

From the birth of the conservation ethic during the nineteenth century in Europe (Delafons 1997) 'Western' interpretations of heritage and approaches to its identification, selection and subsequent management have experienced relative long-term stability (Hudson & James, 2007). Yet over the last two decades the wider heritage discourse has steadily evolved and experienced nuances (Ludwig 2016) aligning with wider international trends in heritage thought (see UNESCO 2003; Bonnici 2009; Meyer-Bisch 2009; CoE 2011 and Sykes & Ludwig 2015). These modifications to the heritage discourse largely relate to notions of inclusiveness, widening not only the definition of heritage itself to include those more intangible aspects, but also widening public participation in its management. Parallel to this shift, many countries have simultaneously witnessed a visible growth in the levels of general public interest in heritage and *social* history (evidenced in the UK by increases in National Trust annual visitor numbers (National Trust 2012), and the popularity of television programmes such as 'The Secret History of Our Streets' and 'Who do you think you are?', for example. Within this evolving context, there are three key approaches to heritage management that warrant particular attention. These include: the material-based approach (which reflects the long-standing principles of Western-based conservation), the values-based approach (which expands on these traditional principles), and the living heritage approach (which challenges the well-established principles of the former two approaches [Poulios 2014]), discussed in more detail below.

Material-based Approach

Originating in Western Europe, the material-based approach to heritage management is often described as the 'conventional approach' (Poulios 2014: 17) and is characterised by Smith (2006) as the 'Authorised Heritage Discourse' or AHD. The AHD has been criticised for revolving around 'materiality and the fabric of the past' and focuses exclusively 'upon processes of designating, listing and registering various "parts" of the historic environment selected by experts as worthy of protection' (Waterton & Smith 2008: 199; DCMS 2003: 10-11). In privileging the physical fabric of the built heritage, this approach has also been criticised for discrediting and silencing alternative conceptualisations of heritage that sit firmly outside this mainstream, tangible-focused interpretation. Consequently, the material-based approach has faced some degree of criticism, particularly from ethnic and minority groups, who seek to 'make visible plural and more subjective contemporary representations of heritage' (Ludwig 2016: 811). As a result of such criticism, the conventional conservation orthodoxy has been challenged to acknowledge the notion that heritage becomes heritage because it is valued as such; immutable intrinsic value is not merely found within the physical fabric of a building.

Values-based Approach

Unlike the material-based approach, the values-based approach focuses on 'the values that society, consisting of various stakeholder groups, ascribes to heritage' (Poulios 2014: 18). Stemming from the Burra Charter (ICOMOS 1999) and adapting to further developments such as the adoption of the Convention for the Safeguarding of Intangible Cultural Heritage (UNESCO 2003) and the Framework Convention on the Value of Cultural Heritage for Society ('Faro convention' 2005), the values-based approach has developed and been advocated internationally (Poulios 2014). While the values-based approach clearly provides the opportunity for a more inclusive understanding of heritage to be applied during decision-making, such an approach is more frequently observed in nations where indigenous and minority communities have vocalised their discontent at the established material-based approach often adopted by state authorities representing majority populations (Smith & Waterton 2009). Despite the powerful rhetoric of the values-based approach, the reality of its implementation, particularly in Western Europe, has been negligible (Sykes and Ludwig 2015; Ludwig 2016). Indeed, when the values-based approach is acknowledged in the UK, attempts are made to merely *shoe-horn* its principles into the deep-rooted, conventional material-based approach operating in conservation practice. In attempting to combine the two approaches, the initial openness and inclusivity sought by understanding heritage values is swiftly diluted due to the restrictions and constraints of the material-based approach (such as the need for tangible evidence, authenticity and scientific fact to validate heritage claims). Such limitations, however, appear less relevant in the living heritage approach; an approach primarily observed outside the legal frameworks of conservation management.

Living Heritage Approach

Living heritage is an approach that is more concerned with 'continuity' and in particular the continuity of a community's connection with heritage '... expressed through (traditional) knowledge, management systems, and maintenance practices; and the continuous process of evolving tangible and intangible heritage expressions in response to changing circumstances' (Poulios 2014: 21). In this regard, a living heritage approach does not necessarily aim to preserve the physical fabric of buildings but instead sees the value of the heritage to be the (intangible) connection between the community and their heritage (Wijesuriya 2005; Poulios 2014). Indeed, living heritage places the emphasis on people. It advocates that 'no matter how different pasts are produced, accessed or consumed, connecting with them is always an activity that is rooted in the present' (Ludwig 2016: 812). As such, living heritage focuses not just on the past (or future generations) but crucially, on the present. According to UNESCO, 'intangible cultural heritage' can also be referred to as 'living heritage' or 'living culture' (UNESCO 2017), and intangible cultural heritage, they argue, 'refers to the practices, representations, expressions, knowledge and skills handed down from generation to generation'. Like Massey (1995), they advocate that this form of heritage plays a particularly fundamental role in legitimising and mobilising current identities, providing communities with a sense of belonging that is continuously recreated in response to their environment (UNESCO 2017). Poulios (2014: 30) however, underlines a key difference between the two terms highlighting that unlike 'intangible heritage', 'living heritage' crucially 'embraces both tangible *and* intangible heritage' [emphasis added]. The concept is not particularly new in the UK, referring mainly to special events and attractions outside the formal/legal heritage management process. Indeed, several events are regularly advertised as such, for example craft fairs and country shows (see Living Heritage Events (2017) for instance), which often include an exhibition of reproduction/replica or restored heritage objects showcased by costumed demonstrators. The appropriation of heritage for entertainment value, however, has received much scholarly criticism, mostly stemming from the heritage industry critique of the 1980s, discussed below.

Disneyfication and the Heritage Industry Critique

A central aspect of the material-based approach to heritage is its concern for authenticity, objective fact and truth. The move towards the *consumption* of heritage in 1980s Britain was therefore heavily criticised for losing the real, authentic sense of heritage and thus damaging its integrity. Historians Patrick Wright (1985) and Robert Hewison (1987) led the critique against heritage in England through their respective publications, 'On Living in an Old Country' (1985) and 'The Heritage Industry: Britain in a Climate of Decline' (1987). The critique was primarily aimed at the economic commodi-fication and 'Disneyfication' of mass heritage tourism (Handler & Saxton 1988; Waitt 2000; Choay 2001), which led to what was considered a 'false' depiction of the past. Hewison (1987: 139) defined the heritage industry as:

> ... a set of imprisoning walls upon which we project a superficial image of a false past, simultaneously turning our backs on the reality of history, and incapable of moving forward because of the absorbing fantasy before us.

The idea that heritage was being manufactured as a bogus commodity be-came a concern echoed by other scholars, leading to the rise of phrases such as the Disneyfication or McDonaldisation of heritage for tourists (Smith 2006; Lowenthal 1985) and derogatory exclamations that, '[...] Britain has been turned into one big theme park' (Lammy 2006: 67). Such criticisms insisted that the commercialisation of reproduction heritage was inauthentic, lacked integrity and sanitised and/or simplified the historical messages of the past. The concept of authenticity, applied globally, is however context-specific and subject to diverse interpretations. The Nara Document on Authenticity of 1994 (1995) for instance, defines authenticity as 'original and subsequent characteristics of the cultural heritage' (Article 9, xxii), and even the 1964 Venice Charter expects the test of authenticity to be applied by individual countries, within the framework of their respective culture and traditions (ICOMOS 1965). This provides space for negotiation and adaptation. After joining the Convention Concerning the Protection of the World Cultural and Natural Heritage in 1985, China recognised and applied the concept of authenticity (*yuanzhenxing* 原真性, literally 'original/real, trustworthy/

nature') to heritage conservation practice (Zhu 2013). A critical question for the Chinese case in the interpretation of authenticity related to 'whether or not the *original* state is essential' (Zhu 2013: 189, emphasis added). Liang Sicheng (1901-1972), a pioneering figure in the preservation and conservation of Chinese architecture put forward the notion of 'restoring the old as it was' (Zhu 2013: 189), however transparency about contemporary additions and restored heritage (new 'old' things) was considered good practice (ICOMOS 1965) and a marrying of these ideas can be observed across China. More recently, notions of 'experiential' (or 'existential') authenticity have further complicated understandings of the term (Wang 1999). Such interpretations of authenticity suggest that one's *experience* of the heritage should be original, real and trustworthy (see Zhu 2013), rather than the originality of the tangible objects themselves or the environment within which such objects are placed. Such diverse and contrasting understandings of a core concept, therefore, raise questions as to the role that open-air museums in the UK and historical theme parks in China (created for people to experience heritage and to serve both educational and entertainment purposes) have played in sustaining the connection between people and their heritage and thus ensuring continuity with the past. The following sections examine and compare an open-air museum founded in England during the 1970s and two historical theme parks opened during the 1990s in China. In doing so, this chapter seeks to understand how the past is selected, (re)invented, disseminated by the creators and/or suppliers of the tourism industries or dictated by consumers' demands (which can also be created); and how heritage is conceptualised in these Disneyfied, often fabricated, fairylands.

Case Study 1: Beamish Museum in Durham, UK

Great Britain, and the Northeast of England in particular, pioneered agricultural developments, especially in livestock breeding as early as the 1820s, but the region is better known internationally for its role in the Industrial Revolution. Indeed, the Northeast of England, now underperforming compared with the UK overall and consequently suffering from comparatively high unemployment rates and low average income brackets (Tighe 2016), once led the world in the industrial production of coal, lead, iron, chemicals, glass pottery and textiles (Beamish Museum 2014). Toward the end of the nineteenth century, Teesside, a conurbation in the Northeast of England around the urban centre of Middlesbrough, was producing one third of the nation's iron output and the shipyards of the Tyne and Wear were producing two thirds of the nation's shipping tonnage (Darsley & Jarman 2011). By 1913 production from the Great Northern Coalfield was at its peak and by 1914 a substantial proportion of British and world trade originated in the Northeast (Darsley & Jarman 2011). So why was the Northeast the birthplace of the Industrial Revolution?

Coal production in the eighteenth century was initially concentrated in the Northeast as a result of favourable geomorphological and geographic conditions. The area not only included coal reserves but also benefitted from relatively shallow pits located along the banks of the rivers Tyne and Wear which made it easy to haul and transport the coal via river to the sea (Beamish Museum 2014). Such natural and locational advantages were further built upon by the man-made development of steam-pumping and the safety lamp, which enabled pits to be sunken to much greater depths and dug farther inland (Beamish Museum 2014). The result of this expansion led to the development of waggonways or 'coal roads' (later to be replaced by railways) and pit communities, housing workers and their families. The Stockton and Darlington Railway became the world's first public steam-hauled passenger railway (opened in 1825) and led to the widespread adoption of railways for the transportation of people and goods, including coal, throughout the country and the world (Beamish 2014). The late nineteenth and early twentieth centuries were thus an era of significant wealth and prosperity in the UK and the Northeast, though destined not to last.

Starting in the 1920s, the region underwent a period of long industrial decline due to the 'relative decline in shipbuilding, the exhaustion of the older parts of the Northeast coalfield and a relative loss of dynamism in some of the engineering sectors' (European Commission 2008: 9). The 1960s in particular saw the closure of 'many small unproductive pits across the region' (European Commission 2008: 10) and this downward spiral was then further exacerbated by the 1980s recession. During this time industry closed 'due to a lack of competitiveness', as well as increased 'internationalisation of markets and low levels of investment in innovation' (European Commission 2008: 11). Privatisation of utilities (energy and water) and lack of investment in the railways were added factors leading to the death of the region's heavy industry, and the mass unemployment and poverty that followed. According to Trimm (2012: 528) 'heritage operated as a compensation for the decline of the British industrial base in the postwar era' and Beamish Museum is a prime example.

The Founding of Beamish Museum

Inspired by museums he visited on his travels around Norway and Sweden, Frank Atkinson was the Beamish Museum's founder and first director.

Atkinson was concerned not only about the disappearance of the Northeast's industries, but also about the Northeast region losing its identity, customs and traditions (Beamish Museum 2014). As a result, he set out to convince the local municipality, Durham County Council, that there was an urgent need to gather and save materials and machinery associated with the dying industries. Such material objects, he suggested, could then be displayed in a new open-air museum, a technique founded by Artur Hazeluis in Sweden (Darsley & Jarman 2011). According to Hewison (1987: 88-89), memorialising early industry in this way was born out of a distinct fear of loss associated not only with the de-industrialisation of the Northeast, but also with the loss of the communities that served such industries.

Atkinson's approach started with a policy of 'unselective collecting' of items that included donations of industrial equipment from shipping, rail and manufacturing industries (Trimm 2012), as well as large donations of everyday items from the general public. This approach was deemed inclusive, enabling a bond to develop between local communities and the museum, actively empowering the former. Following this, Atkinson's next step was to organise the complete removal of several buildings from their original locations in the Northeast and the comprehensive rebuilding of these at Beamish. After several stages of negotiation, leading to an eventual joint agreement signed by eight local authorities in the Northeast, Beamish finally opened its doors to the public in February 1970 (Darsley & Jarman 2011). Beamish was marketed as 'The Living Museum of the North' (Beamish Museum 2014) and was framed as ethnographic and authentic (Trimm 2012) and 'something to be proud of' (Atkinson 1999: 87). As an open-air, living museum, dissemination and consumption of the material and social heritage was very different from conventional exhibitions in traditional museums or visits to open-access castles, monuments and stately homes. Instead, Beamish was designed to bring the history of the Northeast to life through entertainment, interaction and experience.

What and How Is Heritage Presented?

Beamish can be described as operating 'through an ethnographic presentation of a modernizing and industrializing people' (Trimm 2012: 529), where 'people from the past welcome visitors and interpret how the people of the North of England lived and worked' (Dayoutwiththekids 2017). Set over a large, 350-acre site, visitors to Beamish can navigate the site on foot, or can experience the 1920s restored trams and restored and replica buses, driven by costumed chauffeurs to travel around the site. Based on two main time

Figure 5.1   Map of Beamish Museum

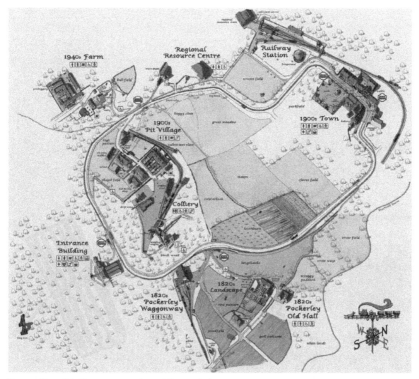

Source: Beamish Museum www.beamish.org.uk

zones, the early 1800s and early 1900s, Beamish presents the 1820s Pockerley Waggonway and the 1820s Pockerley Old Hall, a 1900s pit village, colliery and town (including a public house, various shops, services such as a dentist, solicitor, music teacher, bank, and a school) and a 1940s farm (Figure 5.1 map).

Based around the concept of living heritage, Beamish is clearly not just about the tangible, built heritage, although this is an important backdrop. Instead, the emphasis at Beamish is on people; their way of life, work, recreation and education (Darsley & Jarman 2011). In this respect, Beamish employs many costumed demonstrators who can be found in every building performing the role of shop keeper, bank clerk, tram and bus driver, chemist, teacher, etc. (Figure 5.2). These demonstrators (actors) interact with visitors through serving them, demonstrating aspects of their job, or simply talking to them about their life. In doing so, they seek to give visitors an authentic experience of what life was like during this period.

Advertised as a family day out, Beamish is marketed as an authentic, open-air museum that provides entertainment and education for visitors

Figure 5.2   A costumed demonstrator as a bank clerk

Source: Carol Ludwig

of all ages and interests (Beamish Museum 2014), and as a living museum (i.e., no glass cabinets, labels or interpretive signs), Beamish relies heavily on its costumed demonstrators to disseminate the Beamish story.

Indeed, Beamish's demonstrators appear very knowledgeable about their particular role(s) and explicitly portray a sense of both enthusiastic nostalgia and pride in *performing* what their lives are like. While our visits to each building and demonstrator enabled us to conclude that a reasonably factual presentation of life during this time was disseminated, it was also noticeable that the performance(s) delivered by the demonstrators portrayed positivity and sentimentality, with little or no reference to negative aspects of the time. The primitive dentistry of the time and the fact that female children were not obliged or expected to attend school on 'washing day' was explained with humour. Negative aspects of the period such as the poor environmental and sanitary conditions (pollution, inequality) did not appear to be included in the exhibition as the clear message to be disseminated was about the hard working, pioneering working communities of a modernising and industrialising people at the forefront of history. While museum exhibitions and heritage displays by their nature always involve selectivity, it is important to assess to what extent Beamish's claim to be authentic, is valid.

Authenticity

The concept of 'authenticity' is a very 'Westernised' idea of heritage and is central to the conservation repair orthodoxy of cultural heritage objects across Europe (Pendlebury 2009: 173). In China and Japan, for instance, historic buildings may be frequently demolished and rebuilt with contemporary materials, and may even be moved without diminishing the alleged authenticity of the building or site (Graham 2002), whereas by contrast, restoration in England is repeatedly criticised for delivering 'reproduction heritage', deemed to be 'meticulously researched and beautifully executed fakery, but fakery nonetheless' (SPAB cited in Larkham 1996: 263). In the UK, 'authenticity' tends therefore to be presented as an essential key orienteering point for assessing the validity of heritage claims and, as Hobson (2004: 53) explains, it is deemed to be 'objectively definable and recognisable, given appropriate professional training'. As aforesaid, Beamish as it exists today has developed slowly over the last four decades. It benefits from some *in situ* heritage assets, such as the Mahogany drift mine (Figure 5.3), which is a major heritage attraction (opened in 1855) and visitors can take part in a guided tour of the mine, enabling them to experience the dark, damp and cramped conditions for themselves.

Beamish however has also benefitted from continuous collecting, moving, and restoring of its collection (Darsley & Jarman 2011), and several recent replica new-builds, discussed in detail below. In this context Beamish has experienced some degree of scholarly criticism and scepticism because of its 'reconstructed nature' (Hewison 1987) and is criticised for being 'fabricated from performers or demonstrators "performing the past" and facilities arranged in facsimile' (Trimm 2012: 529; Hewison 1987).

Figure 5.3   Coal works of the Mahogany drift mine

Source: Carol Ludwig

Relocated Heritage

While donations to the museum including artefacts, furnishings, decor and clothing are said to be original and thus authentic, several key built heritage attractions have either been moved to the site and rebuilt and restored or are new replica 'old buildings'. For example, six of the original row of 27 Francis Street miners' cottages (Figure 5.4), originally built in the early 1860s by Hetton Coal Company, were relocated from their original site in Hetton-le-Hole, on Wearside to Beamish and were rebuilt in the pit village in 1976 (Beamish Museum 2014: 18).

Likewise, the school building (Figure 5.5) originally opened in 1892 in East Stanley was relocated to the Museum in 1992 and the 1850s Pit Hill Chapel, originally located near to the Museum's entrance was also rebuilt in the pit village.

In the 1900s town, the Co-op, along with the bakery, originally from Annfield Plain in County Durham, were moved to Beamish in the late 1970s/early 1980s and the latter 'was transformed into an Edwardian bakery' (Beamish Museum 2014: 46). Moreover, six of the 25-home Ravensworth Terrace, originally located in Bensham Bank, Gateshead (Figure 5.6) and built in the 1830s for professionals and tradesmen, were relocated to Beamish in the 1970s and rebuilt between 1980-1985 (Beamish Museum 2014).

The Sun Inn public house is another example of relocation, being moved from Bondgate in Bishop Auckland in 1985, and Eston Church, originally

Figure 5.4   The miners' cottages relocated from Wearside

Source: Carol Ludwig

Figure 5.5   The school building relocated from East Stanley

Source: Carol Ludwig

from Eston, near Middlesbrough is described as 'the oldest and most complex building ever moved by Beamish' (Beamish Museum 2014: 94). Dismantled in 1998, it was subsequently rebuilt at the Museum in 2011/12. While the aforementioned structures were rebuilt using largely the original fabric, other attractions at Beamish only use parts of the original historic fabric and are thus referred to as 'authentic recreations', as explained below.

Figure 5.6   Ravensworth Terrace from Bensham Bank, Gateshead

Source: Carol Ludwig

Authentic Recreations

The masonic hall (Figure 5.7), for instance, is marketed as an 'authentic re-creation' providing 'a unique insight into the world of the Freemasons in the early 20th century' (Beamish Museum 2014: 72). While the frontage has been relocated in 2006 from a former Masonic hall in Park Terrace, Sunderland (originally built in 1869) the demonstrator inside the hall explained that, like several other buildings in the Museum, the masonic hall could not be rebuilt using all of the exact same materials for cost reasons so were instead built to be outstanding representations of the originals. The masonic hall, for instance used wood instead of marble and an original archway detail was removed and simplified for cost reasons.

Replica Buildings

The final category of buildings found at Beamish are replicas or representa-tions of original buildings. The Beamish Motor and Cycle Works (Figure 5.8), for example, opened at Beamish in 1994 and is described in the Beamish Guide book (available for purchase in the souvenir shop) as 'a replica of a typical town garage' (Beamish Museum 2014: 48). Likewise, the Printer, Stationer and Newspaper branch office (Figure 5.9), which opened in the mid-1980s and the Jubilee Confectioners (sweet shop), which opened in 1994 are replicas, designed to represent typical examples. The Confectioners

Figure 5.7   The Masonic Hall in the background

Source: Carol Ludwig

Figure 5.8   The Beamish Motor and Cycle Works

Source: Carol Ludwig

Figure 5.9   The newspaper branch office

Source: Carol Ludwig

Figure 5.10   The chemist and plate photographer

Source: Carol Ludwig

includes a factory where visitors can watch traditional sweets, chocolate and toffee being made 'using techniques and equipment from the era' (Beamish Museum 2014: 68) and these can then be purchased in the shop. The chemist and plate photographer (Figure 5.10) is a new addition to the 1900s Town and is designed to replicate a typical chemist, including dispensary, and photographer's studio. Its design is said to be 'based on a real building in Durham City' (Beamish Museum 2014: 74). These key museum attractions are extremely popular with visitors to Beamish, yet they would all fail to meet the deep-rooted, scientific tangible heritage criteria of the Western conservation orthodoxy or AHD, regardless of how similar they may look to the original buildings. Despite this, the museum and its employees proudly stress the authenticity and accuracy of their performances and displays.

Identity and National Pride

Pride in the perceived authenticity (MacCannell 1973; Ramkissoon & Uysal 2011) of the Museum, is equally matched by pride in the depiction of the past performed by the costumed demonstrators. Indeed, the exhibits (made up of buildings, furnishings, artefacts, etc.) together with all of the employed 'performers' portray an explicit sense of pride, emphasis-ing that the forward-thinking UK, and the Northeast in particular, is the birthplace of many developments in engineering, agriculture and transport (Darsley & Jarman 2011). This positive message reworks and reinforces 'ideas of Britishness' (Trimm 2012: 534) and (re)constructs a shared identity situated around 'nationality and modernity' (Trimm 2012: 529). In doing so, the depiction of the past portrays a nationalisation of British history which is all-inclusive and positive. This sense of greatness, wealth, full employment, and prosperity arguably serves to create a sense of implicit discomfort with the present. Indeed, the demonstrators discuss the achievements of the time, painting a picture of a region that was tough, tenacious, and full of inventiveness and ingenuity (Darsley & Jarman 2011). In doing so, they produce a distinctive gulf/distance between *then* and *now*, and a 'nostalgic longing' (Trimm 2012: 533) is conveyed and encouraged. Moreover, the historical narrative conveyed to visitors is clearly sanitised and simplified. The past is reconstructed using predominantly 'comforting aspects of class and modernity' (Trimm 2012: 530) and the implicit dangers associated with the pit work are included in this narrative only to emphasise the toughness and strength of the Northeast people and the working class.

This sanitised version of the past is clearly designed to ignite a strong sense of pride and national/regional identity, which can individualise the UK and the Northeast (thereby benefiting the tourism industry, discussed below), and just as importantly be passed on to new generations as part of Beamish's educative role.

Education and Tourism

Beamish receives more than 500,000 visitors each year and is the holder of several awards including British Museum of the Year award, Gold Award (2012), Large Visitor Attraction of the Year, Visit England Award for Excellence (Beamish Museum 2014), and in 1987 the European Museum of the Year award (European Museum Forum 2017). Over the last four decades Beamish has continued to expand, with new projects and developments planned for the future, including offering overnight accommodation in an 1820s style coaching inn, and the construction of early industry such as candle-makers, potters and blacksmiths (Beamish Museum 2014). The continued growth of Beamish emphasises its success as a heritage attraction and illustrates the contribution Beamish makes to the UK and regional tourism industry.

Beamish receives international, national and regional tourists, and offers special events and discounts for groups of school children as part of its educative role.

Indeed, marketing material for Beamish emphasises the importance of conveying the history of the Northeast to younger generations in particular. For this purpose, a Regional Resource Centre was set up at the Museum in 2001 and 'many thousands of school children and students come [...] each year' (Beamish Museum 2014: 121). The guide book also emphasises that students 'can explore many contemporary issues through sessions in our historic settings' (Beamish Museum 2014: 121), attempting to develop the continuity link that is so important in living heritage projects between the past, the present and the future.

Summary

The sections above have discussed the particular versions of the past selected and (re)invented at Beamish, as well as the dissemination techniques adopted. They also point to the contemporary purpose(s) of heritage consumption for the UK and the Northeast region in particular.

While Beamish attempts to present the past in an authentic way, as a fabricated construct which has grown through the continuous rebuilding, relocating, restoring and replicating of original buildings, the museum has been subject to some degree of scholarly criticism. While the heritage 'performances' and the exhibits within the museum are largely factual, they have a tendency to omit more negative accounts of the period, carefully disseminating a consistent sanitised narrative based on national/regional pride and identity. While the authenticity and factual nature of Beamish is an important part of the museum's marketing, equally important is the entertainment value Beamish can offer to the whole family. For instance, the museum is heralded as providing not only the opportunity to learn about the region's past, but also a 'family day out'. Beamish's consistently growing tourist numbers confirm the popularity of the museum, regardless of its perceived authenticity or official heritage 'status', and upon leaving the museum, visitors will have gathered a sense of what life was like for working communities involved in these industries and leave with a sense of nostalgic pride. The following sections recount a similar series of events in China, but present a marked difference in the ways in which heritage is conceptualised, commodified and consumed.

Case Study 2: Song Dynasty Theme Parks in Hangzhou and Kaifeng, China

Since the economic reforms began in 1978, the Chinese government has moved away from a socialist ideology and repositioned itself as an entrepreneurial state, promoting economic growth, urban expansion, and globalisation. In response to the state's shift toward entrepreneurialism, local authorities have consequently adjusted their approaches to governance and formulated strategies and policies to prompt development for the purpose of achieving competitiveness domestically and internationally. The trajectory of development and growth in each city has invariably been charted by political leadership and economic enterprise as much as drawn from local resources and cultural heritage. The creation of imaginary Song Dynasty Towns in Hangzhou (1996) and Kaifeng (1998) is a telling example that illustrates how the distant past of China is selected, fabricated, performed and commodified by the local authorities in Hangzhou and Kaifeng to make their city financially more competitive by reclaiming their distinctive identities as imperial capitals of the Song Dynasty (Xu 2008; Wei 2012).

The Inspiration behind Song Dynasty Towns in Hangzhou and Kaifeng

The creation of the two aforementioned theme parks are said to have been inspired by the same historical panoramic scroll 'Along the River during the Qingming Festival', attributed to an otherwise unknown painter Zhang Zeduan (fl. early twelfth century) (Guo 2004; Du 2015; Lin 2015; Li 2016; Ong & Jin 2017). Once thought to depict the ceremonial rituals of the Qingming Festival, the painting has more frequently been understood to portray a panorama of city life in early spring in the capital Bianjing (today's Kaifeng) of the Northern Song Dynasty (960-1126) (Tsao 2003). Despite uncertainty about both the artist and the painting, the theme park in Kaifeng is a materialisation of the painting on what was believed to be its 'original' location and the inspiration for the artist. The Kaifeng theme park was named after the painting in Chinese ('Qingming shanghe yuan'), but named 'Millennium City Park' in English, emphasising its former role as an imperial capital at the turn of the first millennium. The completion of the Kaifeng theme park in 1998, however, fell two years behind the other theme park in Hangzhou, known as 'Songcheng' ('Song City').

Narratives of the creation of Songcheng in Hangzhou have been constructed based on the fact that the city was the capital of the Southern Song

Figure 5.11   Territory of Northern and Southern Song and location of their capital cities Kaifeng and Lin'an

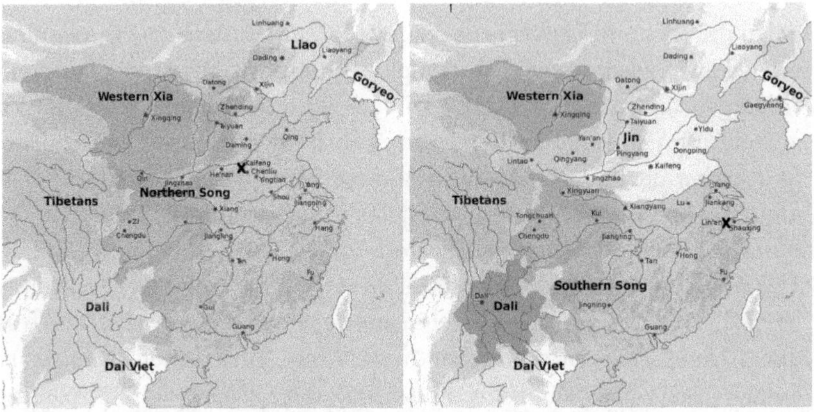

Source: Adapted from Mozzan 2015; https://en.wikipedia.org/wiki/Song_dynasty

Dynasty (1127-1279), although it was not the capital said to be depicted in the historical scroll (Figure 5.11). Both the Hangzhou and Kaifeng theme parks make explicit reference to the historical panoramic scroll on their official websites, and numerous reporters as well as academics have repeatedly associated the two parks with the painting.

The creation of these two parks has drawn much of its inspiration from one of the most iconic Chinese paintings and used it as a blueprint for creating an idealised historical townscape at the end of the 20th century. But whether the urban scenes depicted in the original twelfth-century work were actually of Kaifeng or were instead an idealised portrait of an imaginary city is still debated (Tsao 2003). Whether it was Kaifeng or not, the painting was revered by later scholars and artists, who created a number of replica versions in subsequent dynasties. Later versions, naturally, elaborated on and exaggerated aspects of the earlier versions as well as the original (Figure 5.12).

What and How Is Heritage Presented?

Similar to Beamish, both tangible and intangible aspects of heritage were considered essential to create or, more specifically, invent a make-believe city scene that existed a thousand years ago. The Millennium City Park in Kaifeng has put in a great deal of effort into recreating the architectural landmarks and cityscape depicted in the painting (Ong & Jin 2017). Songcheng in Hangzhou, on the other hand, has prized itself for its theatrical performances,

Figure 5.12   Part of the twelfth-century Song original and an eighteenth-century copy (depicting the City Gate)

Source: https://commons.wikimedia.org/wiki/File:Alongtheriver_QingMing.jpg and https://commons.wikimedia.org/wiki/File:Along_the_River_7-119-3.jpg

which were for the very first time in China staged in a cultural theme park (Du 2015). Both, however, go to extraordinary lengths to simulate scenes of everyday life at that time.

Fabricated Architectural Heritage

Architecture provides an important foundation for the two theme parks to make the experience of travelling back in time more intuitively or perceptually plausible. Whereas the two parks each cover an area of 100 acres, they adopted somewhat different approaches toward architectural 'authenticity'. It is proudly claimed that the buildings in the Kaifeng theme park were built according to a technical treatise on architectural craftsmanship standards, titled *Yingzao Fashi* (State Building Standards) published and enforced by the Song Emperor Huizong (Guo 1998). Buildings and structures in Kaifeng are therefore seen as a material realisation of prosperous and peaceful scenes of Bianjing as imagined or interpreted by *not* the original painter *but* his following imitators. Several temples, palaces and pavilions in the Millennium Park are multi-storey replicas of those depicted in the copies, especially the most refined version created in the eighteenth century but not in the twelfth-century original. The Rainbow Bridge (Hong Qiao), one of the architectural landmarks in the painting, for instance, was made of timber in the original, then replaced by a stone bridge in the 18th-century Qing Dynasty remake (Figure 5.13) and finally realised in the Millennium

Figure 5.13   The Rainbow Bridge in the twelfth- and eighteenth-century paintings

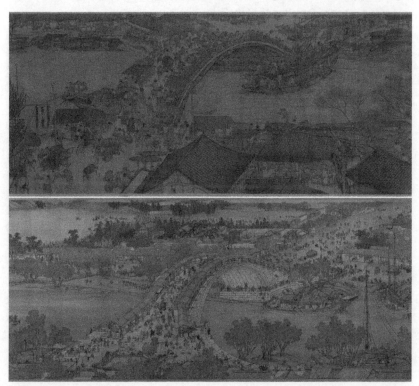

Source: Same as Figure 5.12

Park in steel (Figure 5.14). Some imposing edifices have never appeared in any later copies of the scroll and are newly invented in the Park – as if the theme park itself is another version of the painting in the 21st-century (Ong & Jin 2017). Different from the previous copies, this version is a reinterpretation of the painting for visitors to experience, rather than for emperors to appreciate or collect.

Songcheng in Hangzhou, on the other hand, mainly consists of one or two-storey shops or courtyard houses, with the exception of the City Gate as the only tall building in the park, bearing more resemblance to the twelfth-century painting. However, for a theme park, authenticity tends to be achieved with a minimum of fuss. Rainbow Bridge here becomes a roof-covered bridge with timber truss underneath, ornamentally supporting the reinforced-concrete bridge structure (Figure 5.15). Several places in the park, such as grottos, the ghost house, mazes, etc., are purposely created to fulfil visitor expectations for entertainment, compromising the 'integrity' of the historical theme park.

Figure 5.14   The Rainbow Bridge in Millennium City Park, Kaifeng

Source: Lüsezhuzhu

Figure 5.15   The Rainbow Bridge in Songcheng, Hangzhou

Source: Yiwen Wang

Dissemination of Intangible Heritage

Both of the two parks feature a wide range of activities that are generally associated with traditional arts, craftsmanship or specialities – sometimes without regard to whether they existed during the Song period or not. Costumed demonstrators perform traditional handicrafts, such as the making of hand fans, swords, embroidered textiles, clay sculpture, knots and wood carving. Other traditional skilled occupations, including making tofu, rice cakes, and sugar painting along with various sweets and snack shops also play an important part in simulating and diversifying commercial activities of the time and enrich the tourist visiting experience. The advertisement of Hangzhou's Songcheng (Songcheng Group 2017) vividly encapsulates the aura of the Song Dynasty that it strives to create:

> most food, snacks and drinks provided in the park can be dated back to that era. Visitors will find themselves wandering in an ancient city, surrounded by people from all walks of life in Song Dynasty. They can try their luck in an ancient Chinese style casino, appease their own curiosity by touring in a Song prostitute's boudoir, or buy a rice cake or tofu made on site with tools featuring hundreds years of history.

Although endeavours to evoke associations with the period are noticeably made in both cases, casual references to an unspecified historical period are fairly commonplace. In particular, folklore performances derive inspiration from a wide range of social and religious customs (including marriage, the civil service examinations, dragon and lion dances, riverside markets, etc.); acrobatics and entertainment shows (such as shadow plays, puppet shows, stilt walking, martial arts, cock fights, monkey tricks, face-changing, etc.); or ancient and local legendary characters of the Song (such as the fictionalisation of the patriotic General Yue Fei and the government official Bao Zheng, known as 'Judge Bao' for his unparalleled uprightness and integrity).

These endeavours to recreate a historical scene – be it historically proven or completely fictional – have been recognised by the local government and both parks have been proclaimed by the local heritage authority as a 'Demonstration Site for Chinese Intangible Heritage' (Lin 2015). Indeed, several local craftsman and skilled artisans have been recruited or invited to work in the theme parks on a daily or regular basis to demonstrate or transmit traditional handicraft.

Theatrical Interpretations of the Song Dynasty

Theatrical performance is another manifestation of how heritage is presented in the theme park. Theatrical performances or live entertainment shows have usually appeared in themed hotels or casinos, and its appearance in a historical theme park in Hangzhou was the first in China. The commercial success of Songcheng and the like have led to the support of the Ministry of Culture and the National Tourism Administration to encourage the incorporation of performing arts into the tourism industry by introducing theatrical performances at heritage sites or historical theme parks (Song & Cheung 2010). The last decade therefore has witnessed a growth of theatrical performances in China. These performances vary in types, indoor or outdoor, but are often large in scale, featuring artistic interpretation of historic events, literary works or ethnic folklore.

The advertising slogan of Songcheng emphasises that the park has 'architecture as form; culture as soul' (Songcheng Group 2017) and visitors go there for 'one day in exchange of an experience of a thousand years'. The spectacular theatrical performance, titled 'The Romance of the Song Dynasty' is staged indoor every day at the Grand Theatre (Song & Cheung 2010). Different from traditional performances such as Peking opera, contemporary theatrical performances utilise a wide range of high-tech tools such as laser, lighting, fire, waterfalls and high-definition giant screens, etc. to dazzle spectators with special effects. The local legends, particularly love stories associated with Hangzhou such as the legend of the White Snake and the Butterfly Lovers, are put on the stage and captivate the audience with folk dances and songs, acrobatic feats, sword fights, horse riding and so forth. As noted by Zhan and Kong (2016), the long-lasting popularity of 'The Romance of the Song Dynasty' in Songcheng has derived from its constant 'reinvention' of local legends and anecdotes. Although criticised by Li (2016) for its 'staged authenticity' (MacCannell 1973), most Chinese scholars or critics praise it as a 'must-see in your lifetime' (Zhang 2009; Lin 2015; Wang 2016; Yu & Jiang 2017) or an iconic performance of China 'deserving the title of 'Chinese Broadway' and 'one of the top three theatrical performances of the world' alongside the O show of Cirque du Soleil in Las Vegas and Le Moulin Rouge in Paris (Zhejiang Provincial Tourism Bureau 2015).

In contrast to the indoor performances in Hangzhou, Kaifeng showcases several small-scale outdoor live performances, two large-scale battle reenactments during the daytime and a theatrical performance at night. One of the re-enacted battles is performed on land, depicting a heroic episode in the career of the patriotic general Yue Fei on horseback slaying an enemy. The other battle is performed on water, recreating the epic battle scene on the

Bian River when Song forces resisted the invasion of the Jurchen Jin. After the Song defeat, the capital was moved to Hangzhou. While the two reenactments are designed to evoke emotional responses by creating visual imagery of a selected heroic or tragic episode of the past, the night-time theatrical performance 'The Great Song Dynasty-Reminiscences of the Eastern Capital' is staged on a man-made lake, set to evoke more positive images of the Song Dynasty as a golden era of peace, growth and prosperity, bustling with life and activity. As its advertising slogan goes, the performance is designed to provide visitors with a sensory experience to 'walk into the painting and wander around in the scenes of a thousand years ago' (Songcheng Group 2017).

Rather noticeably, the theatrical interpretations of the Song Dynasty in the two theme parks have not been restricted to the scenes in the painting but cite references to anecdotes and legends that people know well about this particular period from television and radio programmes, and other public media. Intriguingly, only a few critics condemn this 'impressionist' interpretation of the past and the lack of historical accuracy (Li 2016; Zhang 2016), and many instead praise the lavish productions and their contributions to bring Song history back to life.

Authenticity

As elaborated in the case study on Beamish, the pursuit of material authenticity is seen as the primary aim of heritage conservation and has underpinned subsequent conservation practice in the West for many decades. Conversely, seldom have Chinese deemed it essential to validate a heritage claim for tourism industries. This is, in part, because the traditional practice of architectural conservation not only accepted the replacement of building materials and elements, but also welcomed contemporary intervention and alteration of historic structures: to make them larger, taller, stronger or simply better (Qian 2007; Su 2011; Zhu 2015). This also stems from the fact that the Cultural Revolution destroyed many archival records, and post-Mao urban development has demolished many historical buildings and sites, making the pursuit of material authenticity difficult if not unattainable.

Neither Hangzhou nor Kaifeng possess many physical relics of the past, but instead both showcase a complete 'reconstruction' or 'reproduction' of an idealised past depicted in the painting. While both parks proudly claim success in representing the Song Dynasty townscape portrayed on the historical scroll, the authenticity of the twelfth century painting itself remains in question. No archival evidence can indicate the exact date and location that the painting was created. The question as to what extent the painter had faithfully recorded the architectural elements in the capital city and depicted accurately the everyday life of ordinary subjects and their activities in the settings – i.e., with realism and without interpretation – has been fiercely debated by historians (Ong & Jin 2017). Such academic debate on authenticity, nonetheless, would not dissuade people from visiting the park nor preclude visitors from accepting the pseudo-historical settings in the park. As aforesaid, it is discernible that the two theme parks present quite a few notions and understandings about the Song Dynasty that are popularised by the mass media. Having conducted a field survey on visitor perceptions of the architectural design and activities in Kaifeng, Ong and Jin (2017:230) report that the 'simulation of the landscape depicted in the "flat" painting into real 3D space was also found to have gone unchallenged by Chinese visitors' who 'appeared convinced ... that the painting depicts and simulates a real Bianjing'. The historical scroll 'has become iconic to the extent that replicating it on its own is a worthy endeavour because whether or not it is a reproduction of an actual historical landscape and the exact time period in which it was painted would and will not be of importance to visitors' (Ong & Jin 2017:234-235). In these two cases, it can be argued that 'the subjective, "experience-centred" notions of tourist authenticity' has completely overpowered 'the objective, "object-centred" modern notions of heritage authenticity' (Guttormsen & Fageraas, 2011; González Martínez 2017:56).

Identity and National Pride

The theme parks in Hangzhou and Kaifeng have thrived on nostalgic longings for an idealised representation of the distant past on the one hand, and on the other, on the local leadership who are driven to make the city more competitive by branding the city with culture. In the 1990s, Hangzhou and Kaifeng both launched a series of initiatives to protect, reinstate and even 'reconstruct' or 'reinvent' tangible and intangible heritage assets of the city. The two theme parks thrived for the same reason of heritage reconstruction. For cities whose tourism resources are not as globally renowned or competitive as ancient capitals like Beijing (the Great Wall, the Forbidden City) and Xian (the Terracotta Army), any potential cultural resources – be it real, imaginary or fictional – can be utilised, developed and commodified for tourism industries. Hangzhou and Kaifeng both see their past as Song capital cities as a wealth of cultural resource to be tapped. Owing to the absence of physical remains, historical records and shared memories of the capital city, interpretation of the historical scroll in the theme parks has cashed in on the long temporal gap between then and now, creating an idealised landscape for the everyday life of an all-inclusive society from master craftsmen to unskilled prostitutes; or commemorating heroic figures or failures in defending against foreign peoples on the borders of the empire.

Though presented as a mix of the good, the bad and the ugly, the Song Dynasty remains very positively portrayed and perceived in the theme park. The period is well known for technological advances and economic prosperity. It nurtured three of the Four Great Inventions of China, namely gunpowder, printing and the compass, and enjoyed unprecedented economic and population growth as a result of prioritising foreign trade and merchant shipping industries (Temple & Needham 2007; Ropp 2010). The narratives of the past, as depicted in the built environment and landscape, craft activities of costumed demonstrators, historical reenactments or theatrical productions of the two theme parks are, however, heavily based on an idealistic representation of a Han Chinese worldview, while assuming a harmony between Han Chinese and other ethnic minority populations.

Education and Tourism

Admittedly, cultural theme parks can generate a positive impact on contemporary society, as they serve as a transmitter of local customs and traditions and a show window for domestic or international tourists to obtain a quick grasp of local history and experience in person local cultures (MacCannell 1973). In late 1990s China, various theme parks sprang up as an alternative means to satisfy the increasing demand of the new middle class for leisure or to satisfy their curiosity to understand other regions in China or the outside world. Indeed, while Songcheng is considered as a 4A-rated site (Du 2004), the Millennium Park is listed as a 5A-rated tourist attraction – the highest level of recognition awarded to sites of national importance and acknowledging China's history and culture.

The commercial successes of the Songcheng and the Millennium Park have led to the replication of cultural theme parks in other cities. In early years, cultural theme parks burgeoned in historic cities like Hangzhou and Kaifeng where the history of the city can be commodified and sold, or in the regions where ethnic minorities live. In ensuing decades, however, with the further growth of the middle class population and their demand for leisure pursuits, new parks were built in areas that possessed little historical, ethnic, or regional features and therefore had to "borrow" vernacular architecture and cultural performance from elsewhere. Not only have various versions of regional or ethnic cultures in China been displaced to the doorstep of consumers, but exotic cultural themes from abroad have also been brought into the existing well-established parks in order to diversify activities and boost revisits. For instance, Songcheng Group built other theme parks in Sanya, Lijiang, Jiuzhai and Guilin, all of which use the same brand 'Songcheng' and exhibit a mix of architectural features from both the local region and Hangzhou. The 'Romantic Show' in Hangzhou was also replicated in these new parks, with the contents adapted from the romances in the locality – historical, mythical or even fictional. Yu and Jiang (2017) praise highly the success of replicating a Songcheng in Sanya on Hainan Island, in the southernmost part of China, which ironically was originally inhabited by the Li ethnic group but invaded and conquered by Han Chinese during the Song Dynasty. It appears that Chinese scholars in the tourism field have considered positively the use of 'regional cultures' of China – even though 'displaced' and borrowed'– for branding and providing themes for amusement parks, given that they enable visitors to appreciate and identify themselves with their 'Greater China' roots in a broad sense, i.e., from the Han Chinese perspective. When 'cultures' are uprooted from their original time and space and traded as commodities, they run the danger of homogenising a culturally diverse society into a singular whole.

Summary

A fictional version of the distant past was materialised in Hangzhou and Kaifeng, where the history of the city as the capital of a great empire was narrated for the contemporary consumption of heritage and culture. Never have there been attempts to present the past in an authentic way. The Songcheng and the Millennium City Park are both a fabricated 'heritage' in which built environments are misleadingly constructed, and traditional customs, handicrafts and legends are casually performed through subjective interpretation of a famous painting. While both the material and immaterial existence of heritage within the parks are largely fakery, they have won more praise than criticism from scholars and been well-received by visitors. The perceived authenticity outweighs completely the material one. It is believed that the historical theme parks should take on an important role to rejuvenate and bring back to life dying cultural heritage – as evidenced by the designation of the two theme parks as a demonstration site for intangible heritage. The long temporal distance between the Song Dynasty and the present leaves no physical remnants, historical records or shared memories of this particular period of the past, thereby providing ample room for disseminating a sanitised narrative based on Han Chinese identity and an imagined homogeneous national community.

Comparison of Case Studies

Having seen the fabricated construct of the past in the open-air museum and the historical theme parks, the question to be asked is whether it matters if the buildings are original, restored, partly restored or replications? For Beamish, designed by Atkinson to follow a living heritage approach, the intention of the museum is to disseminate an authentic experience to its visitors whereby they learn through being (seeing *and* doing) what life was like during the respective time periods. The creation of the historical theme park in Hangzhou and Kaifeng shares similar goals, but they further capitalise on the city's past as an imperial capital and refashion local identity and cultures for city branding in order to explicitly increase economic competitiveness. Inspired by a historical scroll repeatedly reinvented and reinterpreted throughout history, the two theme parks feature some degree of creativity in reconstructing or reproducing the Song landscape projected by the painting. As Wijesuriya (2005: 37) reiterates, the purpose of a living heritage approach is to maintain continuity, 'even if in certain occasions the fabric might be harmed' or indeed replicated.

Living heritage projects emphasise the intangible connection between 'heritage' and community, rather than the tangible fabric itself (Wijesuriya 2005; Poulios 2014: 23). While this clearly tests existing Western notions of conservation philosophy and may be criticised for 'Disneyfying' the past (Handler & Saxton 1988; Waitt 2000; Choay 2001) or damaging the real purpose and the true meaning of heritage (Hewison 1987; Wright 1985), it is important to understand that how we define authenticity is a contentious issue, just like how we define the very essence of heritage itself. Indeed, the perceived authenticity of the museum and the theme parks appears of little importance to the visitors and demonstrators. Beamish continues to vehemently stress the Museum's authenticity, of which they appear particularly proud. Hangzhou and Kaifeng, on the other hand, have taken their role as a heritage transmitter for granted and never felt the need to make claims on authenticity. This absence of gestures to claim rightful inheritance of heritage has been quite prevalent not only in historical theme parks, but also at heritage sites managed by local authorities.

For living heritage projects, such as that exemplified by Beamish, heritage is conceptualised around and centred on the people and their connections with both material evidence of the past (whether authentic, relocated or fabricated) and immaterial inheritance from the past (such as traditional knowledge, customs and practice that can be transmitted, performed or consumed). This arguable Disneyfication of Britain's industrial history was a preventive measure to save traces of the recent past before it disappeared. It stages a perceived authenticity and serves social, cultural and educational purposes through entertainment, interaction and experience.

Similar to Beamish, the Hangzhou and Kaifeng theme parks have also conceptualised heritage around the people – not merely those who have lived or are living within the city or region, but encompassing a much wider scope and referring to the descendants of Greater China. The connection of this large group of stakeholders (mostly tourists) with China's distant past has relied heavily on a fantasised fabrication of material evidence and immaterial performance. In China, the construction of historical theme parks like those in Hangzhou and Kaifeng has invariably been a joint venture between local political leadership and economic enterprise. Such Disneyfication of China's imperial history has ridden on the burgeoning demand of the new middle class for leisure, and serves cultural political purposes alongside economic, entertainment and educational ones.

Conclusion

The modification to the heritage discourse has widened the definition of heritage to include more intangible or immaterial aspects as well as encouraging consideration of the various values ascribed by stakeholders from all ranks of society. Changing conservation approaches from material-based to values-based in the second half of the 20th century and, more recently, to people-centred living heritage, have expanded significantly the scope of spatial practice of architecture and planning; they have also reformulated, or at least raised new questions about, the principles of selection, interpretation and management of the past. This shift from objective to subjective approaches to heritage management has forged closer links between communities and their pasts. In the process, both tangible and intangible heritage are crucial to connect people and place, sustaining continuity from the past to the present and into the future.

The appropriation of heritage for economic and entertainment values – its commodification – often results in a superficial or false depiction of the past. In Beamish, the appropriation of heritage was set to compensate for the decline of Britain's industrial past and to document the communities that used to serve such industries and their claims on heritage. In a sense, Atkinson can be seen as a philanthropist or patron of the industrial history of the Northeast region. His fear of loss aroused a desire to write the history by saving the physical relics of industrial production and transmitting regional customs and traditions, thereby saving the identity of the region and further the country. The resulting tourism and economic benefits, while clearly important and of value, were secondary. The appropriation of heritage in Hangzhou and Kaifeng, however, has been essentially driven by entrepreneurial endeavours. While Beamish was created with the intent to retain the traces of the city or country's industrial past, the two theme parks in China were designed to evoke a sort of collective national memory of a bygone era. The staged authenticity in the Chinese theme parks depicts society in the past as socially inclusive; but, at the same time, supplemental new stories strengthen an implicit conception of the ethnically exclusive Greater China. Regardless of the authenticity of the sites, both the UK and Chinese case studies show their high value as heritage resources for a multitude of purposes: for reclaiming identities, for political, entrepreneurial, tourism, economic, entertainment and educational purposes. If heritage is for, and inextricably linked to people, we must therefore question what purpose stringent and limiting concepts of authenticity serve in preserving, remembering and transmitting heritage intergenerationally? While we recognise that without such means of 'gatekeeping', it could be argued that anything could become and be listed as heritage, the case studies nevertheless show that to *protect* such valued heritage, the constraints of the Western focus on authenticity, scientific evidence and objective fact, as well as on tangible heritage, are largely outdated and unoperationable for inclusive heritage management. While the people-centred living heritage approach must therefore be recognised for its increasing importance in how we conceptualise heritage and how we interpret the past for contemporary use, we must nevertheless be cautious about the selective nature of heritage practice and exclusiveness that it may consequently bring about.

References

Beamish Museum (2014), *Beamish: The Living Museum of the North*. Peterborough: Jarrold Publishing.

Bonnici, U. (2009), 'The Human Right to the Cultural Heritage – The Faro Convention's Contribution to the Recognition and Safeguarding of This Human Right', in CoE (ed.), *Heritage and Beyond*, 53-59. Strasbourg: CoE Publishing.

Choay, F. (2001), *The Invention of the Historic Monument*. Cambridge: Cambridge University Press.

CoE (2011), *Action for a Changing Society, Framework Convention on the Value of Cultural Heritage for Society*. Strasbourg: CoE Publishing.

Darsley, R. & Jarman, P. (2011), *Beamish 40 Years on Rails: Railways, Tramways and Waggon Ways*. West Sussex: Middleton Press.

Dayoutwiththekids (2017), 'Beamish Open Air Museum', [Online]. Available from: https://www.dayoutwiththekids.co.uk/beamish-open-air-museum (accessed 24 June 2017).

DCMS (2003), *Protecting our Historic Environment: Making the System Work Better*. London: TSO.

Delafons, J. (1997), *Politics and Preservation: A Policy History of the Built Heritage 1882- 1996*. London: Spon Press.

Du, H. (2015), 'The Business Model of the Theatrical Performance of "Songcheng Ancient Love" in Hangzhou', *Knowledge Economy*, 2015 (11): 96.

European Commission (2008), 'Work Package 4: Structural Change and Globalisation: Case Study North East England, UK', [Online]. Available from: http://ec.europa.eu/regional_policy/sources/docgener/evaluation/pdf/expost2006/wp4_cs_north_east_england.pdf (accessed 24 June 2017).

European Museum Forum (2017), 'European Museum Forum'. [Online]. Available from: http://www.europeanmuseumforum.info/emya.html (accessed 24 June 2017).

González Martínez, P. (2017), 'Urban Authenticity at Stake: A New Framework for Its Definition from the Perspective of Heritage at the Shanghai Music Valley', *Cities* 70 (2017): 55-64.

Graham, B. (2002), 'Heritage as Knowledge: Capital or Culture?', *Urban Studies* 39 (5-6): 1003-1017.

Guo, Q. (1998), 'Yingzao Fashi: Twelfth-Century Chinese Building Manual', *Architectural History*, 41: 1-13.

Guo, S. (2004), 'Songcheng: A Successful Model for the Development of Cultural Tourism Resources by Private Enterprises', *China Non-governmental Science Technology and Economy*, 3: 68-69.

Guttormsen, T. S. & K. Fageraas (2011), 'The Social Production of "Attractive Authenticity" at the World Heritage Site of Røros, Norway', *International Journal of Heritage Studies* 17 (5): 442-462.

Handler, R. & W. Saxton (1988), 'Dyssimulation: Reflexivity, Narrative, and the Quest for Authenticity in "Living History"', *Cultural Anthropology* 3 (3): 242-260.

Hanqun, S. & C. Cheung (2010), 'Factors Affecting Tourist Satisfaction with Theatrical Performances: A Case Study of The Romance of the Song Dynasty in Hangzhou, China', *Journal of Travel & Tourism Marketing* 27 (7): 708-722.

Hewison, R. (1987), *The Heritag Industry: Britain in a Climate of Decline*. London: Methuen.

Hobson, E. (2004), *Conservation and Planning: Changing Values in Policy and Practice*. London: Spon Press.

Hudson, J. & James, P. (2007), 'The Changing Framework for Conservation of the Historic Environment', *Structural Survey* 25 (3-4): 253-264.

ICOMOS (1965), *International Charter for the Conservation and Restoration of Monuments and Sites (The Venice Charter)*. Venice: ICOMOS.

Lammy, D. (2006), 'Community, Identity and Heritage', in K. Clark (ed.), *Capturing the Public Value of Heritage: The Proceedings of the London Conference 25-26 January 2006*, 65-69. Swindon: English Heritage.

Larkham, P.J. (1996), *Conservation and the City*. London: Routledge.

Li, Q. (2016), 'Research on the Development of Folk Custom Tourism in Songcheng of Hangzhou Based on the Quality of Tourist Experience', *Tourism Overview* 5: 74-78.

Lin, X. (2015), 'Study on the Design of a Chinese Theme Park from the Perspective of Tourist Experience: The Case of Hangzhou Songcheng', *Jiangsu Commercial Forum* 6: 48-52.

Living Heritage Events (2017), 'Living Heritage Events: Game and Country Fairs'. [Online]. Available from: http://livingheritagecountryshows.com/ (accessed 24 June 2017).

Lowenthal, D. (1985), *The Past is a Foreign Country*. Cambridge: Cambridge University Press.

Ludwig, C. (2016), 'From Bricks and Mortar to Social Heritage: Planning Space for Diversities in the AHD', *International Journal of Heritage Studies* 22 (10): 811-827.

MacCannell, D. (1973), 'Staged Authenticity: Arrangements of Social Space in Tourist Settings', *American Journal of Sociology*, 79 (3), 589-603.

Ong, C. & G. Jin (2017), 'Simulacra and Simulation: Double Simulation at a North Song Dynasty Theme Park', *Tourism Geographies* 19 (2): 227-243.

Pendlebury, J. (2009), *Conservation in the Age of Consensus*. London: Routledge.

Poulios, I. (2014), 'Discussing Strategy in Heritage Conservation: Living Heritage Approach as an Example of Strategic Innovation', *Journal of Cultural Heritage Management and Sustainable Development* 4 (1): 16-34.

Qian, F. (2007), 'China's Burra Charter: The Formation and Implementation of the China Principles', *International Journal of Heritage Studies*, 13 (3): 255-264.

Ramkissoon, H. & S. Uysal (2011), 'The Effects of Perceived Authenticity, Information Search Behaviour, Motivation and Destination Imagery on Cultural Behavioural Intentions of Tourists', *Current Issues in Tourism* 14 (6): 537-562.

Ropp, P. S. (2010), *China in World History*. Oxford: Oxford University Press.

Smith, L. (2006), *Uses of Heritage*. London: Routledge.

Smith, L. & E. Waterton (2009), *Heritage, Communities and Archaeology*. London: Gerald Duckworth & Co.

Song, H. & Cheung, C. (2010), 'Factors Affecting Tourist Satisfaction with Theatrical Performances: A Case Study of The Romance of the Song Dynasty in Hangzhou, China', *Journal of Travel & Tourism Marketing*, 27 (7): 708-722.

Songcheng Group (2017), *'Hangzhou Songcheng Park – Park Overview'* [online] Available from http://www.songcn.com/SongScenic_en/About/ (accessed 15 May 2017).

Su, X. (2011), 'Heritage Production and Urban Locational Policy in Lijiang, China', *International Journal of Urban and Regional Research*, 35 (6), 1118-1132.

Sykes, O., & Ludwig, C. (2015), 'Defining and Managing the Historic Urban Landscape: Reflections on the English Experience and Some Stories from Liverpool', *European Spatial Research and Policy* 22 (2): 9-35.

Temple, R. K. G. & Needham, J. (2007), *The Genius of China: 3,000 Years of Science, Discovery and Invention*. Rochester: Inner Traditions.

Tighe, C. (2016), 'North of England's Economy Undermined by Entrenched Weaknesses', *Financial Times*, March 15 2016, [Online]. Available from: https://www.ft.com/content/d4bcaaba-dbbe-11e5-98fd-06d75973fe09?mhq5j=e1 (accessed 25 June 2017).

Trimm, R. (2012), 'Taking You Back: Region, Industry and Technologies of Living History at Beamish', *European Journal of Cultural Studies* 15 (4): 528-546.

Tsao, H. (2003), 'Unravelling the Mystery of the Handscroll "Qingming shanghe tu"', *Journal of Song-Yuan Studies* 33: 155-179.

UNESCO (2003), *Convention for the Safeguarding of the Intangible Heritage*. Paris: UNESCO.

UNESCO (2017), 'Safeguarding Communities' Living Heritage', [Online]. Available from: http://www.unesco.org/new/en/culture/resources/in-focus-articles/safeguarding-communities-living-heritage/ (accessed 24 June 2017).

Waitt, G. (2000), 'Consuming Heritage: Perceived Historical Authenticity', *Annals of Tourism Research* 27 (4): 835-862.

Wang, N. (1999), 'Rethinking Authenticity in Tourism Experience', *Annals of Tourism Research* 26 (2): 349-370.

Wang, Y. (2016), 'Sanya Songcheng Tourist Area: Root at the Locality and Sustain Glory', *Hainan Today* 6: 31-32.

Waterton, E. & Smith, L. (2008), 'Heritage Protection for the 21st Century', *Cultural Trends* 17 (3): 197-203.

Wei, Y. H. D. (2012), 'Restructuring for Growth in Urban China: Transitional Institutions, Urban Development, and Spatial Transformation', *Habitat International* 36 (3): 396-405.

Wijesuriya, G. (2005), 'The Past Is in the Present: Perspectives in Caring for Buddhist Heritage Sites in Sri Lanka', in H. Stovel, N. Stanley-Price, and R. Killick (eds.), *Conservation of Living Religious Heritage: Papers from the ICCROM 2003 Forum on Living Religious Heritage: Conserving the Sacred*, 31-43. Rome: ICCROM.

Wright, P. (1985), *On Living in an Old Country*. London: Verso.

Xu, F. (2008), 'On the Combination Development of the Local Culture Resource and Creative Economy: A Case Study of Song Cheng Group', *Zhejiang Social Sciences* 9: 63-66.

Yu, S. & Jiang, L. (2017), 'Research on Regional Culture of Tourist Attractions Based on Tourist Demand: A Case Study on "Songcheng Thousand Ancient Love" Theme Park in Sanya', *Modern Business* 12: 47-48.

Zhan, M. & Kong, S. (2016), 'The Experienced Characteristics of Tourism Performance Art: A Comparative Study Based on the Text Mining', *Tourism Forum* 9 (3): 37-43.

Zhang, Q. (2009), 'Operational Mode and Experiences of Tourism Performance in Hangzhou: A Case Study of the Thousands of Years of Love for Songcheng and the Impression West Lake', *Journal of Qingdao Hotel Management College* 1 (3): 24-28.

Zhang, W. (2016), 'Research on the Development of Tourism Entertainment Products in Songcheng: Based on the Perspective of Customer Experience', *West Leather* 24: 76.

Zhejiang Provincial Tourism Bureau (2015), *The Best-Practice Examples of Cultural Tourism in Zhejiang Province*. Beijing: Tourism Education Press.

Zhu, Y. (2013), 'Authenticity and Heritage Conservation in China: Translation, Interpretation and Practices', in K. Weiler and N. Gutschow (eds.), *Authenticity in Architectural Heritage Conservation, Transcultural Research – Heidelberg Studies on Asia and Europe in a Global Context*, 187-200. Switzerland: Springer International Publishing.

Zhu, Y. (2015), 'Cultural Effects of Authenticity: Contested Heritage Practices in China', *International Journal of Heritage Studies* 21 (6): 594-608.

About the Authors

CAROL LUDWIG is a Chartered Member of the Royal Town Planning Institute (RTPI) and Honorary Research Fellow at the University of Liverpool. Her research interests include the theorisation of heritage, the cultural process of identity formation, and community mobilisation in local conservation planning processes.

YI-WEN WANG is an Associate Professor in the Department of Urban Planning and Design, Xi'an Jiaotong-Liverpool University, China. Her research interests lie in the areas of urban conservation and heritage management, focusing on heritage-led regeneration in both urban and rural contexts.

6   Creating Cultural Identity in China

Popularising Archaeological Material and Cultural Heritage

Patrick Wertmann

Abstract

In recent years, China has experienced social, cultural, political and economic transformations. In order to stabilise the country in the midst of dramatic change and to legitimise the continuing rule of the Communist Party, the government has promoted nationalism and the building of a common sense of cultural identity among the people. One of the most familiar and available means to do this is to remind people of China's ancient past. This chapter focuses on the field of archaeology to show how growing interest in cultural heritage work has produced new ways of bringing the past to the people. New ways of making the past accessible to the masses will be introduced in this chapter. These include the construction of new museums, the popularisation of archaeological discoveries, and focus on new target groups through mobile digital museums.

Keywords: archaeological site museum, cultural identity, mobile digital museum, popularisation of cultural heritage

Introduction

In recent years, the Chinese state has faced great challenges due to its unprecedented economic growth, new political contexts, massive demographic changes and a social transformation. To guarantee social, cultural, and political stability, the Communist Party needs to construct political legitimacy, achieved through an increasing emphasis on nationalism and the fostering of a common sense of cultural identity among the people, in particular, through the re-evaluation of China's ancient past. This seems to be a matter-of-course because reverence toward the past is one of the

Ludwig, Carol, Linda Walton, and Yi-Wen Wang (eds), *The Heritage Turn in China: The Reinvention, Dissemination and Consumption of Heritage*. Amsterdam: Amsterdam University Press 2020
DOI: 10.5117/9789462985667_CH06

salient features of China's culture (Ryckmans 2008; Poo 2008; Shepherd & Yu 2013: 15).

When President Xi Jinping visited the special exhibition 'Ancient Capital – History and Culture of Beijing' held at the Capital Museum in Beijing on 25 January 2014, he made the following statement regarding the role of museums and exhibition makers:

> Museum exhibitions on history aim at bearing witness to the past. The presentation of lessons from the past will serve for the present, and they will inspire future generations. Making exhibitions means to compile and revise history. Let cultural relics tell their story, and teach the people about the wisdom of history. Let them inspire our sense of national pride and self-confidence, so to ensure that all the people make China strong and powerful again, and to have the confidence and determination to realise the China Dream. (Capital Museum 2014, author's translation).

This official comment highlights the growing interest in cultural heritage work that can be observed in China today, reflected especially in the construction of new museums, the popularisation of archaeological discoveries, and the focus on new target groups – notably children and families – with innovative means. One very recent example that captures this development is the discovery of the Han Dynasty tomb of the Marquis of Haihun State close to Nanchang, Jiangxi Province. Media coverage exceeds anything seen before. Millions of people followed the live broadcast of the excavation of the main tomb chamber on televisions.

Based on several case studies, this chapter will discuss some of the latest trends driven by growing attention from the Chinese state to the fostering of a common sense of cultural identity among the people, and eventually on the safeguarding of social, cultural and political stability. A construction boom in China has prompted a nationwide *museumisation* and strong competition among museum authorities for innovative approaches, resulting in new museum concepts such as archaeological site museums, mobile museums and new educational programmes. In combination with state-of-the-art technologies such as 3D scanning, new ways have been created for visitors to experience and connect with their cultural heritage, in particular younger people. Examples will be given of the use of new media, i.e., the Internet and educational Apps, which will play an increasingly important role in attracting new target groups, especially younger people, to places and activities that foster engagement with their cultural heritage.

The Creation of a Common Cultural Identity

A collective or *we-identity*, i.e., the awareness of belonging to a certain group or society, can never exist without the individual, whereas the individual is always a social construct defined and shaped in a specific way by the values and standards of a certain culture and time period (Assmann 1992: 130-133). To achieve a stronger sense of community, the individual's awareness of his or her cultural identity thus needs to be strengthened. This collective awareness or identity is typically based on past events and knowledge, which need to be remembered and revered by the people, mediated through symbols such as a common language, rites, fashion, food and monuments to name just a few (Varutti 2014: 90, 96). This process was termed *cultural formation* by Jan Assmann (Assmann 1992: 139). The common sense of identity or community, reached through *cultural formation*, plays a central role for a state as it stabilises social, cultural, and political formations by integrating diverse socio-cultural groups into one system (Lu 2014: 211 ff).

This chapter focuses on Chinese cultural heritage, i.e., cultural relics from museum collections or archaeological sites that initiate this *cultural formation*. Cultural relics are the memory and testimony to the history of Chinese civilisation, and the 'Golden Business Card' of the country and its people, as initially termed in the thirteenth Five-Year-Plan and stated in the opening speech of the 40th International Museum Day celebrated in the Inner Mongolia Museum in Hohhot (Zhongguo Wenwu Bao 2016). The popularisation of cultural relics through a growing number of museums and original curatorial concepts, state-of-the-art exhibition techniques, new media and popular scientific magazines promotes cultural, social and political stability. These developments also foster a sense of common identity among the diverse peoples living in China under a unified central government, in a time of immense social and economic transformation.

The *Museumisation* of China

With reports about the economic rise of China dominating the news, far less attention has been paid by Western media to the equally fast developing culture sector. The on-going construction boom in China, coupled with legislation that requires the excavation of archaeological finds unearthed in this process, has resulted in countless discoveries of ancient artefacts all over the country. In order to protect these in the interests of both the state and the general public, the Chinese heritage sector, in particular the museum industry, has been granted increasing financial support in the past few years. Since 2008, a total of 1,743 museums have received financial subsidies from the state to allow them to reduce or entirely avoid entrance fees. By 2010, these subsidies already amounted to more than two billion RMB (Chinese Museums Association 2010: 67; EUR 271.817.000, according to oanda.com, 22 July 2016). A major reason behind the *museumisation* taking place is the strengthening of cultural identity awareness among the Chinese people and, eventually, the promotion of national unity and stability (Lu 2014: 198 ff; Shepherd & Yu 2013: 20; Varutti 2014: 159 ff). Museum objects and narratives glorify the achievements of Chinese civilisation, and stress in particular the aspects of continuity and unity of the Chinese nation. These are important factors in the legitimisation of the Chinese government as the keeper of Chinese cultural history, and its political and moral heritage (Varutti 2014: 159 ff; Wallace 2008: 398).

Since the opening of the first public museum in Nantong, Jiangsu Province, in 1905, the Chinese museum landscape has undergone a fundamental transformation (Lu 2014, Shepherd & Yu 2013, Varutti 2014, Sigley 2013). This development is apparent in the *Yearbook of the Chinese Museums*, published for the first time in 2010 (Chinese Museums Association 2010). As is the case with most achievements in the cultural sector, the transformation of Chinese museums began with the reform and open-door policy launched under the leadership of Deng Xiaoping in 1978. According to the statistics, there were 349 museums nationwide at this time. By 2013, this number had increased to more than 4,000, with nearly 10,000 exhibitions and 11,177 temporary exhibitions as well as 700 million visitors (according to the Chinese Museums Association 2016, the number of museums increased to 4,692 by the end of 2015. Among them, 3,582 are state museums, and 1,110 are private museums).

These numbers clearly indicate the enormous challenges for museum planners, all the more considering that for a long time the Chinese museum landscape had the reputation of being boring and outdated. In an increasingly leisure-oriented society, museums need to be transformed into places of experience, amusement and education (Wallace 2008: 397). In addition, rising living standards in the large cities, in particular in the economic centres along the eastern seaboard, have led to the emergence of a new educated middle-class that can afford to travel within China and abroad. Based on a recent study, the Chinese middle class accounted for 230 million people in 2012, a number that is expected to rise to 630 million by 2022 (Crabbe 2014: 188). The annual income of a middle class household, according to McKinsey & Company, ranges between 106,000 and 229,000 RMB (c. EUR 13.163 to 28.437,00, according to oanda.com, 1 July 2013), that of a lower class household between 60,000 and 106,000 RMB (Barton, Chen & Jin 2013; approximately EUR 7.450 to 13.163, according to oanda.com, 1 July 2013). According to data issued by the Chinese National Tourism Administration (国家旅游局), the number of Chinese outbound tourists surpassed the 100 million mark for the first time in 2014 (China Tourism Academy Data Centre 2015). Even though this number initially appears large, it represents only seven per cent of the total Chinese population and hence indicates an enormous potential for the growth of Chinese international tourism in the coming years. As this wealthy Chinese middle class experiences other parts of the world, it gains awareness of the importance of preserving local culture and national history for the sake of one's own cultural identity.

A visit to some of the new museums in China quickly reveals that these are not museums in the traditional sense anymore. As places of culture combining the multiple functions of exhibition, education, research, sale and entertainment, their goal is not only to attract professionals, but to make the museum visit become an unforgettable experience for the whole family, from the young to the old. Very often concert halls, theatres and ceremonial halls are integrated into the museum building or made accessible in close proximity. It has become evident in recent years that this development in the Chinese museum sector has turned into a nationwide competition. For instance, each year during International Museum Day, the ten best exhibitions from across the country are announced and rewarded in front of the cameras of the national media. Museum authorities are highly motivated to earn a place among the winners.

New Trends in the Museum Landscape of China

Incentives provided by the Chinese government are aimed at the development of new museum concepts designed to attract and engage people from all levels of society. One of these outreach concepts is the so-called *mobile museum*. As indicated by the name, the exhibits, mostly made of cardboard, are loaded onto a truck to be transported to the doorstep of the visitors, especially to those living in disadvantaged regions with no access to museums. One of these trucks was inaugurated in October 2014 by the Sichuan Provincial Museum (Figure 6.1). By August 2013, it had toured 29 counties and cities within the province, exhibited at 51 stops and counted more than 1,220,000 visitors (Xinhua Net 2013). The mobile museum of the Inner Mongolia Museum is of particular interest as it is the first mobile museum in China that presents entirely digitised objects.

Figure 6.1   Mobile Museum of the Sichuan Provincial Museum, Chengdu

Source: Patrick Wertmann

The Mobile Digital Museum of the Inner Mongolia Museum

According to the *Yearbook of Chinese Museums*, Inner Mongolia counted a total of 78 museums in 2010 (Chinese Museums Association 2010: 267-269). Given the vast size of the Autonomous Region, not all Inner Mongolians have access to them. According to the official introduction of the Inner Mongolia Museum, the mobile digital museum is intended to disseminate knowledge of local culture and history, strengthen cultural identity, ethnic and national unity, safeguard stability in the border regions, and promote social development, especially in these remote areas (Inner Mongolia Museum 2015: 18). Among the target groups of the mobile museum are nomads living on the grassland, soldiers stationed in border regions, old people living in retirement homes or children in remote village schools, many of whom have never before visited a museum. Since its inauguration in May 2013, the mobile museum has travelled 19,000 km to 59 stations in all Banners of Inner Mongolia. An estimate of 90,000 people visited the truck so far (Inner Mongolia Museum 2015: 20).

The truck measures 4 m in height, 2.53 m in width, 16.6 m in length and it houses an exhibition space of 45 square metres (Figure 6.2.1). By combining state-of-the-art technologies, i.e., high-precision 3D scanning, interactive touchscreens, augmented reality, and remote transmission and control,

Figure 6.2   Mobile Digital Museum of the Inner Mongolia Autonomous Region, Hohhot

1 – Mobile Digital Museum Truck; 2-3 – Touchscreen and interactive tool; 4 – Digitised Liao Dynasty painted coffin from the tomb at Tuerji Mountain
Source: Patrick Wertmann

the Inner Mongolia Museum created a completely new type of exhibition from the old-fashioned mobile museums. More than one thousand cultural relics from the collection of the Inner Mongolia Museum were 3D-scanned. These can be now grouped in very short time to form thematic exhibitions. The truck is equipped with ten touchscreens, each of which contains a set of objects, which are complemented by captions in Chinese and Mongolian, images, and sound (Figure 6.2.2 and Figure 6.2.3). The digitised objects can be enlarged, shrunk and rotated by the user just as if handling a real object. Specially trained museum staff accompany the mobile museum to explain the use of the equipment, introduce background information on the relics, give short presentations on various topics, and implement additional educational programmes such as the *Happy Classroom* (see below). Attached to the outside of the truck is a large screen to show educational documentaries.

Instead of viewing the original relics inside the museum's showcases, the visitor can observe the digital 3D object in all its detail from a very close range and from different angles. This might raise the question of authenticity. In the case of museum objects, most visitors still expect to see the real relic. Each relic is one of a kind and should not be reproduced, as only the relic itself can be considered the true and 'authentic' one. As stated by Varutti (2014: 13), however, museum authorities justify the use of replicas in exhibitions from an educational point of view. In this sense, it does not matter whether a relic is original or not, as long as it conveys the same meaning. This also applies to the case of the 3D replicas of the Inner Mongolia mobile digital museum. They are supposed to serve an educational goal, i.e., to teach the people about their local culture and history. In the present case study, a completely new level of authenticity – we would call it virtual authenticity – has been achieved as it enables the visitors to experience the cultural relics as never before. Apart from this, the digitisation is beneficial to the conservation state of the artefacts as they no longer need to be moved or touched for the purpose of the exhibition. One of the most famous objects of the Inner Mongolia Museum, for example, is the Liao Dynasty (AD 906-1125) painted coffin from the tomb at Tuerji Mountain (吐尔基山辽墓). Due to its precarious conservation state, the coffin cannot be placed on display or investigated. After its digitisation, it is now possible for everyone to see the object in full detail (Figure 6.2.4). What is more, the visitor can virtually open the coffin and see all its different layers. Technical drawings and additional explanations supplement the 3D object.

The Transformation of Museums into Educational Institutions

A frequent answer to the latest challenges in the Chinese museum landscape is the architecture of the museum buildings, which impresses due to its innovative and futuristic designs (Jacobson 2014; Figures 6.3 and 6.4). These museums are designed to function as art objects themselves. Without doubt, such buildings bring their visitors under a spell, and they are indeed a 'Golden Business Card' of the local government and people. The exhibition's contents and the curatorial concepts, however, are very often still unaffected by this new trend.

This problem was criticised in an interview by the then President of the Chinese Museums Association, and Deputy Director-General of the State Administration of Cultural Heritage, Song Xinchao, in 2012 (Yang 2012). According to Song, it is not important to take the visitor's breath away by the monumental museum buildings or the number of exhibited relics. It should be more important to carefully develop target group-oriented exhibition concepts with popular scientific approaches. He especially emphasised concentrating on children, who account for one third of all museum visitors at present. He urged forming closer co-operation with schools, for instance, in the form of workshops, and being integrated into the national curricula.

Figure 6.3 The Ordos Museum in Kangbashi, Inner Mongolia Autonomous Region

1 – Outside view; 2 – Inside view
Source: Patrick Wertmann

Figure 6.4   The Guangdong Provincial Museum, Guangzhou

Source: Patrick Wertmann

One museum that successfully began to implement this request was the already mentioned Inner Mongolia Museum with the launch of the educational programme *Happy Classroom* (欢乐大课堂) in 2015. This programme was especially designed to suit the needs of children and youngsters, and to strengthen the museum's function as a supplemental educational institution (Special Committee for Social Education of the Chinese Museums Association 2014: 7-13). Being enjoyable, educational, entertaining, and interactive, the *Happy Classroom* represents a modern alternative to the traditional, often monotonous ways of teaching. The programme can be adjusted according to certain target groups, for instance families and children, kindergartens, elementary and middle schools or universities. It usually begins with a visit to the exhibition halls and continues with a multimedia knowledge quiz competition and interactive activities (e.g., identifying fossils, making ethnic minority clothes, Mongolian wrestling, spinning wool, interactive activities in English). The contents include ancient culture and history, revolutionary history, ethnic minority culture, environment, science and technology, and the history of the Chinese Communist Party. The educational staff of the museum gives lively demonstrations and encourages the students to take part in role-plays and to come out of their shells. The goal is not only to teach the children about their local and national history and culture, but in particular to improve their ability to recognise and appreciate it, and to foster their sense of national identity and patriotism. In order to also enable children from remote areas in Inner Mongolia to enjoy this programme, it is now implemented as an additional programme of the mobile digital museum.

New Media as Means to Disseminate Knowledge: Internet and Educational Apps

Along with the development of new exhibition techniques and educational programmes to spread knowledge of culture and history, and to strengthen cultural identity awareness among the people, another major field in this respect is that of New Media (Wallace 2008: 400). Using the Internet, people can learn about their past without even leaving their homes. A trendsetter in this field is the Beijing Palace Museum, which released a new website in 2016 specially designed for children (Palace Museum 2016). The website includes a number of features such as an animated map of the Forbidden City and guided tours that provide information on the main sites within the palace. Further sections present selected artefacts from the Palace Museum collection or interesting facts about the lives of the emperors. Furthermore, the children have access to games and short videos on various topics related to life within the Forbidden City.

In addition to the Internet, mobile phones and Tablet PCs increasingly dominate the market. A statistic published by the China Internet Network Information Centre (CNNIC) revealed that among the 632 million Internet users, 80.9% access the Internet via their mobile phones (CINFC 2014: 4). According to the Ministry of Industry and Information Technology (MIIT), the number of mobile phone users in China exceeded 1.22 billion at the end of 2013 (Custer 2013). These numbers clearly show the huge potential for this market. By combining traditional contents with state-of-the-art technologies, it is hoped that more people will use these New Media as learning tools.

The Beijing Palace Museum has also achieved a milestone in this field with the release of the first mobile phone App in the cultural sector in May 2014. The App *Painting of Twelve Yinzhen Beauties* (胤禛美人图) designed for iPad in both Chinese and English introduces twelve famous paintings of Chinese beauties, who then guide the user through the luxurious and elegant life of the Qing Dynasty court. According to a statistical survey, this App has been downloaded more than 200,000 times every two weeks since its release (Zhao 2015). More Apps have since been developed and released, among them *The Forbidden City Daily* (每日故宫), *The Forbidden*

Figure 6.5   Touch Media Magic Cards allow visitors to interact with virtual replicas of famous cultural relics

Source: Patrick Wertmann

City Auspicious Symbols (紫禁城祥瑞), and the latest App *The Night Revels of Han Xizai* (韩熙载夜宴图). With the download of the App *Your Forbidden City* (掌上故宫), the user can select from various thematic tours through the Forbidden City that provide, in addition to maps, detailed introductory texts and photographic material. The iPad App *The Emperor's Day* (皇帝 的一天) was launched in October 2014, and designed for children aged nine to eleven. In this App, the users step into the shoes of the emperor to be guided behind the walls of the Forbidden City by a little dragon. They learn about the emperor's everyday life including aspects such as the food he ate, the clothes he wore, the games he played, and the typical duties he had during the course of a day.

Produced by the Touch Culture Media (Beijing) Co., Ltd., Chinese museums such as the National Museum of China, the Emperor Qin Shihuang's Mausoleum Site Museum or the Shaanxi History Museum have released the so-called Touch Media Magic Cards (指触魔卡). A set of ten cards feature a series of objects, which can be scanned with the camera of a mobile phone or an iPad after installation of the specially designed App. Additional background information on the objects is given by a narrator. As in the case of the Inner Mongolia mobile digital museum, the relics appear on the screen as virtual replicas with which the user can interact (Figure 6.5). These differ, however, in that they are in pocket format and hence can be taken away by the visitor.

These cards are just one example of the latest development in the cooperation between cultural institutions and the creative industries. In May 2016,
the State Council announced that it would encourage cultural institutions
to develop creative cultural products (文化创意产品) so as to make culture
and history more approachable and vital for the general public. Again, to
give the Beijing Palace Museum as an example, it now has its own Taobao
channel, on which a large variety of creative cultural products are on sale.

Archaeological Site Museums as Public Places of Cultural Heritage

A new trend in the popularisation of Chinese cultural heritage is linked to
the economic rise of the country, which has resulted in a construction boom
that led to unanticipated discoveries of ancient relics. In order to make the
general public re-experience the exciting moment of the discovery and to
conserve the find situation for later generations, the central and provincial
governments provide significant amounts of financial grants to construct
archaeological site museums. The news about these site museums is received
with great interest by the media, hence they contribute significantly to
the promotion of a growing awareness among the population about their
local and national history and culture. Among the successful examples
of archaeological site museums are the Jinsha Site Museum in Chengdu,
the archaeological site museum of the Nanyue Palace in Guangzhou, and
the Maritime Silk Road Museum in Yangjiang, Guangdong Province. The
latter museum houses the best preserved Chinese shipwreck from the Song
Dynasty (AD 960-1279), the Nanhai No 1, which was transported there in an
unprecedented way inside a huge container after being salvaged from the
seabed (Ma, Xue & Yang 2010). The visitors can now observe archaeologists
carrying out the excavation of the shipwreck. It is worth noting that the
first two museums represent peripheral, but highly sophisticated cultures
that flourished out of the region typically considered the cradle of Chinese
civilisation. These museums are well-suited to the goal of disseminating an
image of China as a multicultural nation of diverse peoples who co-evolved
and prospered in different regions, but who have also always formed an
integral part of a greater and unified *Chinese* civilisation. In this way, local
identities are promoted and given equal rights to be recognised, while
joining together as part of Chinese civilisation, and thus contributing to
national stability (Denton 2014: 39 ff; Shepherd & Yu 2013: 25 ff; Wallace
2008: 398-399, 401-404).

The first private archaeological on-site museum in China is the Tang West Market Museum in Xi'an, Shaanxi Province. Its opening in 2010 represented a milestone in the development of the Chinese museum landscape. As already indicated by the name, the museum was constructed right on top of the archaeological site of the Tang Dynasty West Market, which is often claimed to have been the official eastern starting point of the Silk Roads. The museum forms the core of the so-called Tang West Market project, which was developed by the Xi'an Tang West Market Culture Industry Investment Co., Ltd. (大唐西市文化产业投资集团有限公司), and decided in the framework of the eleventh five-year plan and the twelfth five-year plan of Xi'an City and Shaanxi Province. The gigantic sum of eight billion RMB (approximately EUR 1.090.540.000, according to oanda.com, 22 July 2016) was granted for this project covering an area of 82 acres with a building area totalling up to 1.35 million square metres. The aim behind this project is a completely new approach: combining the preservation and presentation of cultural heritage with modern life and business development. Construction took place in several phases and included the museum itself, an antique and gold market, an art centre, boutiques, restaurants, upper-class residential complexes as well as a hotel and an international trade centre.

According to an official statement of the China Cultural Industry Association (中国文化遗产协会), the Tang West Market project is:

> ... [T]he national sole international business and tourism culture industry project with the subject of Great Tang Culture and Silk Road Culture rebuilt in the former place of west market of Tang Chang'an City, which is the National Cultural Industry Demonstration Base, National AAAA Tourism Attraction and Productive Protection Demonstration Base of National Intangible Cultural Heritage, National Moral Education Demonstration Base and the Model Unit of Chinese Cultural Heritage Protection and Inheritance. (http://www.chncia.org/en/companies-detail.php?mid=4&id=24, accessed: 08 November 2016).

This statement clearly shows the latest trend in the Chinese culture industry: to combine the dissemination and preservation of cultural heritage with business development in order to support local tourism and improve the image and cultural identity of Xi'an, in the case of this project without governmental funds.

The Tang West Market Museum houses a collection of more than 20,000 objects. While most of them were excavated from the archaeological site, others originate from the private collection of the museum founder. The

Figure 6.6   Popular Archaeology, Issue 03/2015

Source: Patrick Wertmann

artefacts are clearly related to the history of the Silk Roads and cover a historical time period of nearly 3,000 years. The archaeological site forms the centre of the museum as it is integrated into the exhibition and provides the visitors a unique glimpse into the excavation works. The permanent exhibition focuses on the trade of the West Market. The museum further includes space for two temporary exhibitions, a bookstore, cafés, restaurants, a cinema and a theatre. The reconstruction of a commercial road built in the style of the Tang Dynasty West Market presents various handicrafts from along the Silk Roads, which the visitors can either buy or produce themselves in the course of workshops offered at specific times.

Growing interest among the Chinese general public towards archaeological site museums was indicated by an article published in the March 2015 issue of the magazine *Popular Archaeology* (大众考古, Figure 6.6). An article by Meng Xianmin dealt with the question of how archaeological remains of antique cities should be presented to the general public, and what importance they have in the promotion of local culture tourism, the economy and landscape design (Meng 2015). Magazines such as *Popular Archaeology* have become increasingly widespread among the general public in China. Like museums, they contribute significantly to the dissemination of national culture and the strengthening of cultural identity. Contributions from the fields of archaeology, culture, historical building research, anthropology and museology are presented to the public in an appealing and easy-to-understand way. The declared mission of the magazine is to arouse the interest of the readers towards their own culture and history, and in particular to make them understand the necessity to preserve their cultural heritage for future generations (He 2015: 2). According to Meng, there is great interest on the part of the general public in city archaeology. The sites and related archaeological work and academic disciplines should be made available to the public. A visit to the archaeological site had to become an experience for the entire family, not only by presenting the excavated relics, but through reconstructions, restoration and especially through inclusion of the visitors. Only then could local history and culture be brought closer to the public.

In the case of the Han Dynasty tomb of the Marquis of Haihun State, the media coverage has exceeded anything seen before. The discovery was one of the key topics reported about in newspapers and especially in popular scientific magazines such as *Chinese National Geography* (中国国家地理), which published a special issue on it in March 2016. The climax, however, was so far reached on 14 November 2015, when the whole nation followed the live broadcast of the opening of the main tomb chamber by archaeologists. A TV host joined by an expert guided the audience through the 90 minute programme. The pressure for the archaeologists must be extremely high under such circumstances, knowing that the entire nation is observing each step they take.

The discovery of the Han Dynasty tomb of the Marquis of Haihun can be regarded as a major breakthrough for the field of archaeology in gaining a public audience. It represents a successful case of how a specialist archaeological topic turned into a topic of wide public interest. Due to contributions made by mass- and social media, whether consciously or unconsciously, the work centred on this archaeological discovery has left the ivory tower and touched the common ground. Because of this newly developed awareness and knowledge of the general public towards archaeology, experts are now faced with a new responsibility, i.e., to share their work results in appealing and easy-to-understand ways.

According to official statements (Nanchang Daily 2016), the next step in the story of the Han Dynasty Marquis is the construction of the archaeological site park *Nanchang Archaeological Site Park of the Han Dynasty Haihun State* (南昌海昏侯国考古遗址公园), and the museum *Nanchang Archaeological Site Museum of the Han Dynasty Haihun State* (南昌汉代海昏侯国遗址博物馆). The ultimate goal is to construct a 5A-level national tourist destination, an archaeological site park, and, eventually, to have the site listed as a UNESCO World Cultural Heritage site

Conclusion

Due to the enormous growth of the Chinese economy in recent years, the state and in particular the Communist Party, is confronted with a fast transforming society expressing new needs and demands. The government needs to take measures to prevent social fragmentation and political instability. A major role in this process is played by the formation and strengthening of a common sense of identity, which is built upon each individual's awareness of his or her culture. According to Chinese tradition, the ruling class focuses on a re-evaluation and the glorification of the past, in particular through the popularisation of archaeological finds and cultural heritage.

This chapter has illuminated the wide range of new developments taking place in the Chinese culture sector, and in particular in the Chinese museum landscape. Immense subsidies granted by the state have led to the construction of museums nationwide. Futuristic museum buildings and state-of-the-art exhibition techniques are used to reach out and attract increasing numbers of visitors. As required by the government, a special focus is placed on children and youngsters by designing educational programmes in line with the national curricula, such as the Happy Classroom programme developed by the Inner Mongolia Museum. Museums have thus gradually been turned into supplemental educational institutions to teach children about their history and culture, and to foster awareness of their cultural and national identity. As shown by initiatives on the part of the Beijing Palace Museum, for example, new media (Internet, Apps) and popular scientific approaches play a further major role in this development process as they attract more than the traditional target-groups. Whereas primarily the economic centres along the Chinese eastern seaboard were initially affected by these changes, the government now puts emphasis on those people living in areas which so far have been less affected – or even unaffected – by the economic boom. By digitisation and the development of new museum concepts, notably the mobile museum, cultural heritage can be moved out of the museum and on to the doorsteps of these people.

Finally, the construction of archaeological site museums across the country is another means to include the local population in the tracing and understanding of their own past and hence to make them connect with their local environment. Very often, this is now done together with social media as exemplified by the discovery of the Han Dynasty tomb of the Marquis of the Haihun State. Future research will need to assess the impact that educational Apps, communication platforms such as WeChat, and popular scientific publications have on the dissemination of knowledge about cultural heritage, and the fostering of a new cultural identity.

Acknowledgments

I would like to thank the Beijing Branch Office of the Eurasia Department, German Archaeological Institute, for supporting this project and for helping me to establish first contacts with the museums mentioned in this paper. I am especially grateful to the colleagues from the Museum of the Inner Mongolia Autonomous Region, Hohhot, in particular Mrs. Wulantuoya and Mr. Li Shaobing for giving me access to the mobile digital museum and for sharing valuable insights into their public educational programmes. Last but not least, I would like to thank the editors of this book, in particular Carol Ludwig and Linda Walton for proofreading and giving valuable comments.

References

Assmann, J. (1992), *Das kulturelle Gedächtnis. Schrift, Erinnerung und politische Identität in frühen Hochkulturen*. München: C.H. Beck.

Barton, D., Y. G. Chen, & A. Jin (2013), 'Mapping China's middle class' [Online]. Available from: www.mckinsey.com/insights/consumer_and_retail/mapping_chinas_middle_class (accessed: 14 January 2016).

Capital Museum 首都博物馆 (2014), 'Rang wenwu chuanbo lishi zhihui 让文物传播历史智慧 [Let cultural relics spread historical knowledge]'. [Online]. Available from: www.capitalmuseum.org.cn/zjsb/content/2016-02/23/content_63186.htm (accessed: 6 November 2016).

China Internet Network Information Centre (CINFC) 中国互联网络信息中心 (2014), 'Zhongguo hulian wangluo fazhan zhuangkuang tongji baogao 中国互联网络发展状况统计报告 [Statistical report about the development of the Chinese Internet]'. [Online]. Available from: www.cnnic.cn/hlwfzyj/hlwxzbg/hlwtjbg/201407/P020140721507223212132.pdf (accessed: 14 January 2016).

China Tourism Academy Data Centre 国家旅游局数据中心 (2015), *2014 nian Zhongguo lüyouye tongji gongbao 2014* 年中国旅游业统计公报 [Statistical Bulletin of the China Tourism 2014]. [Online]. Available from: www.ctaweb.org/html/2015-12/2015-12-17-15-23-83882.html (accessed: 14 January 2016).

Chinese Museums Association 中国博物馆协会 (2010), *Zhongguo bowuguan nianjian 2010* 中国博物馆年鉴2010 [Chinese Museum Yearbook 2010]. Beijing: Science Press.

Chinese Museums Association 中国博物馆协会 (2016), *Di qi jie 'Bo Bo Hui' zhu luntan – 'Sichou zhi Lu yu bowuguan hezuo guoji luntan' zai Chengdu juxing* 第七届"博博会"主论坛－－'丝绸之路与博物馆合作国际论坛'在成都举行 [The Seventh "MPT-EXPO" Symposium in Chengdu on "International Symposium on Silk Road and Museum Cooperation"]. [Onllne]. Available from: www.chinamuseum.org.cn/a/xiehuizixun/20160919/8725.html (accessed: 6 November 2016).

Crabbe, M. (2014), *Myth-Busting China's Numbers*. Basingstoke: Palgrave Macmillan.

Custer, C. (2013), 'China Made 1.2 Billion Mobile Phones Last Year'. www.techinasia.com/china-12-billion-mobile-phones-year (accessed: 14 January 2016).

Denton, K. A. (2014), *Exhibiting the Past: Historical Memory and the Politics of Museums in Postsocialist China*. Honolulu: University of Hawaii Press.

He, Y.A. 贺云翱 (ed.) (2015), *Dazhong kaogu* 大众考古 [Popular Archaeology] 3. Nanjing: Dazhong Kaogu Magazine Press.

Inner Mongolia Museum 内蒙古博物院 (2015), *Bowuguan song dao jia menkou, wenhua huimin ling juli: Nei Menggu bowuyuan liudong shuzi bowuguan xunzhan jishi* 博物馆送到家门口，文化惠民零距离: 内蒙古博物院流动数字博物馆巡展纪实 [Bringing the Museum to the Doorstep, Culture Directly Benefits the People: The Documentation of the Inner Mongolia Mobile Digital Museum Tour]. Beijing: Science Press.

Jacobson, C. (2014), *New Museums in China*. New York: Princeton Architectural Press.

Lu, T. L.-D. (2014), *Museums in China: Power, Politics and Identities*. Abingdon: Routledge.

Ma, H.Z. 马洪藻, G.R. Xue, 薛桂荣, X.Y. Yang 杨昕怡 (2010), *Haishang Dunhuang* 海上敦煌 [Dunhuang in the Sea]. Guangzhou: Nanfang Daily Press 南方日报出版社.

Meng, X. 孟宪民 (2015), 'You Jimo gucheng xiang dao de gudai chengzhi ying ruhe xiang gongzhong zhanshi? 由即墨古城想到的古代城址应如何向公众展示? [Taking the Ancient Jimo Town Site as a Starting Point to Think About How to Present Ancient City Ruins to the Public]', *Dazhong kaogu* 大众考古 [Popular Archaeology] 3: 44-49.

Nanchang Daily 南昌日报社 (2016), 'Buju Haihun Hou Guo yizhi – zaixian Han wenming huihuang 布局海昏侯国遗址—再现汉文明辉煌 [Arrange the Site of the Haihun Marquis-State – Rediscover the Glory of the Han Civilisation]'.

[Online]. Available from: www.nc.gov.cn/xwzx/ncyw/201608/t20160830_821042. htm (accessed: 6 November 2016).

Palace Museum (2016), Palace Museum Beijing, Website for Children. [Online]. Available from: http://young.dpm.org.cn (accessed: 6 November 2016).

Poo, M. (2008), 'The Formation of the Concept of Antiquity in Early China', in D. Kuhn & H. Stahl, (eds.) *Perceptions of Antiquity in Chinese Civilization*, 85-101. Heidelberg: Edition Forum.

Ryckmans, P. (2008), 'The Chinese Attitude Towards the Past'. [Online]. Available from: www.chinaheritagequarterly.org/articles.php?issue=014&searchterm=014_ chineseAttitude.inc (accessed: 14 January 2016).

Segal, A. (2014), 'How China Influences the Internet'. [Online]. Available from: www.forbes.com/sites/adamsegal/2014/11/07/how-china-influences-the-inter net/#2715e4857a0b7039325c0e7f (accessed: 14 January 2016).

Shepherd, R. & L. Yu (2013), *Heritage Management, Tourism, and Governance in China. Managing the Past to Serve the Present*. New York, Heidelberg, London: Springer.

Sigley, G. (2013), 'The Ancient Tea Horse Road and the Politics of Cultural Heritage in Southwest China: Regional Identity in the Context of a Rising China', in: T. Blumenfield & H. Silverman, (eds.), *Cultural Heritage Politics in China*, 235-246. New York: Springer.

Special Committee for Social Education of the Chinese Museums Association 中国博物馆协会社会教育专业委员会, Inner Mongolia Museum 内蒙古博物院, Inner Mongolia Museum Society 内蒙古博物馆学会 (2014), *Zhongguo bowuguan jiaoyu xiangmu shifan anlie – pingxuan*《国博物馆教育项目示范案列》评选 [First Evaluation of the 'Case Demonstration of China Museums Educational Projects']. Beijing: Science Press 科学出版社.

Varutti, M. (2014), *Museums in China. The Politics of Representation after Mao*. Woodbridge: The Boydell Press.

Wallace, G. (2008), 'Archaeology and Society', in R.A. Bentley, H.D.G. Maschner & C. Chippindale (eds.), *Handbook of Archaeological Theories*, 395-407. Plymouth: AltaMira Press.

Xinhua Net新华网 (2013), *Sichuan 'da pengche' liudong bowuguan wie bai wan qunzhong song wenhua* 四川'大篷车'流动博物馆为百万群众送文化 [The great Sichuan mobile museum truck brings culture to a million people]. [Online]. Available from: www.sc.xinhuanet.com/content/2013-09/11/c_117324051.htm (accessed: 14 January 2016).

Yang, M.M. (2012), *5-18 guoji bowuguan, ri mianfei bowuguan: ruhe biancheng da ketang?* 5·18国际博物馆日 免费博物馆: 如何变成大课堂？ [5-18 International Museum Day, Free Museums: How to Turn Them into Large Classrooms?]. [Online]. Available from: www.culture.people.com.cn/GB/87423/17920622.html (accessed: 14 January 2016).

Zhao, Y.Y. 赵莹莹 (2015), *Gugong bowuyuan yuanzhang Shan Jixiang: 'Huangdi' ye yao zhanling shouji APP* 故宫博物院院长单霁翔: '皇帝'也要占领手机APP [Shan Jixiang, Director of the Palace Museum: The Emperor Also Wants to Occupy the Cell Phone APP]. [Online]. Available from: www.news.youth.cn/gn/201503/t20150306_6506672.htm (accessed: 14 January 2016).

Zhongguo Wenwu Bao 中国文物报 (2016), *Shuo zhen lu bao wenmin – di yi ci quan guo ke yidong wenwu pucha chengguo fengshuo* 识珍录宝典守文明 – – 第一次全国可移动文物普查成果丰硕 [Identification, Collection and Registration of Treasures in Order to Preserve Civilization – The Achievements of the First National Survey of Movable Cultural Relics]. [Online]. Available from: www.nmgbwy.com/zydtxq/1304.jhtml (accessed: 25 July 2016).

About the Author

PATRICK WERTMANN is currently research fellow for the project "Sino-Indo-Iranica" at the Institute of Asian and Oriental Studies, University of Zurich. He previously worked at the Beijing Branch Office of the German Archaeological Institute (DAI) and Renmin University, Beijing.

7 The Museum as Expression of Local Identity and Place

The Case of Nanjing

Kenny K.K. Ng

Abstract

This chapter looks at museum representations of the historic city of Nanjing, and explores how the narratives of a relic museum function as a 'memory machine' to reconstruct cultural belonging and identity, generating a bond between people and place that takes on the affective power of 'topophilia'. While such local bonding is crucial for developing an understanding of, and commitment to, heritage preservation, modern museology operates on national and global, as well as local, stages, greatly complicating museum presentations of history and cultural heritage. This chapter argues that the relic museum – as a surviving memorial of the past by saving and displaying its historical objects and artefacts – thus becomes an arena of contestation between top-down state recognition for national and global audiences and bottom-up locally embedded cultural revival.

Keywords: Nanjing, Six Dynasties, relic museum, topophilia, heritage, memory

Introduction

How does a museum tell the stories of a place? Does it tell its stories differently to local inhabitants and to an outsider audience? Like a piece of literature, a museum can be intimately connected with its own city through narratives, images, and symbols. But curatorial practice and exhibition simultaneously involve the processes of contextualisation and de-contextualisation. For example, a historic city with a long tradition and

Ludwig, Carol, Linda Walton, and Yi-Wen Wang (eds), *The Heritage Turn in China: The Reinvention, Dissemination and Consumption of Heritage.* Amsterdam: Amsterdam University Press 2020
DOI: 10.5117/9789462985667_CH07

rich cultural heritage would endow a museum with a great assemblage of objects and texts to materialise an otherwise abstract past. By removing the things from their original contexts and rearranging them in new ways of visual display and perceptions, modern museological practice can contribute to forging individual and collective understanding of a place and its varied identities in past, present, and future.

Yet, to speak of a museum that intrinsically creates an aura of place or 'home' can be a paradoxical statement in itself. The sense of place is customarily understood as a humanistic ideal. For Yi-fu Tuan (1977), 'place' is a fundamental concept in humanistic geography that emphasises human subjectivity and experience rather than the hard logic of spatial science. Tuan defines place attachment as how people relate on an emotional and perceptual level to the places that they inhabit. He coined the term 'topo-philia' (literally 'love of place') to explore the affective bonds between people and settings, environmental perception, attitudes, and value. The material environment, Tuan notes, 'is not just a resource base to be used or natural forces to adapt to, but also sources of assurance and pleasure, objects of profound attachment and love' (Tuan 1990: xii). Tuan's humanistic approach differentiates the 'sense of place' from the abstraction of space as used in social analysis and economic rationality. He develops a notion of space as an open arena of action and movement while place is about stopping and resting and becoming involved. Place is amenable to discussions of things such as 'value' and 'belonging' (Cresswell 2005: 20). Place, as distinct from space, provides a tangible locus of time and living environs to which people and groups have deep emotional and psychological ties. Place 'provides a profound centre of human existence' (Convery, Corsane & Davis 2012: 1) – it is through the individuals' experiences in their sense of place that they define their identities as groups of people, or as citizens in society.

How can museums make sense of place, or how do they welcome and make their visitors feel connected to a place? For most visitors, museum space is a curatorially recreated world of the past and a place that is 'not home'; but it is also where they would like to go precisely because for them the museum is an exotic place and a repository of the unfamiliar past. 'The past is a foreign country' – David Lowenthal quotes L.P. Hartley's opening phrase from *The Go-Between* (1953), arguing that there is a plethora of pasts constantly being redefined and remade to suit our present intentions. Lowenthal notes succinctly that while historical change made present unlike past circumstances, it was not until the nineteenth century that Europeans began to perceive the past as different as 'a congeries of foreign lands shaped by unique histories and personalities' (Lowenthal 2015: 4). Preservation evolved from an antiquarian and individual pursuit into sustained national programmes. Only in the late twentieth century did every country seek to secure its own heritage against despoliation and decay. In China today while accelerating social change, technology, and commercialisation have increasingly alienated the past from contemporary society, both individuals and institutions have sought to recuperate the past as a means of guidance, critique, or escape. The past has become the prime source of personal and collective identity. Hence its relics and objects not only evoke affective feelings and imaginations of bygone times, but also generate discourses and narratives to engage conflicts over history, memory, and heritage. Modern museums thus encounter the challenge of serving as memory houses of exhibits and stories, as attraction spots of leisure and tourist consumption, and also as emblems of shared heritage and communal identity subject to the politics of presentation and interpretation.

The Oriental Metropolitan Museum

Such is the case of the Oriental Metropolitan Museum in Nanjing, known by its Chinese name as the Six Dynasties Museum (*Liuchao bowuguan*), which was built on the archaeological site of palaces and residences historically occupied by a succession of emperors from the third to the sixth centuries. The English translation of the museum's name reflects how the Nanjing government has attempted to position the historic city as the Oriental metropolitan centre on a par with ancient Rome. Its Chinese name, indeed, represents better the historical context of the museum. The Six Dynasties refers to an interval of four centuries (220 to 589 A.D.) after the fall of the Han Empire (206 B.C.-220 A.D.) and before the rise of the Tang Dynasty (618-906), when China was torn by constant civil wars, political strife, and power struggles in the course of rapid dynastic changes. But the hiatus of four centuries was also known as a golden period of cultural reorganisation and regeneration with impressive achievements in the areas of literature, philosophy, aesthetics, and the arts (Juliano 1975: 7). Historically, the cultural renaissance that took place in southern China in the Six Dynasties was a result of the mass exodus of Han literati with their elite culture from northern China to the southland, and subsequent fusions of Han and non-Han civilisations arising from massive multi-ethnic migrations. Han aristocratic families in the north fled from wars and violence to the south, integrating with local people in the south and bringing social and cultural developments to new heights enhanced by the prosperity of an agricultural economy. Culturally, there was a remarkable shift from an imperial worship of divinity to an intellectual embrace of humanism when new philosophies and discourses were born in a chaotic time of explorations of the values of humanity, the meanings of life as well as its transient existence (Wei 2004). Despite constant wars and division, the Six Dynasties was favorably remembered as 'a time of glamor and splendor', excelling in calligraphy, painting, ceramics, carvings and sculpture (Wei 2004: 23). This period also saw a mature development in literary thought and aesthetic consciousness that valorised genuineness and naturalness, and embraced antiquity and tradition with a sense of anxiety and nostalgia for something already lost (Li 2004).

'The museum is the largest collection of cultural relics from the Six Dynasties (third to sixth century) in ancient China, making it vital to preserving the legacy of traditional Chinese culture', remarked the director of the museum, Hu A'xiang from the Department of History at Nanjing University on the occasion of the opening of the Oriental Metropolitan Museum in August 2014 (Lu & Wang 2014). The rapid construction of the museum itself, which took no more than two years to completion after the building project was launched in 2012, was part of China's 'museum boom' of recent decades, one of the means by which China has sought to enhance the nation's 'soft power of culture' (Lu 2014: 196).[1] The idea of building a museum on the site of the Six Dynasties palace came to fruition after an accidental discovery at the beginning of the new millennium. Local archeologists found a royal architectural relic of the Ming Dynasty under a bus station located east of the former Presidential Palace (Zongtong Fu), where Dr. Sun Yat-sen was sworn in as the provisional president of the Republic of China in 1912. Later, from 2007 to 2009 an archeological team discovered the east wall of the palace of Jiankang (one of Nanjing's ancient names) dating back to the Six Dynasties. They found that the foundations of the 25-metre ancient wall were still maintained in good condition (Xu 2010). The discovery led to an ambitious preservation project listed in the Nanjing government's overall three-year plan, with a budget of 200 million yuan (USD 25 million) from the government and private sponsors. The design was developed by Pei Partnership Architects, founded by Chien Chung Pei and Li Chung Pei, sons

---

1   According to the past five-year plan, China was to have 3,500 museums by 2015, a target it achieved three years early. In 2012 a record 451 new museums opened, pushing the total by the end of 2012 to 3,866. By contrast, in America only 20-40 museums a year were built in the decade before the 2008 financial crash. The astonishing proliferation of new museums in China begs the question of filling the abundant spaces with content, and of how the new museums can redefine their roles in society and culture ('Mad about Museums' 2014).

of the internationally renowned architect I.M. Pei. The museum, standing in situ above Jiankang city, presents over 1,200 relics unearthed at the site and artefacts collected in the Nanjing area, including porcelain, pottery figurines, epigraphs, building units, stone inscriptions, painting and calligraphy. Of note are a section of the city wall and the remains of a large-scale drainage facility from the ancient city that are both open to visitors.

City of Memories

Lying on the south bank of the Yangzi River, ancient Nanjing (now the capital of Jiangsu Province) was the capital of the Wu Kingdom (222-280), the Eastern Jin Dynasty (317-420), and the Song, Qi, Liang and Chen kingdoms of the Southern Dynasties (420-589). The museum was built on the ruins of the Eastern Jin capital city of Jiankang, standing as a remarkable cultural heritage project to showcase Nanjing. The city grew in importance during its first millennium of history because of its strategic location along the Yangzi River. It was designated as a dynastic or regional capital a number of times up to the early twentieth century when Nanjing had its last claim as the capital of yet another ephemeral regime, the Republic of China (1927-1937, 1945-1949) prior to its flight to Taiwan. For Chinese people, Nanjing was well-known as 'the capital of the Six Dynasties' or 'the capital of the Ten Kingdoms' (in southern China following the collapse of the Tang) – as China's most favored capital seat and one of the world's historical and cultural centres.[2] The emergence of Jiankang in the Six Dynasties as a wealthy and cultured metropolis constituted a major development in imperial Chinese history as well as representing the height of city building in world civilisations. The rise and fall of the capital city of Jiankang, historically, reflected the course of events during this 'turbulent yet creative age' (Dien 2007: 37). Under the reign of the Liang emperor (502-557), Jiankang underwent massive rebuilding with strengthened city walls and gates, river embankments, and extravagant imperial palaces and parks. Unfortunately, the rebels' invasion and siege of Jiankang in 548-549 brought ruin to the southern capital. When the rebels began to fire on the palace defenders from the city walls, the loyalist troops

2   Nanjing was the capital of Wu during the Three Kingdoms Period, the capital of the Song, Qi, Liang and Chen during the southern dynasties, the capital of Southern Tang Dynasty, Ming Dynasty, Taiping Heavenly Kingdom and the Republic of China. Therefore, it is called 'the capital of ten dynasties'. Since Wu, Jin, Song, Qi, Liang and Chen are all regimes established by the Han people, Nanjing is also called 'the ancient capital of six dynasties'.

sent out arsonists to burn down the palace. During the siege, the rebels found it necessary to demolish wooden buildings to supply fuel. 'Trees were the first to disappear, and by the time the city fell, the only ones left were those in the ancestral temple' (Dien 2007: 43). The fate of Jiankang is by no means unique, as other capital cities were at times destroyed during violent dynastic changes.

Modern archeological studies provide vital information that enables us to reconstruct at least a partial picture of the ancient city and its evolution. The birth of modern archaeology in China, indeed, was tied to a drive to preserve and nationalise heritage. Not unlike its European predecessors, the beginnings of modern Chinese archaeology were related to a new awareness of nationalism born of the 1919 May Fourth Movement (Betts & Ross 2015: 16). After half a century of Western intrusions and raiding of Chinese antiques, the Republican government established after 1911 looked to archaeology as a scientific means to underpin a new national agenda after World War I. Yet, archaeological investigation of ancient Jiankang was limited as the discovered sites and relics of building materials were found lying beneath downtown areas, which has made systematic excavation especially difficult. The fragmented nature of archaeological debris, such as the foundations of city walls and gates, makes it difficult for archeologists and historians to reconstruct ancient city life in China during the Six Dynasties period (Dien 2007: 354). 'The limitations prevent us from presenting a panoramic picture of the Six Dynasties from the archaeological perspective', commented Zhengjin Wei (2004: 17) of the Nanjing Municipal Museum. Textual sources are also limited. While the rich literary records and poetic renderings of the capital written more than a millennium ago gives us insights in the sophistication of elite social life in the capital city, because of their focus primarily on the court and the elite, they tell us little about the everyday lives of urban commoners.

A modern obsession with ruination and the resurgence of heritage preservation in contemporary China are significantly indicative in the new millennium of the understanding of visual articulations of remembrance and nostalgia, as well as their perceived associations between history, culture, and place-making. In *A Story of Ruins: Presence and Absence in Chinese Art and Visual Culture*, Wu Hung (2012: 7-9) examines the images of ruination from Chinese antiquity to modern visuality. He argues that contemporary Chinese art has developed a strong interest in urban ruins. By showcasing examples of painting, photography, installations, performances and films, Wu demonstrates how modern-day Chinese artists reclaim ruins as compelling symbols and narratives to articulate the meanings of ruination, fragmentation, and alienation in modern society. While Wu Hung's study has tracked down a broad array of images of ruination and how these images are differently perceived in pre-modern and contemporary Chinese cultural artefacts, what the author may want to add to his list is the representation of a relic museum both as a monument of ruination and as a memory house of objects of the past. Precisely because of the relic museum's (impossible) mission to salvage the lost objects of a vanished city to reconstruct the past, the sense of ruins and 'emptiness' as translated and denoted by the Chinese term, *xu* (Wu 2012: 26), becomes more pronounced. When the remnant site has few remains to offer, the relic museum that displays restored objects and recollected artefacts *in situ* serves instead to elicit historical memory or emotional and aesthetic responses from an audience.

From the perspective of Western museology, in nineteenth-century Europe fascination with the beauty of ruins gave rise to many national preservation projects. The Industrial Revolution, alongside the developments of increasing urbanisation with demolitions of old structures, communities, and neighbourhoods, spurred 'the romance of ruins' that shaped much of nineteenth-century cultural life, as evidenced in the creation of national museums and cathedral restorations, as well as the Victorian cult of antiquities and ancient civilisations (Betts & Ross 2015: 7). The European sensibility of nostalgia was also intimately related to Romanticism's desire to retain the crumbling pasts. After all, it was the encounter with Roman ruins that inspired Edward Gibbon to write his *Decline and Fall of the Roman Empire* (1776-1789). It is hence thought-provoking to see how current Chinese Communist authorities positioned Nanjing as an ancient Oriental city in world civilisations by drawing a parallel with Rome. According to a promotional report:

> Nanjing was the first city in the world with a population that passed a million, and was called one of the world's two classical civilisation centres, along with ancient Rome ... Nanjing was considered one of the most important 'Oriental metropolitan areas'. It represented the maturity of the agricultural civilisation, which was characterised by peace, balance and respect for nature' (Lu & Wang 2014).

Culturally, Nanjing, including the surrounding southern area known as 'Jiangnan' (meaning 'south of the Yangzi River') or 'Jinling' (the favored ancient name in Tang Dynasty poetry), was a place richly invested with a regional cultural identity. The poetic tradition known as *Jinling huaigu* ('Longing for the Past at Jinling') was rearticulated to celebrate or mourn over imperial Nanjing, rendered both as a land of beauty and leisure and as a place of misfortune and collapse in times of war (Honey 1995). The site poetically denoted as 'Jiangnan' or 'Jinling' became a 'textually imagined world of desire' (Owen 2015: 189). The cultural memories of the place were so endowed with complexly layered literary imaginations that there was 'an overlay of sites, images, and phrases that shaped the way the city was seen' (Owen 1990: 417). One may even find it impossible to think of Jinling or Nanjing as 'an old site and not be caught up in the poetry of the past' (Owen 1990: 454). Such historical formations of poetic moods and images of old Nanjing and the southland were always accompanied by the sentiment of 'lamenting the past' (*huaigu*) in Tang literature, a nostalgia pensively recalling the southern capital which experienced continuous political rebellions and sackings during the Six Dynasties.

For all the multiple literary images and cultural values carried by the historic city, modern Nanjing presents a formidable challenge for museum representation or any representation of its distinctively appalling historical countenance of war and human atrocities in contemporary Chinese history. The most notable of these is the Nanjing massacre of 1937, about which historical memories and literary memorialisation of the traumatic experiences invoke many tensions and contestations. The new millennium has seen a drive to revisit Nanjing's recent pasts in fictional, non-fictional, and filmic forms, including Ha Jin's *Nanjing Requiem* (2011), Yan Geling's *The Flowers of War* (2012) – which has been turned into a recent film adaptation by Zhang Yimou, and most famously, Iris Chang's *The Rape of Nanking: The Forgotten Holocaust of World War II* (1997) – which has spurred a filmic legacy (Feng 2017; Kinney 2012). In addition to these literary novelisations of Nanjing, the establishment of the Nanjing Massacre Memorial Museum in 1985, which is built on a former mass grave where the remains of thousands of victims were exhumed (Williams 2007: 10), bespeaks not only the issue of how the city should represent itself to the public in the form of a memorial museum, but also the question of how individuals are going to wrestle with contradictory images of the city in past and present. Nanjing has been infused with polysemous pasts and memories, erasure and remembrance, with the connotations of creativity and glamour, transience and disintegration, war and devastation. Our concern about museum representation and the city revolves around such key questions: Why is there such a strong perceived need in the new millennium to re-embrace a distant glamorous culture in the museum's display of the past? How can museological practice be integrated into part of the urban fabric to contribute to the city's place-making and self-definition?

Museum Representation: Cultural Site as Place-Making

My study of the city and museums in Nanjing is an outcome of a field trip to Nanjing and Shanghai from 29 December 2016 to 4 January 2017, conducted by a group of students of the City University of Hong Kong under my supervision. Titled 'Field Trip: Investigating Cultural Sites and Industries', the course enabled students to actively investigate cultural sites and industries through visiting cultural institutions and heritage sites in major cities outside Hong Kong.[3] In the Nanjing itinerary, our students visited a number of museums, art galleries, fine art universities, and heritage sites including the Chaotian Palace (the site of holding sacrificial rites to heaven in the Ming Dynasty), the Ming Xiaoling Mausoleum (the mausoleum of Ming emperor Zhu Yuanzhang and a World Heritage site), the Zhongshan Mausoleum (the mausoleum of Dr. Sun Yat-sen), the Nanjing Museum (Nanjing Bowuyuan), and the Oriental Metropolitan Museum.

The Nanjing Museum, built by the Republican government in its capital in 1933, was China's first comprehensive state museum. Supervised by Minister of Education Cai Yuanpei (1868-1940), the museum was the sole large Western-style modern museum in China at that time. While the most emblematic event may have been the transformation of the Forbidden City in Beijing into a public museum in 1925, Nanjing pioneered the building of the first modern museum to actively collect China's national treasures and further paved the way for the concept of public museums in Republican China. These modern museum establishments signaled 'the dismantling of imperial collections and contributed to the establishment of knowledge as a civic right and a public good' (Varutti 2014: 28). The Nanjing Museum – located in a cluster of Nanjing's historical heritage sites (its south gate faces a boulevard leading to the Ming Xiaoling Mausoleum of the first Ming emperor and the Sun Yat-Sen Mausoleum) – with its enormous collections as a storehouse of national treasures, represents the early phase of Chinese modern museology. Ranked as one of the top three comprehensive museums (along with the Beijing Imperial Palace Museum (Forbidden City) and Taipei National Palace Museum), as a repository of national treasures, the Nanjing Museum has also played an important role in reconstructing local culture within the setup of a

3   I wish to thank the student participants in the Program of Culture and Heritage Management of the City University of Hong Kong for their insights in their field reports (see 'City University Student Group' in References). They are: Au Yee Ling, Chan Wai King, Choi Ho Wing, Chow Wing Tung, Ko Yu Tung, Law Lok Kwan, Li Tze Ying, Lok On Yee, Mak Wing Yan, Wong Chlorophyll, Yau Nga Lam.

comprehensive 'cultural palace' of exhibiting some 420,000 holdings of local, national, and international exhibits over time ('Nanjing Museum: A Palace of Culture and Space of Leisure' 2015). Emphasising local culture, the permanent Gallery of History in the museum displays massive numbers of artefacts to illustrate Jiangsu's role in and contributions to Chinese civilisation.

With a different temporal framework and in a relatively smaller size and scale, the Oriental Metropolitan Museum is set up to tell localised stories of the place in a different fashion with a focused theme on Six Dynasties culture and styles of living. On the one hand, the decline of communist ideals and the loss of faith in Maoism of the early 1990s triggered a 'turn to cultural nationalism', which has been connected to newly built museums' 're-evaluation of ancient treasures and cultural features now regarded as the 'core' of Chinese culture and civilisation' (Varutti 2014: 41). On the other, contemporary Chinese museums undertake a new global mission 'to open up to the world and to introduce Chinese culture and civilisation to the widest possible audience' (Varutti 2014: 41).

The buildings and architectural styles of the old and new museums in Nanjing reflect the different historical contexts of their origins. The main building of the Nanjing Museum, designed by master architect Liang Sicheng (1901-1972) in the 1930s, features combined styles of both Chinese and Western architecture. The front section of the hall is a traditional structure built in the style of Liao Dynasty (907-1125) architecture, with the roof covered by golden tiles and looking solemn and magnificent. The exhibition hall in the back is a Western-style flat-roof structure.

Fast forward to contemporary times of global capitalism when China is at the forefront of developing its culture industry, the building of the Oriental Metropolitan Museum is a merger of modern design and traditional style, of museum space and commercial arcade, and of a place of knowledge and leisure. Previously announced that the museum would be designed by Chinese American architect I.M. Pei – whose last signature building in China is the Suzhou Museum (Suzhou Bowuguan) that opened in 2016 in Pei's hometown, the Pei Partnership Architects (managed by Pei's sons and close associates) actually engineered the construction of the new museum in Nanjing. Located adjacent to the historic Nanjing Presidential Palace on the east end of Changjiang Road, the Oriental Metropolitan Museum is connected with the Nanjing Hanfujie Plaza within a commercial complex of a hotel and shopping mall. In their descriptions, the architects adopted an approach of environmental harmony to limit the building height to 21 metres so as to preserve the natural daylight for adjacent buildings and throughout the complex (Pei Partnership Architects 2008-2013). The whole

Figure 7.1   Oriental Metropolitan Museum

Source: Kenny K.K. Ng

design ventures to maintain a balance between nature and urban and commercial culture. Omnipresent glass walls are instituted in interior spaces to mingle the inside with outside, and fuse the historical exhibits inside the museum with the urban environment outside. On the ground floor, the hotel lobby and the museum atrium are separated by glass walls to allow for transparency between the two components.

The museum is organised as an L-shaped structure with a Chinese garden in the heart of the complex. The exterior of the museum is built as an integrated structure by the use of two materials: a beige limestone covering the walls is said to recall the colour tone of the Six Dynasties period, and the glass of the fenestrations and skylights as state-of-the-art building patterns. The double-height museum entrance is carved underneath the museum's stone façade, with the all-glass canopy resting above the entryway to frame the main entrance as a monumental atrium and an inviting hallway for visitors.

At the entrance gallery visitors are led by the staircase to go down to Level B-1, the hall of the Ancient Relic Wall displaying architectural remains of ancient Jiankang. Building fragments of the city are housed in glass covers in separate display boxes: some of the highlights are a rammed earth wall of 25 metres wide, which was excavated near the current site of the

Figure 7.2   Remnant site of Jiankang City

Source: Kenny K.K. Ng

Figure 7.3   Exhibition hall, Oriental Metropolitan Museum

Source: Kenny K.K. Ng

museum, and the remains of drainage ditches that reveal the waterways and canal systems crucial to the city's domestic use, transportation and self-defense. The exhibition hall is illuminated by a somber and warm yellow light, spacious enough to allow an audience to leisurely roam around the geometrically arranged display boxes. Through viewing the remains of the past in their specific configurations within the hall, visitors feel invited to wonder about and reimagine daily life in the ancient city. Yet, the relic museum faces the challenge to preserve the unpreserved heritage, and to resurrect the past through spectacle and feeling.

If the exposure of architectural objects *in situ* gives the audience a sense of emplacement with illustrated knowledge of the past in connection with the fragments, modern museology has more to do with a displacement strategy of detaching the artefacts from their historical contents and contexts, counting on audience contemplation of the way objects are displayed. The grand staircase at the end of the atrium leads visitors to Level 2 of the mezzanine which houses the permanent galleries of archaeological artefacts not merely as material culture *per se* but more importantly as objects charged with aesthetic values and multiple meanings pending the audience's appreciation and deciphering. One example of this kind of display is the 'Chicken-spouted Vessel' (*Qingci hu*), a celadon vessel commonly used by the upper class in the Six Dynasties for wine drinking as well as for religious purposes in burials. The Chinese illustration emphasises the shape, function, and colouration of the vessel – that is, on the practical and aesthetic values of the object in daily life. Without much elaboration on either archaeological or historical knowledge about the artefact, the brief English illustration ends, 'This is one of the typical celadon in Six Dynasties'. Compare this with an earlier 1975 catalog of the object compiled by the China House Gallery in New York, which provides detailed epistemological, archaeological, and historical frameworks with dating for the same object in three long paragraphs. As the middle paragraph goes, 'Ewers of this type begin to appear in the fourth century, reflecting a new direction in the development of green glazed stonewares; vessel forms move away from their dependence on Han bronze prototype. The venerable *hu* (vessel) shape has been transformed by adding a handle and perky spout like a chicken's head with a cock's comb. Spout and handle lend the stout but controlled well-known form of the body a lightly spontaneous and whimsical spirit' (Juliano 1975: 30). Seemingly, the modern Chinese museum has adopted a visually oriented and aesthetic approach that alienates the objects from their contexts of creation and use by posing them in more spectacularly pleasing fashions. A similar aesthetic mode of presentation is used for the remaining celadon vessels, figurines, the eaves tiles of buildings, and the like.

Figure 7.4   Chicken-spouted vessels

Source: Kenny K.K. Ng

The museum's emphasis on aesthetics and visual spectacle favors the creation of a past civilisation in the atemporal realm of universal beauty, that is, recreating a contemporary vision of Six Dynasties culture and more significantly, of a provincially southland culture in the environs of Nanjing as Chinese civilisation writ large. In addition to presenting Nanjing and its

Figure 7.5   Chicken-spouted vessels, displayed in broken pieces

Source: Kenny K.K. Ng

Figure 7.6   Display of figurines

Source: Kenny K.K. Ng

Figure 7.7   Display of eave tiles

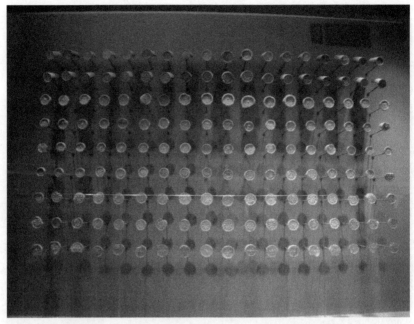

Source: Kenny K.K. Ng

past as a hidden gem in Chinese culture, as well as transcending the place and historical context, this new mode of museology can be understood as an ongoing transformation of modern Chinese museums and cities at large on their paths to commercialisation, commodification, and consumption. As Marzia Varutti suggests, 'Chinese museums are facing a vast array of challenges, not least a growing domestic appetite for cultural consumption and the scrutiny of increasingly informed, cosmopolitan and consumption-oriented audiences (2014: 162). 'Aestheticisation' is one of the strategies that museums deploy to meet such challenges. Visitors are invited to buy objects in the museum shop as simulacra of Beauty, the Past, or the Ethnic 'Other'. Trying to appeal to a consumption-oriented and pleasure-seeking urban audience (along with foreign visitors), galleries are crafted as interior courtyards with soothing sounds and sights of bamboos, hanging scrolls of calligraphy, stone seats and ponds to provide reclusive moments of intimacy for individuals to sit down, view, and contemplate the exhibits. This simplicity and modesty of interior spaces and architecture are functional in forging a new 'museum effect', in which an audience is lured through sensations to feel and experience the way of living in the past in its reconstructed glamor and beauty instead of learning the bloody histories through words.

Figure 7.8   Interior court, Oriental Metropolitan Museum

Source: Kenny K.K. Ng

Coda: Museum as City Restoration

The innovative construction of the Oriental Metropolitan Museum is characteristic of different forms of public and private heritage initiatives in present-day Chinese cities, where rapid urban development and fast demolition of old structures and neighbourhoods in a historic city like Nanjing has actually intensified discoveries of old sites and antiques buried underneath the city for more than a thousand years. The current museum site had already been bought by a private medicine company (Shenghe yaoye) in 2007 to be developed into a huge commercial and entertainment arcade in the heart of the city (Tao 2010). During the process of demolishing and construction, workers dug up architectural debris, which were studied and identified by archaeologists as belonging to the ancient city of Jiankang. Thanks in part to the private developer, which sacrificed a portion of its commercial interests in the land to compromise with the government, the current site has been turned into the present museum and commercial complex.

This happy achievement of a new museum project, however, has to rely crucially on individuals' emotional and ethical commitments to community and the tradition of a place. At the same time, the project shows how private visions and capital are inextricably tied to the government's emphasis on linking cultural tourism to city development. Heritage policy and practice in China, on the one hand, are overwhelmingly driven by 'developmental and political considerations', and 'new museums are becoming a major symbol of metropolitan status' (Evans & Rowlands 2015: 290). On the other hand, particularly in urban China, historic preservation and urban planning can be antithetical concerns that undermine each other (Wang 2015), and the preservation of heritage and local identity has become a thorny issue for private developers, community activists, and local governments. For instance, a recent controversy arose in connection with the debris of the fourteenth-century Ming Dynasty palace, which is believed to lie beneath the city. This site risks being eradicated from community memories due to a huge real estate project currently underway on top of the old sites; alarmingly, at the moment there has been no sign of the government stepping in or halting the project to reconsider any preservation alternatives (Lin 2015). What an irony for a city to fall prey to the loss of its architectural remnants due to growing urban reinvention, when Nanjing is still touted by tourist agencies as showcasing many well-preserved historic locations such as 'the longest Chinese city walls in existence' (Mote 1977: 136), a monumental construction traced to the Ming Dynasty founder.

As a historic dynastic, regional, and national capital, and a metropolitan city today, Nanjing was among the first to be listed by the State Council of China as the country's 'Famous Historic and Cultural Cities' (*Lishi wenhua mingcheng*), later followed by a series of the state's documented plans to preserve the city's historic streets and zones, cultural relics, and architectural and archaeological heritages. In 2010, local activists fought for the establishment of the 'Measures for the Protection of the Historic and Cultural Landmarks of Nanjing' (*Nanjing shi lishi wenhua mingcheng baohu tiaoli*) in their bid to protect the old city and its cultural and historical values. For all the public attention paid to promoting heritage preservation together with urban development, the city has been subject to irrevocable processes of modernisation and urbanisation accompanied by relentless construction and destruction. It begs the question of which parts of the past should be selected, protected, and used in heritage policies to generate new meanings and identities of the city. As my students put in their concluding report (City University Student Group 2017):

> The regulation showed the effort of the local professionals who considered Nanjing's cultural assets as important properties. It is also essential for them to protect any historical remains and evidences of Nanjing. These cultural assets are important in supporting the narration of Nanjing's

story and identity. Heritage conservation is the backing for constructing and re-imagining local identities. Debates in mass media concerning demolition and conservation of old city structures have offered local residents important lessons to think about the meaning of the city they inhabit. The Nanjing people are proud of the city as the ancient capital of the Six Dynasties, which has become a brand name for Nanjing for the press and tourist agency, and Nanjing's many heritage sites have become great resources and commodities for tourist consumption.

Modern museology serves as a 'memory machine' to reconstruct cultural belonging and identity, generating a bond between people and place that is an entrenched affective power of 'topophilia'. Our students believe that local bonding is crucial in conceiving the Chinese notion of heritage and in preservation of the built environment. If the museum functions to restore local communities' perceptions of their cultural pasts and values, so much the better; and it is even better if the restored heritages can be transmitted to future generations. But heritage reconstruction in museums has more to do with the locals' self-definition and self-reinvention of their pasts to engage with audiences who are non-local residents, foreign tourists, people who go there as travelers or on temporary assignment (like our students in their field trip), or even the younger native generation who have fewer emotional affiliations with the city's past and tradition. Remnants of the past, material and non-material ruins alike, constitute real or imagined heritages and may well aid as marketing instruments in branding and reinventing an old Chinese city like Nanjing. The new Oriental Metropolitan Museum demonstrates what Kirk Denton has observed about history museums in the postsocialist PRC today, which have moved beyond the Mao narratives of didactic nationalism and class struggle 'to both tell new stories and retell old stories in ways that speak to more contemporary concerns' (Denton 2014: 3). It reflects changes in the perception of modern museums as warehouses of the country's extraordinary cultural pasts within China's changing dynamics of memory politics. A selective discourse of history – in this case the glamour and beauty of Six Dynasties civilisation – is used as the means of place-making and place-branding for a renewed city. And changing exhibition practices that are tied to the new narrative of a 'history of the local' (Denton 2005: 565) facilitate and legitimate state directives to showcase the place as a nation with a rich cultural past on a par with other ancient civilisations in world history.

Our field trip and post-tour study of the fragmented images of Nanjing and its evolution from past to present have recalled Boyer's *The City of*

Collective Memory, a study of European cities with their historical imagery and complex representations. There are different layers of historical time superimposed on each other in European cities, but they can no longer offer a synthetic order for us to grasp, nor a reconstruction of history we can collectively assume. Refuse of urban and architectural traditions 'bear witness again and again that something has vanished from our present-day cityscapes that we seek to regain and to review' (Boyer 1994: 6). In this sense, modern museums can act as media and interpreters to restore debris and fragments in their new display and staging, presented as traces from the past to reawaken forgotten memories. The relic museum is a figure of speech for the fragmented city of memories, becoming an arena of contestation between top-down state recognition and bottom-up locally embedded cultural revival. We should, however, allow modern-day museum spectators their agency, acknowledging the participatory role they play in their unscripted encounters with the relics and artefacts. It is indeed the elusive nature of the unfamiliar objects relocated and reconfigured in the museum displays that appeals to audiences and causes their reflection about the precarious nature of existence, encouraging them to reframe their memories and identities in affiliation with the place.

References

Betts, P. & C. Ross (2015), 'Modern Historical Preservation: Towards a Global Perspective', *Past and Present* 226 (suppl. 10): 7-26.

Boyer, M. (1994), *The City of Collective Memory: Its Historical Imagery and Architectural Entertainments*. Cambridge, MA: MIT Press.

City University Student Group (2017), 'Constructing Local Identities in Heritage Conservation and Museum Industry: Nanjing and Hong Kong', Unpublished Report, Program of Culture and Heritage Management, City University of Hong Kong.

Convery, I., G. Corsane, & P. Davis (2012), 'Introduction: Making Sense of Place', in I. Convery, G. Corsane, & P. Davis (eds.), *Making Sense of Place: Multidisciplinary Perspectives*, 1-8. Woodbridge: Boydell & Brewer.

Cresswell, T. (2005), *Place: A Short Introduction*. Malden, MA: Blackwell Publishing.

Denton, K. (2005), 'Museums, Memorial Sites and Exhibitionary Culture in the People's Republic of China', *The China Quarterly* 183 (Sept.): 565-86.

Denton, K. (2014), *Exhibiting the Past: Historical Memory and the Politics of Museums in Postsocialist China*. Honolulu: University of Hawai'i Press.

Dien, A. (2007), *Six Dynasties Civilization*. New Haven: Yale University Press.

Evans, H., & M. Rowlands (2015), 'Reconceptualizing Heritage in China: Museums, Development and the Shifting Dynamics of Power,' in P. Basu & W. Modest (eds.), *Museums, Heritage and International Development*, 272-294. New York: Routledge.

Feng, P. (2017), 'Remembering Nanking: Historical Reconstructions and Literary Memorializations of the Nanking Massacre', *Inter-Asia Cultural Studies* 18 (1): 75-91.

Honey, D. (1995), 'Before Dragons Coiled and Tigers Crouched: Early Nanjing in History and Poetry', *Journal of the American Oriental Society* 115 (1): 15-25.

Juliano, A. (1975). *Art of the Six Dynasties: Centuries of Change and Innovation*. New York: China House Gallery.

Kinney, D. (2012), 'Rediscovering a Massacre: The Filmic Legacy of Iris Chang's *The Rape of Nanking*', *Continuum: Journal of Media & Cultural Studies* 26 (1): 11-23.

Li, W. (2004), '*Shishuo xinyu* and the Emergence of Aesthetic Self-Consciousness in the Chinese Tradition', in Z. Cai (ed.), *Chinese Aesthetics: The Ordering of Literature, the Arts, and the Universe in the Six Dynasties*, 237-276. Honolulu: University of Hawai'i Press.

Lin, S. (2015), 'Surprise! Old Sites of the Ming Palace in Nanjing Are Turned into Real Estate Developments Worth Billions of Dollars' [Jing! Nanjing Ming Gugong yizhi jingcheng qianyi kaifa an], Chinatimes.com (Sept 9). [Online]. Available from: www.chinatimes.com/realtimenews/20150909003092-260409 (accessed April 2017).

Lowenthal, D. (2015), *The Past Is a Foreign Country – Revisited*. Cambridge: Cambridge University Press.

Lu, T. L-D. (2014), *Museums in China: Power, Politics and Identities*. New York: Routledge.

Lu, Y., & G. Wang (2014), 'Oriental Metropolitan Museum Opened', *Chinese Social Sciences Today*. [Online]. Available from: www.csstoday.com/Item/859.aspx (accessed April 2017).

'Mad About Museums' (2014), *The Economist* (Jan 6). [Onlline]. Available from: www.economist.com/news/special-report/21591710-china-building-thousands-new-museums-how-will-it-fill-them-mad-about-museums (accessed April 2017).

Mote, F. W. (1977), 'The Transformation of Nanking, 1350-1400', in G.W. Skinner (ed.), *The City in Late Imperial China*, 101-153. Stanford: Stanford University Press.

'Museum in Nanjing Displays Relics from Six Dynasties' (2014), *China Daily* (May 15). [Online]. Available from: http://www.kaogu.cn/en/News/Academic_activities/2014/0815/47196.html (accessed April 2017).

'Nanjing Museum: A Palace of Culture and Space of Leisure' (2015), in 'The Best in Heritage Event'. [Online]. Available from: presentations.thebestinheritage.com/2015/Nanjing-Museum (accessed April 2017)

Owen, S. (1990), 'Place: Meditation on the Past at Chin-ling', *Harvard Journal of Asiatic Studies* 50.2 (Dec): 417-457.

Owen, S. (2015), 'Jiangnan from the Ninth Century On: The Routinization of Desire', in P. Wang & N. Williams (eds.), *Southern Identity and Southern Estrangement in Medieval Chinese Poetry*, 189-206. Hong Kong: Hong Kong University Press.

Pei Partnership Architects (2008-2013), 'The Six Dynasty Museum and Nanjing Hanfujie Plaza Complex'. [Online]. Available from: www.peipartnership.com/projects/type/cultural/the-six-dynasties-museum-and-nanjing-hanfujie-plaza-complex (accessed April 2017).

Tao, W.Z. (2010), 'Nanjing is Going to Build a Six Dynasties Relic Museum' (Naning jiangjian Liuchao yizhi bowuguan), *Xiandai kuaibao* (Jan 24). [Online]. Available from: news.qq.com/a/20100124/000127_1.htm (accessed April 2017).

Tuan, Y. (1977), *Space and Place: The Perspective of Experience*. Minneapolis: University of Minnesota Press.

Tuan, Y. (1990), *Topophilia: A Study of Environmental Perception, Attitudes, and Values*. New York: Columbia University Press.

Varutti, M. (2014), *Museums in China: The Politics of Representation after Mao*. Woodbridge: Boydell Press.

Wang, M. (2015), 'Historical Layering and Historic Preservation in Relation to Urban Planning and Protecting Local Identity: City Study of Nanjing', Masters Thesis. University of Pennsylvania.

Wei, Z. (2004), 'The Six Dynasties: A Time of Splendor', in Nanjing shi bowuguan (Nanjing Municipal Museum), *Liuchao fengcai* (*The Six Dynasties: A Time of Splendor*), 14-26. Beijing: Wenwu chubanshe.

Williams, N. & P. Wang (eds.), *Southern Identity and Southern Estrangement in Medieval Chinese Poetry*, 189-206. Hong Kong: Hong Kong University Press.

Williams, P. (2007), *Memorial Museums: The Global Rush to Commemorate Atrocities*. Oxford: Berg.

Wu, H. (2012), *A Story of Ruins: Presence and Absence in Chinese Art and Visual Culture*. Princeton: Princeton University Press.

Xu, S. (2010), 'I.M. Pei to Design Relic Museum', *Global Times*, Jan 18. [Online]. Available from: www.globaltimes.cn/content/499059.shtml (accessed April 2017).

About the Author

KENNY K. K. NG is Associate Professor of Film Studies at the Hong Kong Baptist University. His publications include *The Lost Geopoetic Horizon of Li Jieren: The Crisis of Writing Chengdu in Revolutionary China* (Brill, 2005), and numerous articles on Chinese literary and visual culture and Cold War cinema.

Section 3

History, Nostalgia, and Heritage:

Urban and Rural

8   The Role of History, Nostalgia and Heritage in the Construction and Indigenisation of State-led Political and Economic Identities in Contemporary China

Andrew Law

Abstract

Over the years interlocutors have pointed to the role of elites in the selective utilisation of history, memory, nostalgia and heritage within modern China; particularly, scholars have pointed to the role of Confucianism, humiliation history and totalitarian nostalgia within these hegemonic processes. However, with the exception of work on Shanghai, there is a paucity of investigations on the role of local elites in the utilisation of local historical-geographic discourses within contemporary China. Acknowledging this lacuna in the extant literature, this chapter argues that 'local elites' – defined as coalitions of local officials, developers, commercialists and/or urban conservationists – are increasingly coming together to utilise local histories, memory, nostalgia and heritage as a tool of urban marketing and place-branding. To unpack this argument, this chapter therefore explores local state coalitions dedicated to urban development in the cities of Shanghai, Wuhan and Xi'an.

Keywords: selective remembering, nostalgia, heritage, Shanghai, Wuhan and Xi'an

Introduction: History, Nostalgia, Heritage and the Chinese State

Debates on the use and abuse of history, memory, nostalgia and heritage have been longstanding in contemporary discussions of China

Ludwig, Carol, Linda Walton, and Yi-Wen Wang (eds), *The Heritage Turn in China: The Reinvention, Dissemination and Consumption of Heritage*. Amsterdam: Amsterdam University Press 2020
DOI: 10.5117/9789462985667_CH08

(Feuerwerker 1968; Unger 1993; Duara 1995; Wang 2001; Horner 2009; Macmillan 2009; McGregor 2010). In recent years a growing number of researchers have examined the ways in which history, nostalgia and heritage have been utilised by elites (particularly governmental elites) in the construction of Chinese identities and subjectivities. Literature in this area has often focused on the role of Confucianism in the production of new forms of Confucian identities both as a mode of national and international identity making (in the construction of pan-Asian Chinese subjectivities) and as a form of party political identity making (Yu 1984, 1987; Brook 1997; Ong 1997a, 1997b, 1999; Zurndorfer 1997, 2004; Bell 2008; Barr 2011; Kallio 2011; Johnson 2016). From a different perspective, another group of writers have pointed to the role of humiliation history as a central tool in the construction of new 'humiliation subjects' in the present era (see Gries 2004, Broudehoux 2004, Callahan 2010, Macmillan 2010, Wang 2012, Law 2014). Here 'humiliation history', which actually has its origins in the 1910s-1920s, can be understood as an instrument in the production of a particular discourse of Chinese historical identity that encourages Chinese subjects to see themselves as victims of a century of humiliation (Callahan 2010: 19);[1] Moreover, along with historical discourses of Confucianism and humiliation, in the post-Maoist era other scholars have also pointed to the role of revolutionary, Maoist and/or totalitar-ian selective history and nostalgia in the contemporary moment (Wu 2006, Yang & Lee 2007, Barmé 2009). Wu Jing in particular has pointed to revolutionary nostalgia (which emerged in the 1990s) as that historical discursive production which has:

> glorified the past and present contributions of the ruling party, creating a new cross medium genre called 'the mainstream melody' (Zhuxuanlu). Media products belonging to this genre ranged from novels, theatrical plays, music and operas, to films and television dramas. Not surprisingly many of these products relied on excavating the 'gold mine' of 'revolution-ary classics' (Wu 2006: 361).

1   As commentators have explained, the century of humiliation is posited as that historical epoch which began with the Opium Wars in the mid-nineteenth century (1840s) and ended with the 'liberation' of the Chinese nation from imperialism and civil war by the contemporary administration in 1949. As interlocutors have opined, whilst the origins of this discourse predates the PRC, in the end humiliation discourse has served a critical part in a discursive justification and ideological legitimation of the contemporary Chinese state (Broudehoux 2004; Wang 2012; Law 2014).

However, whilst much of this research has focused on selective national histories, nostalgia and heritage, there is less research on the way local and specific historical geographical discourses are taken up by local Chinese elites. An exception to this is work by scholars in urban studies who have examined the utilisation of 1920s and 1930s colonial history, nostalgia and heritage by a series of commercial, development-based and state-led actors within the cities of Shanghai and Beijing (Zhang 2000, Pan 2001, 2005; Broudehoux 2004, Wu 2006, Ren 2008, Janson & Lagerkvist, 2009, Law 2012). These studies have noted that an assemblage of state-led and non-state-led actors have sought to market a 'Golden Age' of the 1920s and 1930s in a bid to revive the economic and cosmopolitanism legacy of the colonial Republican city. Thus, as Wu Weiping has contended:

> Today, after more than three decades of cultural drought, Shanghai's reserve of cultural heritages is still significant. Most apparent among them is the array of physical attributes, including the Bund, architectural landmarks, and streetscapes in the former concession areas. As the country gradually opens up to the world and undergoes market reforms, Shanghai is renewing its cosmopolitan reputation and transforming its physical environment. Cultural strategies become an integral part of the modernization drive Shanghai has launched, to recreate a sense of place and to put the city back on the map of great world cities (Wu 2004: 61).

Although the work on Shanghai (and a smaller body of work on Beijing) has improved and developed the field, arguably a broader picture of the way history, heritage and nostalgia has been utilised by local Chinese elites (through cities) is missing in the extant literature. Moreover, whilst Shanghai has often been understood as a unique case, I want to suggest that in other Chinese cities 'elites' (meaning growth coalitions of the state, commercialists and private developers) have also sought to utilise history, nostalgia and heritage in a bid to construct economic and cosmopolitan globalised (capitalist) identities. Rather than adopting the notion of 'elites' as a general category, I argue that the recent utilisation of history, nostalgia and heritage in Chinese cities has been of critical importance to local state-led growth coalitions of officials, developers, commercialist and/or local conservationists. Critically, my point here is that whilst the extant literature can treat the idea of elite history/nostalgia/heritage as a general trend, the strategic use of history, nostalgia and heritage by state-led growth coalitions (of officials and developers) can be regarded as a very specific form of urban branding and urban development strategy. In this regard, the historical/ nostalgia and heritage branding that took off in Shanghai is now being read as a distinct urban branding strategy (regarded as a successful one) in other Chinese cities.

This chapter will reassess the writing on Shanghai regarding the elite growth coalitions of state and non-state that reside within it. In addition, responding to the lack of research on the interior cities of China,[2] this chapter will also examine state-led growth coalitions within the central city of Wuhan and the northwest city of Xi'an. In exploring the use of history, nostalgia and heritage by assemblages of state and non-state agents, I will argue that common themes around the construction of identities and space can be found. Specifically, I contend that *local* history, memory, nostalgia and heritage has been of increasing interest to state-led growth coalitions because it allows local administrations/developers to create a sense of uniqueness and/or a sense of place. Mirroring Shanghai's historic/nostalgic/heritage-based urban branding, I will further claim that elite growth coalitions in Wuhan and Xi'an have also drawn upon selective discourses of history, nostalgia and heritage with the intention of constructing 'deep' (or indigenous) economic and cosmopolitan identities which seek to root and reinforce discourses of global capitalism and international cosmopolitanism within the historical fabric and identity of their locale.

Furthermore, reflecting upon all three of the cases explored in this chapter (Shanghai, Wuhan and Xi'an), I will argue that material sites – including urban landscapes, city centres, historically themed shopping malls and different forms of town and urban-city arrangement – are also critical to the reinforcement of economic and cosmopolitan identities. The employment of history, memory, nostalgia and heritage by the local state has very real material outcomes for the built environment (or urban landscapes) and the conservation of certain heritage sites. Thus, an implicit argument here is that discourses of history, memory, nostalgia and heritage are absolutely critical to an understanding of the ways in which the construction and management of physical urban space (and indeed heritage-based urban landscapes) take place in the contemporary moment.

2   Indeed, arguably the extant literature in Chinese and urban studies has often prioritised research on coastal cities, including Shanghai and Beijing. Whilst there has been a shift of research emphases, I would argue that more work needs to be done to explore the multifaceted nature of central, southern and western Chinese cities.

THE ROLE OF HISTORY, NOSTALGIA AND HERITAGE

Theoretical and Methodological Approaches: Conceptualising History, Nostalgia, Heritage in the Chinese State and Discourse Analysis

Concepts surrounding notions of 'history', 'nostalgia' and 'heritage' are often separated in academic literature as very different subjects of study (Lee & Yang 2007). However, thinking through these terms via certain post-structuralist assemblage theories, arguably 'history', 'nostalgia' and 'heritage', when utilised by agents, can often become an assemblage of historic signi-fiers, imaginaries, factual accounts, physical heritage and/or knowledges (Delanda 2010); furthermore, when aligned, arguably these assemblages of knowledge can play an important role in the political construction of identities, subjectivities, places and spaces. When I use the terms 'history', 'nostalgia' and 'heritage', I am also utilising these conceptualisations through Foucault's ideas of power/knowledge and *governmentality* (Foucault 1991). Indeed, as Oakes contends, 'a governmentality approach to heritage [and in the theoretical case I am proposing here the concepts of history and nostalgia] is concerned less with what heritage is in terms of its content and more with how it is instrumentalised as a vehicle for governmental power and what sorts of political rationalities its use in this way generates' (Oakes 2016: 4). Drawing upon these theoretical approaches, this chapter contends that history, nostalgia and heritage can be viewed as a collective instrument of power through which governmental influence is exercised in the construction of particular kinds of subjectivities. In this regard, whilst particular forms of Chinese historicising, memorialising, nostalgia and heritage practices might have their beginnings in non-hegemonic movements, in the hands of the Chinese state an assemblage of 'historical knowledge' is utilised with the expectation of constructing contemporary identities and futures.

Theorising the Chinese State

The second concept explored in this chapter is the idea of the Chinese state. Conservative and certain forms of neo-Marxist representations of the Chinese state have often sought to represent it as a *homogenous actor* that has clear goals and drives, or unifying principles (Jacques 2009). Other writers, however, have drawn attention to a much more complicated picture that hints at an image of the Chinese state as a multidimensional *heterogeneous actor* divided by differing motivations, contradictory goals and/ or very dif-ferent and varying geographical needs (Chao & Dickson 2001: 10). Moreover, in taking a heterogeneous conceptual approach, increasingly writers have begun to explore the effects of neo-liberal politics and economics upon the actual makeup of the state. Scholars have noted that in the reform period the Chinese state has become increasingly decentralised, deregulated and marketised as a result of increasing privatised discourses, paradigms and agendas.[3] Consequently, Ho Chung (2001) has argued that

> China's reform of the last two decades may be epitomised at the changes towards decentralisation, marketisation and privatisation. Through decentralisation, the extent of which seems to have so far been the largest among the three, a wide range of decisional authority was devolved from the central government to the provinces below for the sake of promoting local incentives and initiatives for reform. Through marketisation, state plan-controls were significantly weakened and principles of competition and comparative advantage were diffused. Through privatisation, the extent of which remains quite limited, individual and non-state property rights as well as foreign capital have gradually increased their influence over China's economy (Ho Chung 2001: 46)

In simple terms, this increasing decentralisation of the Chinese state has seen serious shifts in China's political economy. Indeed, and quoting Walder (1995) as Wu Fulong has advocated, through 'economic decentralization, the locality arose as a substantial entity of interest ... now local government sees a hardening of budgets and thus acts like an industrial firm. Special development zones and industrial parks are set up to attract foreign investment' (Wu 2009: 423). Before the reform era (beginning in 1978), as Wu Fulong has contended, the economy was characterised by 'State-led industrialization' which saw the Chinese state 'controlling resource allocation' and the reproduction of its 'work unit system' (Wu 2009: 424). However, after the reform period the local Chinese state became more entrepreneurial and the local state specifically utilised cities as key sites of 'accumulation' (Wu 2009: 424). An important aspect of this new economic mode is that cities and new forms of place-based marketing (or urban branding) have become critical to the new regime of accumulation. As Wu has contended, '[t]he development of flagship and ostentatious consumption landscapes is

---

3   However, in making this claim I do not want to suggest that the contemporary Chinese state is now straightforwardly analogous to regular western neo-liberal states such as the UK and United States. Indeed, as scholars have continually proffered there is no clear relationship between the contemporary Chinese state and neo-liberalism (see, for instance, Keith et al. 2014).

used by the city government to "sell places"' (Wu 2009: 423). Whilst there have been many different types or forms of urban branding – including eco-branding, creative branding and more recent smart or high tech urban branding – recently commentators have pointed to the growing appeal of 'historic' and 'cultural' branding. You-Tien Hsing (2011) has commented that:

> On the cultural front, [Chinese] cities compete with one another for the recognition by the national government as a 'distinctive historical and cultural city' or more ambitiously, for the title of UNESCO World Cultural Heritage Site. Leaders invest heavily in rebuilding ancient city walls, restoring ruins, temples and traditional housing compounds and commercial streets, and complete them with museums, handicrafts workshops, and folk theatres. They also produce place-promotion TV dramas and films that are set in historical periods and shot in restored heritage sites (You-Tien Hsing 2011: 4).

Below I examine in more detail the emergence of several new examples of this historic local place branding; moreover, rather than just creating distinctive or unique places (as You-Tien Hsing suggests), these new forms of historic branding regimes can also serve to reproduce particular forms of marketised discourses, identities and local historic narratives which are of undoubted attractiveness to foreign and domestic investors.

Methodological Approaches: Data Sets and Discourse Analysis

The data that follows are based upon three case studies of local state-led growth coalitions in the cities of Shanghai, Wuhan, and Xi'an. These three case sites provide illuminating examples of the ways in which history, nostalgia and heritage have been drawn upon intensely by the local state. The data from these three case studies are comprised of a mixture of primary and secondary sources, although the section on Shanghai is chiefly based on secondary sources. However, some data has been gathered from primary sources via two concurrent studies examining growth coalitions in Wuhan and Xi'an.[4] The data in these two studies include mainly information from government documents, interview surveys and visual spatial analyses. Whilst the collection of governmental documents came via government

---

4   The first of these studies was conducted by an independent scholar Qianqian Qin and myself (Law and Qin 2017). The second study was conducted by Alastair Bonnett, Yang Yang and myself (Law, Bonnett & Yang 2017).

websites and from information gathered via planning/development-based exhibition showrooms, the visual surveys involved mass photographic surveys of these two cities.

In this process of visually mapping entire urban spaces as well as photographs, sometimes visual field sketches were made to try to understand the complexity of the landscapes and material spaces that had been produced by coalitions of the local state and their associated developers. Likewise, the author and (sometimes hired) fieldworkers also conducted a small number of interviews with officials and cultural agents (including local academics, planners, and heritage/conservation specialists) who worked as advisors or spatial producers in the construction of new forms of historic local identities. Interview data has not been used in these studies due to issues of ethics and confidentiality. However, statements and opinions drawn from interviews have shaped and influenced the nature of the author's ideas, findings and interpretations and the way the data is represented below.[5]

Textual Analysis, Urban Landscapes and Senses

The primary and secondary sources examined in this study were scrutinised through *discourse analysis*. Whether through secondary sources (the literature reviews conducted in this writing) or primary sources (development brochures, government statements or interviews), this chapter has sought to utilise what Fairclough has described as discourse analysis, which refers to an 'oscillating analysis' that focuses on specific texts and a focus on 'the relatively durable social structuring of language that is itself one element of the relatively durable structuring and networking of social practices' (Fairclough 2003: 3). However, this chapter also develops a particular form of visual investigation inspired by the writings of Lynch (1960), Emmison & Smith (2000) and Rose (2016). As well as examining texts and symbolic media, the visual messages, codes and texts inherent within the design, organisation and layout of public spaces and urban landscapes were also subjected to investigation (Lynch 1960; Duncan 1990; 2004; Emmison & Smith 2000: 166; Rose 2016: 226-241). This methodological approach seeks to interrogate public spaces as places through which 'political practices and individual intentions' are realised (Duncan 1990, 2004: 5). In more practical

---

5   In the main, officials and cultural agents were very difficult to meet and so the interviews that have taken place are very small in number and are not representative. However, some of the insights given to this author by the interviewees have certainly contributed to my understanding of the issues.

terms, this involved the reading of urban landscapes as having 'punctuation marks' or spaces in which historic, nostalgic and/or heritage-based signifiers and materialities were constructed and reproduced. By making extensive field sketches and by taking numerous photos, this author sought to analyse these marks in the landscape, which included statues, physical heritage sites, water foundations, nostalgically themed malls and signs and a whole range of commercial ephemera and simulacra that inhabited these spaces.

Furthermore, in some instances the data developed in these studies were also concerned with what Rose has described as another more implicit aspect of discourse analysis, which refers to the 'material practices of institutions' (Rose 2016: 192). Thus, at times, the primary data collected in Wuhan and Xi'an also involved a careful understanding of the *actual spatial layouts* of particular 'historic' urban landscapes and/or the layout of exhibitions within planning halls – what Rose calls the technologies of layout (Rose 2016: 238); finally on occasion the researchers also drew upon more *sensual analyses* of the urban landscapes in question. Inspired by the theoretical commentaries of interlocutors such as Pink (2009) and Low (2015), this author also took a series of analytical walking tours through the urban heritage landscapes of Wuhan and Xi'an so as to experience and document a series of sensory registers that had been inserted into the landscape by developers: these sensory registers often included visual displays, sights, sounds, smells, 'heritage shows', light shows, water fountains and phantasmagoria.

1920s and 1930s Colonial Nostalgia

In recent years numerous scholars have conducted research on the growth of Republican and colonial nostalgia within the city of Shanghai (Zhang 2000; Pan 2001; 2005; Wu 2006; Ren 2008; Janson & Lagerkvist 2009; Law 2012). This nostalgia has strong popular consumer-based roots; thus, in an essay 'Shanghai Nostalgia: Post-revolutionary Allegories in Wang Anyi's Literary Production in the 1990s', Zhang argues that:

> Indeed, contemporary Shanghai nostalgia emerges with the postsocialist urban consumer masses and their obsession with searching for a classical moment of Chinese bourgeois modernity, whose feudal and colonial birthmarks are now indistinguishably mingled with commercial logos and signs. As a commercially viable fashion in China's newfound mass cultural industry and an emotional valorization of the semiautonomous intellectual discourses in the 1990s, nostalgia can be considered as a

sentimental Chinese response to a global ideology, whose singularity lies precisely in its homesick longing for a futurological utopia hinged on some earlier or more classical phase of world capitalism, on something Shanghai once was or at least could have been. In the Chinese context, the last trend seeks to replace the incomplete, unsettled, and open-ended project of Chinese modernity with an empathic projection of the present onto the larger constellation of historical ages in which revolution and socialism are to be erased or suspended as a violent interruption (Zhang 2000: 335-336).

However, whilst the growth of this nostalgia might have emerged from an initial wave of alternative consumerism, other writers have proposed that increasingly this nostalgia has been assimilated by 'post-Deng social and political elites' (Pan n.d.: 1). Thus, as Jansson & Lagerkvist have implied, the construction of Republican and colonial nostalgia is something that has been subsumed within the place-branding strategies of local growth coalitions: urban coalitions of state (planners, politicians, conservationists) and non-state commercial actors (including retailers, artists and entrepreneurs). Thus, Jansson & Lagerkvist write:

> In order to turn this increasingly global city into a leading commercial hub of East Asia, planners and politicians, commercial interests and entrepreneurs have jointly encapsulated the city by employing a Shanghai nostalgia for the Golden Age of the 1920s and 30s (Pan 2005) and by calling for a retroactive future gaze, reminiscent of the inter-war era, planners and policy makers create a hyper-real sense of futurity, inclusive of futures past and futures never fulfilled (Jansson & Lagerkvist 2009: 43).

Moreover, as Wu Jing has written:

> With a strange turn of fate, turn of the century Shanghai found it necessary to excavate a past that was once deemed shameful and alien – that is, the memory of a city of commerce, adventure, entertainment, fashion and the most up-to-date modern experiences of the times. In urban planning, international banks returned to the old colonial-style buildings where they used to be before they were forced to evacuate the city in 1949. The municipal government renovated old entertainment centres and shopping areas, including parks, movie theatres and coffee bars, trying to recover the charm of city life in an era when being modern was once again the imperative of the day (Wu 2006: 366-367).

In short, in moving from popular consumption to state-led consumption, the local municipal government and these related commercial movements have worked in tandem to produce a very concrete nostalgic imaginary of Shanghai from the 1920s and 1930s. Arguably such measures can be read as a way of individualising the city: that is, nostalgia has been used by this growth coalition to give the city a unique character, which can in turn attract tourists and of course investors. However, arguably, like the other cities we will explore in the following sections, the branding of Shanghai has not simply occurred to create a unique or distinctive place; indeed, rather than uniqueness alone, interlocutors have also suggested that Shanghai has been constructed with the intention of creating 'deep' historical economic and cosmopolitan identities.

Thus, in his 'Shanghai nostalgia: historical memory, community-building and place-making in a late socialist city' (2001), Pan points to the Xin Tian Di (meaning the New Heaven and Earth) in Shanghai as a project with political implications. He contends that the development, which was paradoxically supported by 'district officials', represents a form of political rebuilding[6] since it was founded on the 'once hallowed ground of Maoist China ...' where the first Chinese Communist Party (CCP) congress was held in 1921. As Pan notes:

> Since the founding of the Chinese Communist Party (CCP) [in 1921] was supposed to represent a new era with the promise of creating a new heaven and earth for the Chinese people, the establishment of Xin Tian Di there proclaimed the post-socialist triumph of capitalism over communism right at the heart of [the] CCP's birthplace (Pan nd: 15).

Furthermore, in recent writing on Shanghai and the cultural industries, Wu Jing has contended that:

> In the renewed effort to connect China to the worldly process of modernisation again, old Shanghai becomes a possible mirror image for a future China. The nostalgic caressing of a once-existing modernity drives home the following questions: Was there an internal drive to modernity in China? Did semi-colonial Shanghai offer an indigenous example of modernization? (Wu 2006: 367).

What these quotes demonstrate is a clear story of local economic and governmental anxiety over the marketing of Shanghai. Rather than being

---

6 See also Bevan (2006) on the political symbolic implications of rebuilding.

'stuck' in the 'backwaters' of Maoist communism, the drive to rebrand the history of Shanghai and to create an imaginary of 1920s-1930s bourgeois modernity is critical to a new era of global capitalism, where business leaders and city officials have desperately tried to create a new image of the city as historically prosperous, cosmopolitan and modern: a city now truly unfettered by the shackles of Maoist communism. But, these readings of Shanghai also suggest that business leaders and the local government are simultaneously trying to construct a language of futurity: an identity that, as Wu Jing rightly indicates, points to a 'mirror image for a future China' (Wu 2006: 367). As Hanchao Lu has written:

> Longing for the past used to be the most watched sentiment in China, for it was directly associated with the perceived danger of 'restoring capitalism' (fuzi ziben zhuyi), the lethal accusation in Mao's time that eventually ignited the Cultural Revolution. Today 'restoring capitalism' remains taboo in China's political lexicon, but the virtual capitalism in many aspects of Chinese lives has been justified by the officially sanctioned notions of 'socialism with Chinese characteristics' and China being at the 'preliminary stage of socialism'. It is against this background that the Shanghai nostalgia represents a similar kind of wrangling with ideological justification and legitimacy, an essential feature of China's future (Lu 2002: 170).

Wuhan's Urban Growth Coalitions: Ming and Qing Identities and the Construction of Mercantile Capitalisms

Unlike in Shanghai, research on the use of history, nostalgia and heritage by local growth coalitions in Wuhan is relatively sparse, although investigations into urban profiling and urban conservation in the city do exist (Han & Wu 2004, Huan et al. 2008). Acknowledging these gaps in the research, Qianqian Qin and this author (Law & Qin 2018) have recently conducted a study on place-making and urban branding in the city that has utilised visual analysis, interviews with local planners and government officials, and the textual analysis of documents, brochures and other resources associated with an increasing branding programme for the city (Law & Qin 2018). As Law and Qin (2018) demonstrate, the local government of Wuhan has drawn upon a very selective narrative of history and heritage relating particularly to the Hankou district of the city. For readers unacquainted with the city, the Hankou area is one of three districts that make up the city (the other two being Hanyang and Wuchang). Historically, as William T. Rowe has pointed out, Hankou can be associated with an indigenous Chinese (although ethnically diverse) merchant port culture. Thus, ostensibly, whilst an uninformed observer might assume that the colonial intervention in Hankou was the starting place of the city's merchant capitalism, in two extensive volumes of economic history, Rowe very persuasively asserts that the mercantile industries and transport links that formed in Hankou were primarily indigenous (see Rowe 1984, 1988).

As our own research shows, rather than simple historic-based regeneration, this 'indigenous' Ming and Qing mercantile port history and culture (and an implicit narrative of Ming and Qing mercantile capitalism) has been important to the development and branding of the city. Specifically, one area within Hankou, Hanzheng Street, seems to have been of particular interest to local officials since it is understood to have been a key site in which indigenous Ming and Qing port mercantile practices took place. A review of one of the brochures associated with the redevelopment of this area reveals a series of interesting discourses associated with the construction of a new Wuhan central business district – analogous to the Pudong area in Shanghai. The new CBD area which is built on the (now increasingly redeveloped) Hanzheng Street site has been utilised by officials to construct a new *discursive language* of the city which is pregnant with nostalgia for an indigenous moment of Chinese capitalism:

> From Ming Dynasty, Hanzheng street led business trade, humanistic fashion; made 'Hankow' one of the four most famous towns in Ming, Qing Dynasties and tens of thousands of merchants rich; after the reforming and opening up, it has even become the cradle of China's private economy, the pioneer leading open and enlivened markets, also has become a gilded signboard in the heart of market practitioners, consumers with the biggest commodity trading volume in our country (Wuhan Urban and Rural Construction Group; n.d. C. 2013: 24)

This nostalgia for Ming and Qing mercantile capitalism is not only connected to redevelopment projects but can also be associated with a range of other sites and spaces that serve to reinforce this historic/heritage reimagining of the city (Law & Qin 2018). Thus, in some areas of the city, including a Riverside Park, (situated alongside the Hankou bund) statues of port workers have been assembled which reproduce and reinforce the historic presence of a mercantile world gone by (but that is still haunting the city).

Furthermore, at Wuhan's citizens' home, which is a multi-purpose local governmental centre, a very large planning exhibition Hall (located on level two of the citizens' home) also reinforces this historic mercantile discourse through a plethora of display boards which cover the city's history and heritage. Though the exhibition does in fact cover many historical periods, noticeably, the displays on the Han River and the Hankou area reinforce the wider mercantile narrative (see Law & Qin 2018). Thus, on one display board named 'Hanzheng Street the most prosperous area in Chu', narratives surrounding the mercantile aspects of this area are reinforced through poetic text that encourages readers to reflect on the unique history of this space:

> In this area with many rivers and lakes, people make business on the boats and live in bamboo houses. During the Wanli period in Ming Dynasty (from 1573 to 1620), there were towns within the vicinity of Hanzheng Street in Hankou. The shops and brokers' storehouses welcomed merchants from all places. At the end of the Ming Dynasty and the beginning of Qing Dynasty, Hankou became the national trade and commercial centre, known as one of the four most famous towns along with Zhuxian town in Henan, Jingde Town in Jianxi, and Foshan Town in Guangdong. The prosperity of trade and commerce helped form the unique culture of business, clubhouse[s], hometown associations, business associations and government offices in Hanzheng Street ... It was the origin of the Hankou Culture with profound business heritage of Old Hankou (Display Board, entitled 'Hanzheng Street the most prosperous area in Chu', level 2F, City History Exhibition Hall).

In this way, through a range of actual regeneration projects, urban statues and exhibitions, the Wuhan government has seized on the opportunity to hint at a rich indigenous commercial history of the city (a commercial history that also implies a world of domestic trade). Furthermore, this history is of course being used to underpin the commercial branding of the city in the present.

Xi'an's Urban Growth Coalitions: Zhou, Qin, Han and Tang Identities and the Construction of Early Global Capitalisms, Cosmopolitanisms and Modernities

As in Wuhan, research on local nostalgia in Xi'an has been fairly sparse, although numerous social, cultural, political, and planning, conservation and economic histories do exist on the city (Holledge & Bishop 2000, Wang

2000, Yin et al. 2004, Will 2013). An exception to this, however, is the work of William Feighery (2008, 2011) who notes that in recent years, local networks of government officials and developers have sought to market Xi'an through a nostalgic discourse of the Tang Dynasty. Here, as Feighery proposes, often the impulse for this new Tang branding has been marked by a keen desire amongst officials and developers to market the city for the purposes of tourism and the tourist economy. As Feighery states:

> The decision to pursue the articulation of Xi'an's Tang heritage, as opposed to that of other important periods of Chinese history, stems from a belief that for many Chinese, the Tang Dynasty represents one of the most advanced and enlightened periods of Chinese history. Thus, there is strong support in official circles for replicating the splendour of the Tang Dynasty ... This can be viewed as part of the process in China whereby tourism, market commercialisation and commodification have collaborated to invent a landscape of nostalgia upon which to build a sense of national identity (Feighery 2008: 328).

However, Feighery also suggests that the marketing, as well as commercialisation, of the city in this way meets the needs of the mainly Han (majority ethnic) tourists who come to visit the city. Problematically, as Feighery rightly proposes, the construction of the city through a Han-centric style lens means that many of the more complex and multi-ethnic rich histories and heritages of the ethnic minority communities – mainly the Hui Muslim community – that live in the city are negated. With reference particularly to the Lianhu district, Feighery suggests that Tang branding (and a series of urban plans that have supported the themisation of the area) has subjugated and silenced 'the rich local traditions of the local Hui population' (Feighery 2011: 44). However, whilst Feighery's research is important (particularly in terms of differing ethnic interpretations of the city), it stops short of a fuller analysis of the extensive nostalgic branding that has taken place in the city.

Taking Feighery's work further, from 2013 onwards, Bonnett, Yang and myself (see Law, Bonnett & Yang 2017) have sought to explore in further detail the utilisation of the city's history, nostalgia and heritage by the local state and its associated development and commercial networks. Like Feighery, our research has focused on the construction of identities and place-branding strategies within the city. However, our preliminary findings so far also demonstrate that, rather than just 'Tang' branding (although we recognise the prominent role of Tang branding in the city), a broader 'ancient' and multi-dynastic or 'imperial nostalgia' has taken hold of city

officials, commercialists and developers in the construction of new kinds
of local identities and urban landscapes. Along with the Tang Dynasty, the
Zhou, Qin and Han dynasties have also played a major role in the discourses,
visions and imaginaries of government and development actors. Moreover,
rather than nostalgia for particular historical epochs alone, arguably the
government and its agents have also demonstrated a really keen interest
in the revitalisation of a discourse of the Silk Road and in some cases the
actual materialisation and conservation of certain heritage sites relating
to the Silk Road. Thus, in a glossy state-produced tourist brochure from the
1990s, official commentators on the city's heritage drew upon a plethora of
historical discourses, nostalgia and signifiers:

> Xi'an may be a shade less glamorous and sophisticated than many of
> its counterparts in today's world, but it is catching up rapidly thanks to
> the policy of reform and opening up to the outside world. By carrying
> forward the enterprising spirit of the forefathers of the Zhou and Qin
> ages and inheriting the openness and magnanimity of the Han and Tang
> dynasties, the ancient city of Xi'an is transforming itself into a modern
> metropolis with an impressive setup of commerce, trade tourism, science
> and technology and education. Xi'an today is striving to rejuvenate the
> glory of Han and Tang days, reopen the Silk Road to the world today, and
> emerge once again as a booming international town. Xi'an an old city
> with a glorious yesterday, certainly will have a very promising tomorrow
> (Foreign Affairs Office, Xi'an Municipal Government, 1996: Introduction).

In these statements a very specific narrative of the city as having a deep
historic enterprising past is revealed; moreover, as with the branding
strategies of Shanghai and Wuhan, the sub-text of these discourses is that
a longitudinal enterprising spirit is in the process of being rejuvenated once
again. In the economic development of the city, the local government has
given increasing powers to an emerging growth coalition known as the
Qujiang New District Administrative Committee (QNDAC). This administrative committee, originally set up to advance the economic prospects of
Qujiang (a then poorly performing economic area), now seems to have a
major role in the management and development of some of the wider city's
major heritage sites (and heritage sites that exist outside the city in Shaanxi
province more broadly). Supporting the findings of Feighery, the QNDAC
has been absolutely central to the construction of a series of 'Tang branded'
commercial landscapes that have transformed the Qujiang district area from
a series of sparse farmlands to a multi-level mega-shopping commercial area

which contains numerous shopping malls, attractions and heritage sites. Detailed visual surveys of the Qujiang area – via visual mapping and sensory observation – reveal the symbolic prominence of commercial sites such as the Great Tang Mall. The Great Tang Mall lies in close proximity to Wild Goose Pagoda, a key Buddhist temple in Xi'an's Tang and Silk Road history. Importantly, then through a range of statues (referencing the achievements and the cosmopolitanism of the Tang Dynasty), a grand stone frieze, (in front of Wild Goose Pagoda) restaurants, commercial signs, Tang branded billboards and hotels, branding the Great Tang Mall evokes Tang culture and history and speaks to a new language of the past and the present to reinvigorate the city's prospects for the future.

However, whilst the heavy Tang branding of the city and the Qujiang district strongly speaks to a language of nostalgia, a closer look at the documentation, pamphlets and public statements created by the QNDAC illustrates a much broader and complex picture. Thus, in the annual reports of the QNDAC, readers might find the following statements:

> What is the cultural brand of the Xi'an city? The answer is 'ancient capital.' This is because Xi'an is recognized nation-wide and internationally as an ancient capital of both China and the world. To summarize the whole rationale of using 'ancient capital' as Xi'an's brand, it will come to the conclusion of the unbreakable connection between Xi'an and its name as an ancient city. In other words, being an ancient capital is the source of power for Xi'an in development …
>
> … The soul of the ancient capital of Xi'an is the root culture [(root culture meaning here Chinese culture)]. Xi'an and the Tang Dynasty once were the focus of the world desired by everyone, as well as the hearth of the spirit and culture of the entire nation (minzu) … If Xi'an is the crown jewel of the Chinese historical culture, then Qujiang must be the diamond on the jewel (QNDAC, 2003).

In contrast to the more explicit revivalist overtones of the other texts we have examined, these texts evoke more localist discourses with references to Qujiang and the city as an 'ancient capital'. Texts such as these hark back to the Tang period when Xi'an, or Chang'an as it was known, was the imperial capital; they therefore hint at a subtext that Xi'an is in fact the real authentic historic capital of China (and not Beijing). Such texts also suggest an administration highly confident in the status of their locale as a competitor to other prominent cities within China. Moreover, with its multiple references to internationalism and the world, these texts also implicitly reference the city's traditional dynastic status as the eastern starting place of the Eurasian Silk Road. The branding of Xi'an in this way further indicates that this city should not be understood as a 'backwater' or parochial interior city whose fortunes have been cast aside by post-Maoist industrial decline. Rather as these discourses suggest, Xi'an, with its deep roots in a prestigious, economically prosperous ancient past (mainly in the Tang Dynasty), is in fact the heart or spirit of the entire Chinese nation. As this text implies, the greatness of Xi'an is not simply being defined in terms of the city's potential economic development; rather what is at stake here (and the many other texts, that Law, Bonnett and Yang have surveyed in their current project) is that the city's cultural, national and international status will be restored once again.

Conclusions: Mediating History, Nostalgia and Heritage through the Local State in the Construction of Political and Economic Identities

Utilising literature that examines the relation between discourses of history (nostalgia and heritage) and elites, which include commercialists, developers and the Chinese state, I have argued that there is a paucity of research on the role of elites in the construction of local historical-geographical discourses. However, an exception to this is work conducted by scholars on Shanghai (and to a smaller extent Beijing) and the utilisation of 1920s and 1930s Republican history, nostalgia and heritage by the city's growth coalitions (coalitions of the state, commercialists and developers). Within the context of Shanghai in the 1920s and 1930s nostalgia has been of particular interest to local elites because it allows local agents to construct economic and cosmopolitan discourses that symbolically refer to internationalism, worldliness, capitalism and modernity.

The use of historical discourses to create economic and cosmopolitan identities and narratives is not something unique to elites in Shanghai, but may also be a factor in the production of new forms of local identity and branding in other Chinese cities. Secondly, and moving away from a general analysis of 'elites' (whether commercialists, developers or officials), this chapter has also proposed that for a more concentrated analysis, scholars might begin to focus upon state-led growth coalitions – coalitions actively directed by state-led forces in the pursuit of a historic/nostalgic/heritage urban branding strategy.

In addition to Shanghai, this chapter has explored amalgamations of the local state and urban specialists (including planners, urban designers and conservationists) in the cities of Wuhan and Xi'an. In these urban centres, like Shanghai, the administrations have also drawn upon local histories, nostalgia and heritage with the intention of producing detailed economic identities. In the case studies of Wuhan and Xi'an, the local state in particular has used selective discourses of history, nostalgia and heritage to elicit global (cosmopolitan) capitalist, cosmopolitan and sometimes modernist indigenous Chinese identities. Moreover, in examining these selective histories, we also suggested that city officials are harking back to these dynasties with the intention of creating a rejuvenist economic language of the city; that is, the past is being used to revitalise the economic fortunes of the present and the future. However, along with economic narratives, in the marketing of the city, we also noted that official texts display a very strong sense of local pride within which local officials and developers market Xi'an as an 'ancient capital'. What is at stake here are discourses of local pride, wherein city officials are also seeking to highlight the cultural and political 'status' of the city both domestically and internationally.

Finally, the actual material urban landscapes (whether real or imagined) have served a crucial role as marketing instruments in the branding of these cities. This was exemplified in Wuhan by the construction of nostalgic statues and, more fundamentally, by the complete reconstruction of Hanzheng Street in the Hankou area. In Xi'an, the complete reconstruction of the Qujiang area has now been branded very vociferously through the language of the Tang Dynasty. The construction of particular forms of historical branding does not end with discourse alone. Rather, the manufacture of historical branding has very real and/or tangible effects on the material urban environments and landscapes of Chinese cities: from the conservation of heritage, to the erection of statues and/or the absolute total malling of rejuvenated historic landscapes.

In sum, then, within Shanghai, Wuhan and Xi'an local history is being utilised to fulfil local economic and political needs. History, nostalgia and heritage are being marketed to sell places and to make Chinese cities seem competitive within both domestic and international landscapes. But, whilst the marketing of local places is highly understandable in the neo-liberal climate of the local Chinese state, especially in economic terms, (indeed, such practices are not uncommon in Western cities), the sometimes monolithic historic heritage branding of these cities does however raise certain questions. First, in the process of using history, nostalgia and indeed heritage in the construction of 'deep' global capitalist cosmopolitan Chinese identities (and the regeneration and marketing of Chinese urban space), we might ask, what happens to complex and dissonant histories in Chinese cities?

Second, issues over the construction of these histories in urban areas with Chinese ethnic minorities also raises questions around the silencing and/or assimilation of alternative ethnic histories that exist in and around Chinese cities. Indeed, for example whilst Xi'an is understood as a key example of a longitudinal or 'deep' Chinese capitalism and cosmopolitanism, arguably the economic and cosmopolitan prowess of this site is also very much dependent upon the nomadic ethnic communities who travelled to the city during the history of the Silk Road (and the flows of diverse peoples who live in and who travel to the city in the present). As Feighery has warned, the Hui Muslims, who form an important part of the city's history, seem to be highly underrepresented by 'governmental authorities who prioritise the articulation of tangible heritage for tourism consumption' (Feighery 2008: 333).

Finally, since some of these historic economic heritage branding schemes are so powerful in their material actualisation and transformation of urban landscapes – especially in Xi'an – questions about the value of these spaces to different stake holders need to be continually asked. Thus, though there are no doubt economic benefits from new forms of physical historic urban branding, interlocutors are continually drawing our attention to the plight of social actors who have to be relocated and financially compensated as a result of living in proximity to historic areas or heritage sites (Feighery 2008: 332). In this regard, much more research needs to be conducted on the use of history, nostalgia and heritage by the local Chinese state, because the construction of particular historical branding regimes seems to be having a series of 'knock on' consequences for the people who are living within these spaces. Moreover, as this chapter has suggested, for those communities that often have different or non-economic (perhaps even parochial) historic cultures a growing neo-liberalisation of local history, nostalgia and heritage may also serve to erase and/or silence the history and cultural heritage of a broad range of subaltern (and/or 'economically redundant') Chinese subjects.

References

Abramson, D. B. (2011) 'Places for the Gods: Urban Planning as Orthopraxy and Heteropraxy in China', *Environment and Planning D: Society and Space* 29: 67-88.
Barmé, G. (2009) '1989, 1999, 2009: Totalitarian Nostalgia', *China Heritage Quarterly* 18. [Online]. Available from: http://www.chinaheritagequarterly.org/features. php?searchterm=018_1989nostalgia.inc&issue=018 (accessed 1 November 2016).

Barr, M. (2011) *Who's Afraid of China? The Challenge of Chinese Soft Power*, London and New York: Zed Books.

Bell, D. A. (2008) *China's New Confucianism, Politics and Everyday Life in a Changing Society*, Princeton and Oxford: Princeton University Press.

Berg, P. O. and E. Bjorner (2014), *Branding Chinese Mega-Cities: Policies, Practices and Positioning*. Cheltenham and Gloucester, UK: Edward Elgar Publishing Ltd.

Bevan, R. (2006), *The Destruction of Memory: Architecture at War*. London: Reaktion Books.

Brook, T. (1997). 'Profit and Righteousness in Chinese Economic Culture', in T. Brook & H. Luong, (eds.), *Culture and Economy: The Shaping of Capitalism in Eastern Asia*, 27-44. Ann Arbor: University of Michigan Press.

Broudehoux, A. M. (2004), *The Making and Selling of Post-Mao Beijing*, London: Routledge.

Callahan, W. (2010), *China, the Pessoptimist Nation*. Oxford: Oxford University Press.

Chao, C-M. & B. Dickson (eds.) (2001), *Remaking the Chinese State: Strategies, Society and Security*. London: Routledge.

Delanda, M. (2010), *Deleuze: History and Science*. New York & Dresden: Atropos Press.

Duara, P. (1995), *Rescuing History from the Nation: Questioning Narratives of Modern China*. Chicago: University of Chicago Press.

Duncan, J. (1990; 2004), *The City as Text: The Politics of Landscape Interpretation in the Kandyan Kingdom*. Cambridge: Cambridge University Press.

Emmison, M. & P. Smith (2000), *Researching the Visual*. London: Sage.

Fairclough, N. (2003), *Analysing Discourse: Textual Analysis for Social Research*. London: Routledge.

Feighery, W. (2008), 'Heritage Tourism in Xi'an: Constructing the Past in Contested Space' in J. Cochrane (ed.), *Asian Tourism Growth and Change*, 323-334. Oxford & Amsterdam: Elsevier.

Feighery, W. (2011), 'Contested Heritage in the Ancient City of Peace', *Historic Environments* (23) 1: 37-45.

Feuerwerker, A. (1968), *History in Communist China*. Cambridge, MA and London: The MIT Press.

Foreign Affairs Office of Xi'an Municipal Government (ed.) (1996), *Xi'an: An Ancient Capital of Many Splendours*. Shenzhen and Sanwang: China Tourism Press.

Foucault, M. (1991), 'Governmentality', In G. Burchell, C. Gordon & P. Miller (eds.) *The Foucault Effect: Studies in Governmentality*, 87-104 Chicago, IL: University of Chicago Press.

Gries, P. (2004), *China's New Nationalism: Pride, Politics, and Diplomacy*. Berkeley: University of California Press.

Han, S. & X. Wu (2004), 'City Profile Wuhan', *Cities* (21) 4: 349-362.

Ho Chung, J. (2001), 'Reappraising Central-Local relations in Deng's China' in Chao, C-M. & B. Dickson (eds.), *Remaking the Chinese State: Strategies, Society and Security*, 46-75. London: Routledge.

Horner, C. (2009), *Rising China and its Postmodern Fate, Memories of Empire in a New Global Context*, Athens and London: The University of Georgia Press.

Huan, H., B. Smolders, & J. Verweij (2008), 'Cultural Heritage Conservation in Historic Wuhan', Conference paper for the 44th ISOCARP Congress.

Jacques, M. (2nd ed.) (2012), *When China Rules the World*. London: Penguin.

Jansson, A. & A. Lagerkvist (2009), 'The Future Gaze: City Panoramas as Politico-Emotive Geographies', *Journal of Visual Culture* (8)1: 29-53.

Johnson, I. (2016), 'China's Memory Manipulators', *The Guardian* 8 June 2016. [Online] Available from: https://www.theguardian.com/world/2016/jun/08/chinas-memory-manipulators (accessed 12 July 2016).

Kallio, J. (2011) *Tradition in Chinese Politics: The Party-State's Reinvention of the Past and the Critical Response from Public Intellectuals*. The Finnish Institute of International Affairs. FIIA Report 27.

Keith, M., S. Lash & A. Rooker (2014), *China Constructing Capitalism: Economic Life and Urban Change*. London: Routledge.

Law, A. (2012), 'Post-colonial Shanghai: An Urban Discourse of Prosperity and Futureority', in M. Desai & M. Rajagopalan (eds.), *Colonial Frames/ Nationalist Histories*, 285-304. London: Ashgate.

Law, A. (2014), 'Humiliation Heritage in China: Discourse, Affectual Governance, and Displaced Heritage at Tiananmen Square', *in* I. Convery, G. Corsane, & P. Davis (eds.), *Displaced Heritage: Responses to Disaster, Trauma and Loss*, 165-173. Woodbridge, UK: The Boydell Press.

Law, A., A. Bonnett, & Y. Yang (2017), 'The Historical Branding and Management of Cultural Heritage in Xi'an: Cultural Nationalist and State-led Discourses of Humiliation and Rejuvenation in the Shaping of Historic Urban Branding in the mid-Western Chinese City of Xi'an'. Unpublished monograph.

Law, A. & Q. Qin (2018), 'Searching for Economic and Cosmopolitan Roots: Historical Imaginaries and "Hankou Merchant Port Nostalgia" in the Central Chinese city of Wuhan 武汉.' *Journal of the Faculty of Architecture, Middle East Technical University* [Online]. Available from: https://eprint.ncl.ac.uk/214143 (accessed 15 August 2018).

Lee, C. K. & G. Yang (2007), *Re-envisioning the Chinese Revolution*. Washington, D.C.: Woodrow Wilson Centre Press.

Low, K. E. Y. (2015), 'The Sensuous City: Sensory Methodologies in Urban Ethnographic Research', *Ethnography* 16 (3): 295-312.

Lu, H. (2002), 'Nostalgia for the Future: The Resurgence of an Alienated Culture in China', *Pacific Affairs* (75) 2: 169-186.

Lynch, K. (1960), *The Image of the City*. Cambridge, MA: Technology Press.

Macmillan, M. (2009), *The Uses and Abuses of History*. London: Profile Books.

McGregor, R. (2010), *The Party: The Secret World of China's Communist Rulers*. London: Penguin Books.

Oakes, T. (2000), 'China's Provincial Identities: Reviving Regionalism and Reinventing "Chineseness"', *The Journal of Asian Studies* (59) 3: 667-692.

Oakes, T. (2016), 'Villagizing the city: turning rural ethnic heritage into urban modernity in southwest China', *International Journal of Heritage Studies* 22 (10): 751-765.

Oakes, T. & D. Sutton, D. (2010), *Faiths on Display: Tourism, Religion, and the State in China*. Plymouth: Rowman & Littlefield Publishers.

Olds, K. (1997), 'Globalizing Shanghai: the "Global Intelligence Corps" and the Building of Pudong.' *Cities* (14) 2: 109-123.

Ong, A. (1997a), 'A Momentary Glow of Fraternity: Narratives of Chinese Nationalism and Capitalism', *Identities* (3) 3: 331-366.

Ong, A. (1997b), 'Chinese Modernities: Narratives of Nation and of Capitalism', in A. Ong & D.M. Nonini (eds.), *Ungrounded Empires: The Cultural Politics of Modern Chinese Transnationalism*, 171-202. London: Routledge.

Ong, A. (1999), *Flexible Citizenship: The Cultural Logics of Transnationality*. Durham and London: Duke University Press.

Ong, A. and Nonini, D. M. (1997), Ungrounded Empires: The Cultural Politics of Modern Chinese Transnationalism. London: Routledge.

Pan, T. (n.d.). '"Shanghai Nostalgia": Historical Memory, Community-Building and Place-Making in a Late Socialist City.' [Online]. Available from: http://mumford.albany.edu/chinanet/past_conferences/conferences/Tianshu.doc (accessed 9 August 2016).

Pink, S. (2009), *Doing Sensory Ethnography*. London: Sage.

Qujiang New District Administration Committee (2003), *Qujiang Incidents (Qujiang Shibian)*. [Online]. Available from: http://www.qujiang.com.cn/info/1052/5928.htm (accessed 12 December 2014).

Ren, X. (2008), 'Forward to the Past: Historical Preservation in Globalizing Shanghai', *City and Community*, (7) 1: 23-43.

Rose, G. (2016), *Visual Methodologies: An Introduction to the Interpretation of Visual Materials*, 4th edition. London: Sage.

Rowe, W. (1984), *Hankou: Commerce and Society, 1796-1889*. Stanford: Stanford University Press.

Rowe, W. (1988), *Hankou: Conflict and Community in a Chinese City, 1796-1895*. Stanford: Stanford University Press.

Unger, J. (ed.) (1993), *'Using the Past to Serve the Present': Historiography and Politics in Contemporary China*. Armonk, N.Y.: M.E. Sharpe.

Walder, A. (1995), 'Local Governments as Industrial Firms: An Organizational Analysis of China's Transitional Economy', *American Journal of Sociology* 101 (2): 263-301.

Wang, E. Q. (2001), *Inventing China through History: The May Fourth Approach to Historiography*. Albany: State University of New York Press.

Wang, Z. (2012), *Never Forget National Humiliation*. New York: Columbia University Press.

Wu, F. (2009), 'Neo-urbanism in the Making under China's Market Transition', *City* (13) 4: 418-431.

Wu, F., J. Xu, & A. Gar-On Yeh (2007), *Urban Development in Post-Reform China: State, Market and Space*. Abingdon: Routledge.

Wu, J. (2006), 'Nostalgia as Content Creativity: Cultural Industries and Popular Sentiment', *International Journal of Cultural Studies* 9 (3): 359-368.

Wu, W. (2004), 'Cultural Strategies in Shanghai: Regenerating Cosmopolitanism in an Era of Globalisation', *Progress in Planning* 61: 159-180.

Wuhan Urban and Rural Construction Group (n.d., C. 2013) *Hanzheng Street Cultural Tourism Business District*. Wuhan: Wuhan Urban and Rural Construction Group.

Yu, Y. (1984), *Cong jiazhi xitong kan Zhongguo wenhua de xiandai yiyi* [*The Contemporary Significance of Chinese Culture from the Point of View of its Value System*). Taipei: Shibao wenhua chuban qiye.

Yu, Y. (1987), *Zhongguo jinshi zongjiao lunli yu shangren jingshen* [*The Modern Chinese Religious Ethic and the Spirit of Merchants*). Taipei: Lianjing chuban gongsi).

Zhang, X. (2000) 'Shanghai Nostalgia: Post-revolutionary Allegories in Wang Anyi's Literary Production in the 1990s', *positions: east asia cultures critique* (8) 2: 349-387.

Zurndorfer, H. (1997), 'China and "Modernity": The Uses of the Study of Chinese History in the Past and Present', *Journal of the Economic and Social History of the Orient* (40) 4: 461-485.

Zurndorfer, H. T. (2004), 'Confusing Confucianism with Capitalism: Culture as Impediment and/or Stimulus to Chinese Economic Development'. Paper presented at the third conference of the Global History Economic Network, Konstanz, Germany.

About the Author

ANDREW LAW is Senior Lecturer in Town Planning at Newcastle University, UK. His research is concerned with the use and abuse of history, selective remembering and nostalgia within the built environment; recently, his work has explored these issues in relation to the PRC.

9 Local Voices and New Narratives in Xinye Village

The Economy of Nostalgia and Heritage

Marina Svensson

Abstract

The present chapter is influenced by critical heritage scholars who understand heritage as a 'process' rather than a particular object, place or practice, or, differently put, understand heritage as a verb and as something that both discursively and materially transforms places and practices. It illustrates the complex and changing rural heritagescape in China through a case study of Xinye village in Zhejiang province. The focus is on how the heritagisation process has involved and given rise to multiple stakeholders and actors with different social and cultural capital in and outside the village, and the different ways they engage with and make sense of heritage. It pays particular attention to how the heritage is mediated and visualised on film, analysing a range of different TV productions, and how performance and entertainment are essential aspects of the heritagisation process.

Keywords: heritagisation, mediatisation, performance, film, rural heritage

Introduction

This chapter is influenced by the work of critical heritage scholars who pay particular attention to issues of power and agency in heritage work and understand heritage as a 'process' rather than a particular object, place or practice, or, differently put, understand heritage as a verb and as something that both discursively and materially transforms places and practices (e.g., Harrison 2013; Harvey 2001; Smith 2006). The heritagisation process almost

Ludwig, Carol, Linda Walton, and Yi-Wen Wang (eds), *The Heritage Turn in China: The Reinvention, Dissemination and Consumption of Heritage*. Amsterdam: Amsterdam University Press 2020
DOI: 10.5117/9789462985667_CH09

inevitably puts heritage on display and draws our attention to issues of performance, mediatisation, and entertainment/spectacle (Haldrup & Bærenholdt 2015). The chapter will illustrate the complex and changing rural heritagescape in China through a case study of Xinye village in Zhejiang province, which the author has regularly visited since 2003.[1] The focus is on how the heritagisation process has involved and given rise to multiple stakeholders and actors with different social and cultural capital in and outside the village, and the different ways they engage with and make sense of heritage. The chapter addresses both top-down and bottom-up processes and interactions as well as changes over time. It pays particular attention to how the heritage is mediated and visualised on film, analysing a range of different TV productions, and how performance and entertainment has come to constitute an essential aspect of the heritagisation process.

Official Heritage Making and Processes of Change in Rural China

Chinese heritage policy is shaped by the country's political context and socio-economic developments, which today also is heavily influenced by the international heritage discourse in UNESCO (for general discussions on the Chinese heritage policy see for example Blumenfield & Silverman 2013; Svensson & Maags 2018). In the post-1949 period imperial sites and cultural practices associated with the earlier cultural and political elite were vilified and destroyed, whereas the revolutionary heritage was celebrated and protected. The death of Mao Zedong in 1976 paved the way for the CCP's ideological shift away from class struggle and revolutionary re-modelling of society to a new nationalistic discourse that takes pride in the country's long history and rich traditions (Madsen 2014). The new vocabulary and way to conceptualise the past in terms of cultural heritage (*wenhua yichan*) has changed how historical sites and cultural traditions are imagined, valued, interpreted, mediated and used. While there is still a strong emphasis on the revolutionary heritage, China's imperial history, vernacular heritage, local traditions, and different cultural practices are now also celebrated. China's signing of the UNESCO Intangible Cultural Heritage Convention in

---

1   I have made several trips since 2003 and conducted interviews with different actors. I have stayed in the village during the Chinese New Year and also attended the temple festival on several occasions. I have gathered additional information from academic works, the Ye Genealogy, and other works made by villagers, as well as obtained news and information from the village websites and the social media WeChat group.

2003 and adoption of the concept of intangible heritage (*fei wuzhi wenhua yichan*) domestically has unleashed further changes and a stronger interest in traditions and cultural practices (see, for example, Bodolec 2013, Maags 2018, Orbinger 2011). The intangible heritage includes a wide range of traditions and handicraft, ranging from traditional opera, to acrobatics, to papermaking and different ritual and religious festivals. It means that many cultural practices, including religious rituals, which in the past were seen as 'superstitious' practices now are celebrated as heritage (Gao 2014; Liang 2013). It is important to remember that heritage is as much about the present and the future as about the past, and that it serves contemporary goals and needs, including to strengthen CCP's legitimacy and foster modernisation and economic development (Madsen 2014; Svensson & Maags 2018). Although the heritagisation process in China is very top-down in character there are also bottom-up developments and a strong interest in local history and celebration of place-based identities among Chinese citizens.

After the CCP took power in 1949 it eliminated old power elites in the countryside such as lineages and religious associations, as well as eradicated or appropriated their symbolic and material manifestations such as temples and ancestral halls (Svensson 2012 and 2016). The economic reforms and ideological relaxation after 1979 unleashed a cultural revival in the countryside where people quickly took the initiative to rebuild and renovate temples and ancestral halls and revive different cultural practices. These religious and cultural activities are today embedded in and shaped by an evolving ideological, socio-economic and political environment where heritagisation is one important manifestation. In the 1990s, vernacular buildings, including ancestral halls, and well-preserved traditional villages, were discovered by scholars and experts and listed as officially protected sites (*wenwu baohu danwei*) by heritage authorities at different levels of the administration. In 2003, a special category of historic townships and villages was created, and in 2012, the ministries of culture, construction and finance joined forces to further promote and protect traditional villages with the announcement of the first batch of 327 traditional villages. Tourism has had a strong impact on the heritagisation process (e.g., Zhu 2012). Domestic tourism has grown rapidly in China as a result of growing incomes, more leisure time, and longer public holidays, and the tourism industry is now an economic sector of great importance to many local governments and rural communities (Oakes & Sutton 2010; Chio 2014). Rural tourism includes visits to historic villages, famous temples, scenic areas, and so-called *nongjia le* (small peasant restaurants or inns). Many local governments see tourism development as a promising way to generate economic growth, lift villages out of poverty, and promote modernisation. Most villages that have developed tourism offer short tours of the village where village history, architectural features, and geomancy (*fengshui*) are showcased, in some cases also complemented with exhibitions of traditional handicraft and performances. In some cases, religious pilgrimage and local temple festivals that have been transformed into intangible heritage are important attractions in rural heritage tourism (for different examples see Liang 2013; Chen 2015; Oakes & Sutton 2010; Zhu 2012).

The Chinese state has thus since the 1990s come to re-evaluate vernacular architecture and traditional villages as well as to co-opt lineages, ancestor worship and other rituals within a framework and narrative of cultural heritage (Svensson 2012). Yang (2004) has shown how the re-building of temples, graves, and ancestral halls in the Wenzhou area involve both negotiations and challenges to earlier state projects, whereas other scholars such as Chen (2015), Gao (2014), Madsen (2014), Svensson (2012, 2016) and Zhang & Wu (2015) more explicitly discuss how lineages and rural communities negotiate with, appropriate, and make use of the official cultural heritage discourse when claiming legitimacy for their own history and cultural practices.

History, Architecture and Cultural Life in Xinye Village

Xinye village in Jiande municipality, Zhejiang province, has around 3000 inhabitants and is a one-surname village where more than 90 per cent belong to the Ye lineage. Their ancestors arrived already in the early thirteenth century and over the centuries have thrived and expanded into several branches. There are today around 200 traditional buildings dating in some rare cases from the Ming Dynasty but mostly originating from the late Qing Dynasty and the Republican period. There were many ancestral halls of different sizes in the village, and six bigger ancestral halls remain and are used by the different lineage branches. There is also a major temple, the Yuchuan Temple, in the village, a pagoda, called *Tuanyun* or *Wenfeng*, and a Temple to the Literary God (*Wenchang ge*). The village is clustered around several dams and is surrounded by mountains. It is often said that the mountains and dam resemble a pen and an ink stone and symbolise the literary ambitions of the Ye family. Since transportation in the past was not so convenient the village is quite well preserved although many new houses have been built since the 1990s.

After 1949 the ancestral halls were taken over and used for different purposes, including as a granary, and the focal hall, which was used as a school already before 1949, continued to be used for that purpose until 2002 when a new school was built. Parts of another ancestral hall, the Youxu hall, have been used as a small shop, teahouse, and assembly room for the Old People's Association. It was only in the early 1980s that ancestor rituals and religious worship were revived. As in many other places in Zhejiang province the Ye lineage regained control over their ancestral halls and collected money for renovation, and then also revived the ancestor ceremonies during the Chinese New Year. This was a bottom-up affair with no support or encouragement from the government. In the 1980s, older women began to renovate the Yuchuan Temple collecting small donations from devotees. When I visited the village for the first time in 2003, some local women had also begun to turn parts of the Temple to the Literary God into a temple. This is perhaps not so surprising since the adjacent Earth God Shrine (*Tudi ci*) had been added as late as 1919, and as temples in China develop over time and often come to include many different deities. The village women paid for and begun to install a range of gods, including the 18 Arhats (*Luohan*), and turned one part of the building into a small communal kitchen. People from neighbouring villages also donated money and the temple was inaugurated in 2004. But when tourism later took off, all these statues apart from the Earth God were removed and the building turned into an exhibition space (discussed below).

The village's temple festival (*miaohui*), known as *sanyue san* (third day of the third month) as it takes place on that day, was revived in 1985. It is closely related to ancestor ceremonies as the gods protect the lineage and the village. Members of the lineage walk to the temple, which is around two kilometres from the village centre, and receive (*ying shen*) the three major gods that are carried on a sedan chair in a procession through the village. The sedan chair with the gods is then taken to the branch ancestral hall in charge of the festival where it is kept until next year when it is returned to the temple. During the festival a big table with offerings is set up in the ancestral hall and senior members of the lineage officiate at the ceremony and other lineage members come to worship. The festival is also a market event where local businessmen arrive in the village and set up shop, selling everything from household equipment, clothes, DVDs, to medicine. The temple festival has traditionally attracted villagers from the surrounding villages, and villagers from Xinye will also visit other villages in the neighbourhood when they organise their temple festivals. Many family members try to come home to take part in the festivities, particular those belonging to the branch in charge of the festival that year. This lineage branch will invite and pay for an opera troupe that will perform Wu Opera twice a day for six days. In

2004 when I first visited the temple festival the opera was still held in the Youxu Ancestral Hall, but due to tourism the festival had in 2013 become a bigger affair and the opera had to be held on a makeshift stage outside the Chongren Ancestral Hall in order to accommodate all the visitors and tourists. It is mostly Wu Opera that is played and popular in villages in this part of Zhejiang but in the past the village also had its own *Kunqu* opera troupe, often referred to as village *Kunqu* or *Cao Kun* (grassroots *Kunqu*) due to its simplified form.

The Heritagisation of Xinye: New Actors and New Stories

It was at first only the architectural qualities of Xinye's different buildings and the traditional layout that attracted the attention of experts and heritage bureaus. They were not much interested in the rituals that took place in the ancestral halls or in the religious life of the village. In 2000 Xinye village became a provincial level protected site (*wenwu baohu danwei*), and in 2010 it was nominated to national level historic village (*lishi wenhua mingcun*). In 2011 the village was listed as a national level protected site, and in 2012 it was included in the first batch of traditional villages. The early listings did not radically change the village and its cultural life, and in fact some destruction took part of its original layout as new houses continued to be built and some old houses were neglected. The heritage listing however resulted in some official funding for the restoration of the major ancestral hall, but it did not interfere with the lineage's own use during the Chinese New Year. Later the joint policy of the ministries of culture, construction and finance also included large-scale investment in protection and in 2016 restoration of a number of old residences began in the village.

Many temple festivals organised by lineages and local communities have in recent years been listed as intangible cultural heritage, and this status was also bestowed on Xinye's temple festival in 2009. As a result, the temple festival has undergone major changes between 2004 when I first visited the village and 2013 when I last visited the festival. It has grown in size, type of visitors, and involvement from the local government and the tourism company. In 2010, the local government decided to brand it as a 'farm cultural festival (*nongye wenhua jie*),' and also added some new elements (on rebranding and heritagisation of religious and temple festivals see Liang 2014 and Chen 2015). The festival today attracts a large and heterogeneous group of people apart from the Ye lineage members and villagers from neighbouring villages. In 2013, I noticed many tourists and amateur photographers from different photography associations that were attracted by the spectacle of the festival and its visual qualities. The heritagisation of the festival has thus changed it from a local affair for the lineage to a larger cultural event that is consumed by outsiders, and although it is still managed by the lineage, the local government and the tourism company are heavily involved in its promotion.

The Hangzhou cultural bureau in 2009 also put the local *Kunqu* opera on the municipal list of intangible cultural heritage. A group of old men were selected as transmitters (*chuancheng ren*) and charged with the work to transmit knowledge to the younger generation. Ye Zhaobiao, one of the transmitters, has for example been involved in a project to teach opera to school children and middle-aged women in the village but this has proved a difficult task. It does not seem likely that the local opera will be possible to revive after so many years of neglect and in view of new economic realities and young people's lack of interest in these traditional cultural activities.

Voice and Agency in the Local Community: Diverse Actors and a Changing Environment

A wide and growing range of individuals and groups are today talking about and engaging with the cultural heritage. However, they play different roles and have different impacts. Many experts and scholars are appointed by and work in close cooperation with government bodies, although there are also informal networks of enthusiasts, intellectuals, and activists who through their writing, art, and different activities celebrate heritage in different ways. Another category consists of people working in different kinds of media and cultural industries, such as journalists, photographers and filmmakers. In some cases, people who long ago have left their villages still retain a close connection with them, or in recent years have become more engaged and shape heritage work in their home villages (personal observations in several villages, including in Xinye, see also Nitzky 2013). They may be involved in documenting local history in writing or through documentary film, or take part in different heritage events and promote traditional handicrafts. In other cases, intellectuals and artists, the most famous example being artist Ou Ning, have settled in villages where they have no previous ties and engage in different types of rural reconstruction projects that also often pay attention to heritage issues, including restoring historical buildings, engaging in different cultural festivals, and helping to preserve and develop local handicraft (Wainwright 2014). Local communities, including lineages, and transmitters of intangible heritage who personify and embody traditions, are crucial for the survival and performance of everyday cultural practices in the village.

In the case of Xinye one can identify a range of different individuals and groups who in various ways and capacities are involved in discovering, documenting, narrating and managing the cultural heritage, and where new groups and constellations have appeared over time. The Ye lineage, dominated by a group of older men, were the initiators behind work to reclaim and renovate the ancestral halls in the 1980s and revise the genealogy in 2001, and they continue to be active in documenting family and village history and managing ancestor ceremonies and the temple festival. The Xinye Ye lineage is also linked with a larger network of Ye lineage members. In 2000, the World Association of the Ye Lineage (*Shijie Ye shi lianyi zonghui*) was established at a meeting in Henan, although it is formally registered in Hong Kong. It is currently involved in work to compile a comprehensive genealogy. In 2009, the Hangzhou, Jiaxing, Huzhou, Jinhua, and Quzhou section of the association was set up and held its first meeting in Xinye. Both the World Association and many local sections publish their own magazines that document important events and celebrate individual family members' achievements. In 2010, the Jiande Ye Lineage Old Culture Study Association was set up and formally registered with the local civil bureau. It has also launched its own publication. The organisation aims to document the Ye lineage in all villages in Jiande, and the magazine publishes articles on different events, famous historic figures as well as contemporary lineage members who have made exceptional contributions to society and the lineage. It mainly draws its membership among older people, including from the Old People's Association (OPA). Members of OPA are among the most active in the different lineage associations and in the management of ancestral halls, and are also in charge of maintaining the upkeep of the genealogy.

Many of the most active villagers have worked outside the village, several as teachers, and retired to the village and now spend their time documenting lineage and village history. In 2011, when I spent the Chinese New Year in the village, one of the men, Ye Ruirong, was documenting and photographing ancestor portraits that some families had been able to save and which they put up in their home during this time of the year. He has continued to collect much material and during my latest visit in 2016 showed me the 20 volumes he had put together thus far that he had self-printed. Some other villagers have also put together a book on the village that was self-published in 2009, and in 2010 by a publishing house (Li 2010). These books provide information about lineage and village history as well as traditional beliefs and local stories. While the genealogy and the villagers' own writings focus more on lineage history and local events, other books situate Xinye within a larger narrative of Chinese traditional culture and values. In Li (2010) the village is thus described as 'a living example of farm culture (*nonggeng wenhua yichu huo biaoben*)', a description that is also reiterated in different media and film productions. Another distinctive group of people, albeit overlapping with those mentioned above, are those who recently have been listed as transmitters, such as Ye Zhaobiao who learned and were involved in the village Kunqu opera group before it was disbanded in the mid-60s, and now has helped the cultural bureau to write down the old opera.

A group of younger people, again mostly men, who have left the village, are also active in documenting and celebrating local history. One man, Ye Zhiheng, a professor of classical literature in Hangzhou, has for many years been working on an academic book about the history of the village as part of a bigger state-sponsored project to document villages in Zhejiang (Ye 2016). His main motivation is a concern that knowledge about village history and traditions is rapidly disappearing and the need to provide a more correct and in-depth history of the village than that found in the media and in tourism promotional material. Another man, Ye Guichang, working as a chemistry teacher in a school in the township, in 2008 set up a website with news and information about the village's history and traditions.[2] He uses the website to provide information on history, local architecture and traditional festivals. He also publishes news, information on village affairs and official policies related to heritage and tourism in the village. The website enables people who have left the village to stay in touch and continue to engage with the lineage and with village life. It also connects the village with strangers and tourists interested in local history and rural traditions. The website in a sense serves as a digital archive of the very process of heritagisation. In 2015, Ye Guichang also set up a WeChat group, *Xinye wenhua yanjiu hui*, with some 92 people who mostly live outside the village and use the platform to stay in touch, share news about the village, and interact on other issues.

Other villagers engage in the heritagisation process in a more down-to-earth manner through their work in the tourism sector, for example selling souvenirs, operating guesthouses and restaurants, as well as producing and

---

2   The first website was set up in 2008: http://www.xinyecun.com/ ; and in 2013 it moved to a new site: http://www.xinyecun.net/

selling local products and food. Local products, for example a local wine, are also celebrated as intangible heritage, and an exhibition of the local winemaking opened a couple of years ago. Heritage tourism has thus resulted in more people becoming involved in performing, selecting and marketing heritage, which contribute to the commodification of Xinye's heritage. The way they perform heritage departs from earlier cultural practices that mainly were confined to ancestor ceremonies and religious practices. Local actors are thus involved in several types of bottom-up activities to document and celebrate local heritage, including some that are based in traditional practices such as compiling genealogies and transmitting knowledge about and taking part in ancestor ceremonies, and others that are a reaction to or stimulated by the heritagisation process and tourism development.

Local communities are not passive in the transformation of the countryside and its heritage. Many lineages have for example appropriated the language of heritage and patriotism, and one can find placards in ancestral halls that show that the halls have been nominated as 'patriotic education base (*aiguo jiaoyu jidi*)'. This is an example both of the state's co-option of lineages as well as the lineages' own negotiations with the state and appropriation of state ideology (Svensson 2012). At the 2013 temple festival I discovered that among the traditional symbols and decorations in one of the ancestral halls hung a colourful electric placard inscribed with the new slogan 'China Dream' launched by President Xi Jinping. To embed and claim the temple festival to be part of the China Dream shows the lineage's ideological awareness and appropriation of a key political slogan. After Xinye's success in getting Hunan TV to record the popular reality-show *Baba qu na'r* (Where is Daddy Going?) in the village in 2014, many signs and placards, including life-size cardboard figures of the main stars, were put up at different sites. The use and mixture of traditional symbols, official propaganda, entertainment and commercial advertisements show the complex and multi-layered environment in which heritage is embedded, performed and narrated.

Although an increasing number of individuals celebrate different aspects of their heritage, there are some missing voices and topics in the heritagisation process. Male voices who dominated in the patriarchal lineages also dominate the newly emerging heritage communities and networks and in the writing of local history. The exhibitions set up by the tourism company also tend to privilege male voices and experiences, whereas women's history and roles in the village are largely invisible. Women's handicraft, production of different foods, and engagement in different types of rituals and everyday religious life are thus often ignored and not celebrated as heritage albeit very central to the life and development of the village. Some women who have stayed behind in the village to take care of small children, grandchildren and elderly parents are today however finding a new place for themselves as growing tourism has encouraged households to open small restaurants and inns. One woman, who together with her husband was among the first families to open a small inn and restaurant in the village, has received awards for her skills and proudly taken part in several competitions, and has also been interviewed in the media.

Discovery and Commodification: The Role of Experts and Tourism Companies

Local actors are increasingly involved with, dependent on, and inspired by a range of outside actors, including experts, heritage bureaus, tourism companies and the media. One of the first outsiders to have a big impact on preservation efforts and the heritagisation of the village was professor Chen Zhihua of Qinghua University. Professor Chen has worked on different preservation plans in Zhejiang province and elsewhere, and his books on rural architecture and traditional villages are a valuable source of information. He first came to Xinye in 1989 when he was working in neighbouring Zhuge village. His book on Xinye (first edition in 2003) provides rich information about lineage and village history, local cultural practices, economic life and architecture, including detailed drawings of the different buildings and beautiful photos of the village. His high praise of the village and its unique features helped convince the provincial heritage bureau to list the village as a protected site. Experts at the provincial heritage bureau have since played an important role and provided advice and funding.

There had been an abortive attempt to set up a tourism company in 2001, but for a variety of reasons tourism never took off at the time. It was not until 2010 that a tourism company, established by the township but with the village having 20 per cent of the shares, was established in the village. Since then they have helped promote the village and worked to attract visitors. The works by experts such as Chen Zhihua are not so easily accessible, although on sale in the tourism office, whereas media reports, tourism promotional material and popular books on rural heritage and village tourism have proliferated and shaped many Chinese citizens' perceptions about village life. This more visual and popular work, including TV programmes and films discussed below, embeds the heritage of Xinye within a larger narrative of historic villages and a traditional literati and farming culture that feeds on nostalgia and contributes to the aestheticisation of heritage and the visual consumption of the past.

When I first visited Xinye there were no signs or information about the different ancestral halls and other buildings. Most of the ancestral halls were also closed, apart from during the Chinese New Year when ancestor ceremonies took place there, except for Youxu Ancestral Hall which partly was used as a meeting place for the Old People's Association where senior citizens came to drink tea, play cards and mahjong. One of the large and well-preserved buildings collectively owned by the village, Shuangmei Hall, was then equipped with a TV set, a range of newspapers, as well as a small library, all of which was open to every villager. This building has now been renovated as a tourist site only accessible with an entrance ticket and no longer serves the villagers (the library has been moved elsewhere).

It was not until 2013 that tourism really took off, with investment in new signs, a big tourism office, and the opening up of several ancestral halls and buildings, including The Temple to the Literary God, Youxu Ancestral Hall and West Hill Ancestral Hall, to visitors who only could enter if they had bought the entrance ticket to the village. The tourism company and the local government have spent quite a lot of money upgrading infrastructure in the village, at the same time as strict zoning has been enforced, resulting in the demolition of some new houses and the setting aside of an area for new buildings outside the village centre. The tourism company has also invested heavily in tourism promotion, including setting up a website.[3] The promotion is now paying off and during high season and weekends the village receives an increasing number of visitors; according to the tourism office, there were 200,000 visitors in 2015 (personal communication). The village is also using its increasing fame to host many different events and meetings. In April 2016, the Zhejiang Family Inn Association for example held a meeting in the village. The Hunan TV reality show *Baba qu na'r?* (Where is Daddy Going?) definitely put Xinye on the tourist map. It resulted in an influx of tourists, particularly families with small children and young fans of the stars in the show. There have been some attempts to integrate the stories and adventures from the show into the tourist experience, although it has mostly been a question of setting up signs at the different sites the stars visited with references to what they did. The recent growth in tourism has encouraged many villagers to open inns, restaurants, and souvenir shops. In 2010 there were only three inns but by 2016 there were as many as twenty.

3   http://www.xinyegucun.com/

Mediatisation and Visualisation of Heritage: Nostalgia for the Past and Site of Entertainment

In recent years, the role of the visual in the construction, production and consumption of cultural heritage has received more attention (Waterton & Watson 2010). The visual representations of the past take different forms, and can, for example, be found in museums' use of photography, film, and new media displays, in TV documentaries, and in films made by independent filmmakers, anthropologists and local communities. There are thus many different actors involved in the mediatisation and visualisation of the heritage, including ordinary citizens, amateur photographers, heritage bureaus, tourism companies, media organisations, including TV producers, and independent filmmakers. In Xinye it is mainly photographers' associations, the tourism company, and different TV crews that have been active. But it is interesting to note that with the growing use of smartphones and cheap DVD cameras, ordinary citizens are also actively documenting cultural practices and village life on still photos and film. Ye Ruirong, a retired teacher and avid recorder of the village, has, for example, been active in documenting village life and changes through photography. During my first visit to the temple festival the event was mainly recorded by professional filmmakers (see further below), but in 2013 I noticed many villagers and other visitors using smartphones and film cameras to document the event. Photography is quite popular in China, and rural scenes and historic villages have become a favourite topic (e.g., Schaefer 2010). Local photographers' associations often travel to villages to take photos and are also invited to document villages or participate in different photo festivals in villages. In 2013 some famous photographers were invited to the temple festival in Xinye, and the village also aims to attract photographers through setting up the Xinye Old Village Photography Base. In 2015 when I visited the village there was an exhibition in the Youxu Ancestral Hall that mainly exhibited photography portraying an aestheticised vision of a tranquil and peaceful rural life. Internet and social media are also important tools for mediatisation and used by both official actors and ordinary citizens. One example is the website established by Ye Guichang that includes a lot of visual material. He publishes his own photographs and when I spent Chinese New Year in the village in 2010 he also uploaded some of my photographs.

In recent years numerous TV programmes on Chinese history, traditions, and cultural issues have been made and broadcast, and they are quite popular. They are part of the heritage turn in China and speak to a nostalgia for a lost rural life – far from the images of exploited peasants narrated in the early years of the PRC – prevalent among some in the urban middleclass. The way these programmes focus on and narrate traditional values also speak to contemporary needs and attempts to reinvigorate the Chinese nation. In the following I will discuss four different films/TV programmes and their narratives and aesthetics. The first one is a 39 minute film made by Hangzhou TV and directed by Mao Xiaolu in 2004. The second is a 15 minute promotional film that one can buy in the tourism company but which is part of a series of films on villages in Zhejiang. The third is a 30 minute film produced and screened on CCTV 4 in 2015; and the fourth is the reality show *Baba qu na'r* made by Hunan TV in 2014. They exhibit different forms and aesthetics and present slightly different narratives and voices. The Hunan TV production has without doubt had the biggest impact on the village in terms of visibility and tourism promotion.

In 2004 I ran into a team from Hangzhou TV led by Mao Xiaolu, a writer and director, that was making a film about the village as part of a series of films on six traditional villages in Hangzhou. The series is called 'Memory Home' (*Jiyi jiayuan*), and the choice of title shows how the village is constructed as a site of memories and home to traditional values. The film provides a detailed overview of the lineage history from the arrival of Ye's ancestors, including some of the more important family members and their achievements, the geomancy of the village as well as its architecture. It also shows the temple festival and discusses its meaning. The film provides a narrative of a lineage that has devoted itself to 'farming and education (*gengdu*)' over the centuries which symbolises traditional rural life and values. The mode of storytelling is very traditional with a male voice-over that narrates the story of the village accompanied with aesthetically pleasing images of the village. No villagers are speaking in the film, and their lack of voice denies them agency in telling their own story and how they have preserved the village and maintained cultural practices. The village is depicted as traditional and unchanged, the preferred focus in many of these kinds of films, despite the fact that it has undergone many changes, including disruption of traditional life during the Cultural Revolution, and, since the reform period, it has seen a big out-migration and the influx of new values and ways of living. There is nothing in the film about the difficulties villagers encountered in the past, or any of the struggles they face today, and for all its historical detail it is quite ahistorical. The purpose is to celebrate an imagined rural life rather than give an in-depth and accurate historical analysis or to problematise the contemporary situation and the preservation of traditions.

The promotional video used by the tourism company is much shorter, 15 minutes, and its narration is very fragmented and built around different scenes, many of them staged.[4] This video also has a male voice-over that narrates the scenes in a highly artificial way to the accompaniment of soft traditional music. The video does not provide much historical information and also relatively little about the village's architecture. It begins with some seductive and picturesque images of the landscape and of a man ploughing with his ox in the early morning sun. The impression one gets from the images is one of a quiet and peaceful rural life where the 'dream of farming and reading (*gengdu mengxiang*)' continues to be pursued. Villagers are performing and acting out different scenes, a marriage scene, drinking tea in an old mansion, writing calligraphy, playing *erhu* at a dam, and worshipping in the ancestral hall. It is obvious, at least for somebody who has visited the village, that the majority of these scenes are staged, and that people have been dressed up for the occasion. The village is described as dreamlike, reinforced by the title of the video *Menghui gucun, ganwu Xinye* (Dreaming of the old village, feeling Xinye), or as the English title on the video itself runs, 'Dream back to ancient village Xinye'. The impression the viewer gets is of an unchanged and charming rural way of living, and of a village that is described as *gulao he shenmi* (traditional and mysterious). The fact that the video makes use of aesthetically pleasing photos and staged scenes underlines its nostalgic view of rural life. Its goal is to sell an imaginary and picturesque village and the filmmakers are not interested in the more complex historic reality and contemporary challenges on the countryside.

In 2015 CCTV 4 broadcasted a series that celebrated rural heritage, *Jizhu xiangchu* (Remember Nostalgia) where Xinye was one among a total of sixty villages selected and portrayed in 30 minute programmes.[5] The programme on Xinye has the subtitle, *du ke xiushen* (reading can cultivate one's moral character), and focuses on the Ye lineage's emphasis on education. The film begins with a scene at the start of the school semester when the pupils gather for a ceremony in the Temple to the Literary God called 'picking up the pen ceremony' (*kai bi li*) and read a text that one of their ancestors had composed on the importance of learning and education. The film describes the yearning for education through both historical examples and interviews with a range of people such as school children, a man who started a library, and a man from the village who became a professor. The film has no voice-over but is shaped by the reporter who is walking around and talking with

4   The film is part of a series of films on villages in Zhejiang and reportedly took five years to make at a total cost of 8 million yuan. See the production's website at www.mhgc.com.cn
5   The part on Xinye was first broadcast on 17 January 2015, see http://tv.cntv.cn/video/VSET10/c231aa97a40a4b8aa2563cfde3994c00

various people in the village. The film has been carefully crafted in order to tell one particular story, that of the high importance put on education, and should be seen in the context of the other films in the series that depict and exemplify other valued aspects of Chinese civilisation and traditions. It is a very selective, and slightly distorted, slice of Xinye's history, and it is obvious that the emphasis on education also speaks to contemporary concerns and aspirations in Chinese society.

Baba qu na'er? (Where is Daddy Going?) is a quite different sort of TV programme that aims more to entertain than inform, although there are certain educational lessons to be learned. It is originally a South Korean show that has been adapted by Hunan TV and recorded in the village in 2014 with several famous artists and superstar basketball player Yao Ming. The village has tried to make the best of this promotional opportunity and huge boards and signs inform visitors about the TV programme, now firmly placed in the history of the village, and the places where the stars visited or lived while they stayed in the village. The book about the Xinye episode is also available for sale in the tourism shop. In the reality show famous fathers take their children on a trip of adventure and fun games. The history and heritage of the village is more of a quaint backdrop to the stars and the games. There is only very superficial interaction with the village and its history. The stars sleep in the old houses and engage in some activities such as for example reading the classics in the Temple to the Literary God. The reality-show has attracted many families with small children and some young fans of the stars to the village. They travel not so much in search of Xinye, or an imagined rural past, but in the footsteps of the stars and are attracted by the show's playfulness. The reality show illustrates the manifold ways heritage can be used and repackaged, and that it sometimes only serves as a colourful background for entertainment and play. The combination of heritage and entertainment/play is not new, as it is a feature of many different historic and cultural theme parks in China, and in other attempts to recreate historical events through games and play.

Conclusion

Rural communities, including lineages and transmitters, today have to navigate a new heritage discourse and landscape. This can be both em-powering and disempowering, and it sometimes changes people's cultural practices and lives. Lineages continue to play an important cultural and political role in Zhejiang province where people maintain a strong sense of family-based and placed-based identities. Some lineages have been able to boost their status and cultural capital by having their halls listed as heritage and appropriating the language of cultural heritage and patriotism. In tourism promotion and in the media Xinye village is said to represent the quintessential Chinese village, Confucian virtues and the traditional 'farming and reading' (*gengdu*) spirit, at the same time as its rich architecture and pleasing aesthetics are celebrated. For the Ye lineage, historic buildings such as ancestral halls represent family history and past achievements and continue to be used during the Chinese New Year and other times of the year. As a result of the heritagisation process and growth in tourism the village has, however, undergone some changes in terms of management of these sites, at the same time that outsiders and tourists now also visit the ancestral halls. But ancestor ceremonies and religious life for now mostly continue in parallel to tourism, without either official support or direct interference.

An increasing number of villagers and former villagers are today engaged in documenting their own history and traditions, in part inspired by the general heritage boom in society, and often without much contact with official bodies or the tourism company. The grand narrative of 'farming and reading' in the films promoting the village and celebrating rural life in the past is quite remote from village life today. There are very few people left in the village who depend on farming, and education is more a way out of the village for young people. Nonetheless, people in Xinye village do not reject the official heritage discourse or object to the depiction in the media and on film, and instead seem quite happy to embrace even the more imaginary and invented aspects of tradition as it helps promote the village and brings economic benefits. The Ye lineage and different individuals in Xinye are actively negotiating with and appropriating the new ideological field and the economic space that the heritage turn has created. Heritage and tourism are deeply embedded in the cultural life and social and economic struggles and developments in the Chinese countryside today.

References

Blumenfield, T. & H. Silverman (eds.) (2013), *Cultural Heritage Politics in China*. New York: Springer.

Bodolec, C. (2013), 'The Chinese Paper-Cut: From Local Inventories to the UNESCO Representative List of the Intangible Cultural Heritage of Humanity', in R. F. Bendix, A. Eggert & A. Peselman (eds.), *Heritage Regimes and the State*, 257-264. Göttingen: Universitätsverlag, 2nd revised edition. [Online]. Available at http://www.oapen.org/download?type=document&docid=611230] (accessed 19 May, 2017).

Chen Z. (2015), 'For Who to Conserve Intangible Cultural Heritage: The Dislocated Agency of Folk Belief Practitioners and the Reproduction of Local Culture', *Asian Ethnology* 74 (2): 307-334.

Chen Z., et al. (2003), *Xinye Cun* [Xinye Village]. Shijiazhuan: Hebei jiaoyu chubanshe.

Chio, J. (2014), *A Landscape of Travel: The Work of Tourism in Rural Ethnic China*. Seattle: University of Washington Press.

Gao, B. (2014), 'How Does Superstition Become Intangible Cultural Heritage in Postsocialist China?', *positions: east asia cultures critique* 22 (3): 551-572.

Haldrup, M. & J.O. Bærenholdt (2015), 'Heritage as Performance', in E. Waterton and S. Watson (eds.), *The Palgrave Handbook of Contemporary Heritage Research*, 52-68. Basingstoke, Hampshire: Palgrave Macmillan.

Harrison, R. (2013), *Heritage: Critical Approaches*. London: Routledge.

Harvey, D. (2001), 'Heritage Pasts and Heritage Presents: Temporality, Meaning and the Scope of Heritage Studies', *International Journal of Heritage Studies* 7 (4): 319-338.

Li Y., ed. (2010), *Gucun Xinye* [The Old Xinye Village]. Tianjin: Tianjin guji chubanshe.

Liang, Y. (2013), 'Turning Gwer Sa La Festival into Intangible Cultural Heritage: State Superscription of Popular Religion in Southwest China', *China: An International Journal* 11 (2): 58-75.

Madsen, R. (2014), 'From Socialist Ideology to Cultural Heritage: The Changing Basis of Legitimacy in the People's Republic of China', *Anthropology & Medicine* 21 (1): 58-70.

Nitzky, W. (2013), 'Community Empowerment at the Periphery? Participatory Approaches to Heritage Protection in Guizhou, China', in T. Blumenfield & H. Silverman (eds.), *Cultural Heritage Politics in China*, 205-233. New York: Springer.

Oakes, T. (2013), 'Heritage as Improvement: Cultural Display and Contested Governance in Rural China', *Modern China* 39 (4): 380-407.

Oakes, T. & D. Sutton (eds.) (2010), *Faiths on Display: Religion, Tourism and the Chinese State*. Lanham, MD: Rowman and Littlefield.

Obringer, F. (2011), 'Chinese Medicine and the Enticement of Heritage Status', *China Perspectives* 3: 15-22.

Schaefer, W. (2010), 'Poor and Blank: History's Marks and the Photographies of Displacement', *Representations* 109 (1): 1-34.

Smith, L. (2006), *Uses of Heritage*. London: Routledge.

Svensson, M. (2012), 'Lineages and the State in Zhejiang: Negotiating and Reinventing Local History and Heritage', in A. Bislev and S. Thøgersen (eds.), *Organizing Rural China*, 157-172. Lanham, MD: Rowman and Littlefield.

Svensson, M. (2016), 'Evolving and contested cultural heritage in China: the rural heritagescape', in A. Matsuda & L. Mengoni (eds.), *Reconsidering Cultural Heritage in East Asia*, 31-46. London: Ubiquity Press. [Online]. Available from: http://www.ubiquitypress.com/site/books/10.5334/baz/ (accessed 7 May 2017).

Wainwright, O. (2014), 'Our cities are insufferable: Chinese artists go back to the land', *The Guardian*, 2 December 2014. [Online]. Available from: https://www. theguardian.com/artanddesign/2014/dec/02/chinese-artists-rural-rebellion-xi-jinping (accessed 7 May 2017).

Waterton, E. & S. Watson (2010), *Culture, Heritage and Representation. Perspectives on Visuality and the Past.* London: Routledge.

Yang, M. (2004), 'Spatial Struggles: Postcolonial Complex, State Disenchantment, and Popular Reappropriation of Space in Rural Southeast China', *Journal of Asian Studies* 63 (3): 719-755.

Ye, Z. (2016), *Xinye gu cunluo yanjiu* [Research on old village Xinye]. Hangzhou: Zhejiang daxue chubanshe.

Zhang, Y. & Z. Wu (2015), 'The Reproduction of Heritage in a Chinese Village: Whose Heritage, Whose Pasts?', *International Journal of Heritage Studies* 22 (3): 228-241.

Zhu, Y. (2012), 'Performing Heritage: Rethinking Authenticity in Heritage,' *Annals of Tourism Research* 39: 1495-1513

About the Author

MARINA SVENSSON is Professor of Modern China at Lund University, Sweden. She writes on human rights, digital developments, media and cultural heritage in China. She co-edited *Chinese Heritage in the Making: Experiences, Negotiations and Contestations* (Amsterdam University Press, 2018).

Section 4

Appropriations and Commodifications

of Ethnic Heritage

10 'Even If You Don't Want to Drink, You Still Have to Drink'

The Yi and Alcohol in History and Heritage

Joseph Lawson

Abstract

This chapter considers the history of alcohol in Nuosu Yi society in relation to the formal codification of a Yi heritage of alcohol-related culture, and the question of alcohol in Yi health. The relationship of newly invented tradition to older practice and thought is often obscure in studies that lack historical perspective. Examining the historical narratives associated with the exposition of a Yi heritage of alcohol, this study reveals that those narratives are woven from a tapestry of threads with histories of their own, and they therefore shape present-day heritage work. After a brief overview of ideas about alcohol in contemporary discourses on Yi heritage, the chapter then analyses historical texts to argue that many of these ideas are remarkably similar to ones that emerged in the context of nineteenth and early twentieth century contact between Yi and Han communities.

Keywords: Nuosu, Yi, alcohol, Liangshan, drinking song

Introduction: Yi History, Tradition, and Alcohol

It is widely accepted that a significant part of what we think of as heritage or tradition is invented, or at least recreated, according to present-day concerns and ideas. But the relationship of newly invented tradition and its associated discourses to older practice and thought is often obscure in studies that lack historical perspective. This chapter considers the history of alcohol in Nuosu Yi society in relation to the formal codification of an

Ludwig, Carol, Linda Walton, and Yi-Wen Wang (eds), *The Heritage Turn in China: The Reinvention, Dissemination and Consumption of Heritage*. Amsterdam: Amsterdam University Press 2020
DOI: 10.5117/9789462985667_CH10

Yi heritage of alcohol-related culture, and the question of alcohol in Yi health. It explores the historical narratives associated with the exposition of an Yi heritage of alcohol, showing that those narratives are woven from a tapestry of threads with histories of their own, and they therefore shape present-day heritage work, as much as the latter seeks to impose its own reconstructions of the past. Following a brief overview of ideas about alcohol in contemporary Yi society, it then analyses historical texts to argue that many of these ideas are remarkably similar to ones that emerged in the context of nineteenth and early twentieth century contact between Yi and Han communities. Discussion of alcohol in contemporary Yi society is often characterised by the notion that Yi drinking habits have been disturbed by either commercialisation or contact with Han culture in the recent past. This allows the recovery of a traditional drinking culture to be positioned as a way to reconcile the contemporary celebration of alcohol with concerns about its effects on the health of Yi communities. The chapter demonstrates that the idea of a recent rupture in drinking habits brought on by contact with Han or commercialisation is itself an old one, older than narratives about a recent transformation of drinking culture suggest. This raises the question of whether contemporary heritage discourses are really inventing tradition, or if they are not re-articulating already long-established ideas.

Composed of various indigenous peoples of the upland Southwest, the Yi 彝 are one of China's larger officially recognised ethnic groups (*minzu*). There are some eight million Yi in China today, with considerable variation in language and culture between different Yi groups. This chapter concentrates mostly on the Nuosu Yi of Sichuan's Liangshan, with some reference to Yi groups in Yunnan. Before the 1950s, Nuosu society was organised around self-governing clans, each of which had a caste identity – principally one of the 'hard-boned' elite *nuoho* and *nzymo* castes, or 'soft-boned' *quho*, who were considered of lesser social rank. There were also slaves, who lacked a lineage identity, but who might become *quho* over several generations. Since the 'Democratic Reforms', a radical program initiated in 1956 to spread collectivisation to the non-Han peoples of Sichuan's west and southwest peripheries, Yi society has undergone substantial change, though caste and lineage identities remain extremely important for the Nuosu Yi. In recent years, the preservation of Yi heritage has become a matter of increasing concern.

It is common for anthropologists and Nuosu themselves to note the importance of alcohol in Nuosu society. As Thomas Herberer comments: 'the Liangshan Nuosu Yi perceive themselves as "*lao da*", the heartiest drinkers among all Yi groups, and look down on other Yi and Han on this account.

Being able to hold one's drink is perceived as a sign of superiority, particularly in comparison to non-Yi, and as part of the ethnic identity' (2007: 171, 204). A common aphorism, repeated in many discussions of the difference between Han and Yi, is that 'Alcohol is for the Nuosu what tea is for the Han' (Jia 2014: 215; Herberer 2007: 203; Mahei & Li 1994: 286). A commenter on *Yizu ren wang* 彝族人网 (Yi people online) a popular website with a wide range of Yi culture related content and a forum used by Yi people to discuss topics of particular relevance to Yi writes that 'It's as if the Yi live for drinking and their friends. Especially young guys, who drink like money and life don't mean anything' (Suomaecho 2011). An album of 'Yi drinking songs' produced by the Sichuan Music Recording Publishing House features Nuosu pop singer Jidi Kangshi 吉狄康帅whose image combines Nuosu-styled clothing with the long uncovered hair of a Chinese rock star, and whose lyrics mix Nuosu and Chinese language in a similar way. On one song, Jidi enthusiastically sings lines from what is presented as Yunnan folk song: 'It doesn't matter if you like it or not, you still have to drink' (*bu guan ni xihuan bu xihuan, ye yao he*) (2002). The same song forms part of the greeting at the Solar Calendar Square Park in Chuxiong in Yunnan, a theme-park/museum complex that showcases aspects of Yi heritage for tourists (Harrell & Li 2003: 379).

Not for nothing does the song say that alcohol consumption is compulsory. Alcohol was and is a highly important component of many social, political, and judicial ceremonies in Yi societies. It is traditionally consumed at important ceremonies such as marriages, to seal agreements, including land trades, and during the mediation and resolution of disputes. Nuosu customary law specified schedules of payments to be made to victims of crime, the most minor and common of which was the sacrifice of livestock and provision of alcohol (Cai & Mi 2014: 135-136). Ritual consumption of alcohol was and is treated extremely seriously as a way of making a vow. Nuosu scholar Liu Yu notes that 'They [Nuosu] viewed liquor as equal in value to 'duty' and life. Thus, people who drank together could not possibly go back on their word' (Liu 2001: 116). Various other aphorisms similarly weigh the value of liquor against the lives of humans and livestock.

Although the general place of alcohol consumption in Yi society is about as far from being endangered as it is possible to be, in recent years those concerned with the preservation of Yi heritage have become worried about the possible disappearance of traditional alcohol production techniques and consumption culture. The authors of a recent volume on the intangible heritage of the Yi note that: 'There are now fewer and fewer people who understand traditional brewing techniques, and as a component of the intangible heritage of the Yi people these should be protected carefully' (Jia

2014: 227). Concerns such as these have meant that alcohol-related culture has been included on formal lists of Nuosu heritage. In June 2014 the Sichuan government published its fourth list of 'intangible cultural heritage' in the province, containing 36 items, many of them associated with minority ethnic groups (Sichuan sheng wenhua guan 2015). One of the items on the list was a technique for fermenting oat-based alcohol from Liangshan's Huidong County. Other alcohol-related heritage on the same list included two other fermentation techniques, and three distillation techniques. This was not the first official listing of alcohol or alcohol-related culture as part of Yi heritage. In 2008, the State Council (*guowuyuan*) published its second list of national-level intangible cultural heritage, which included a 'Yi drinking song' from Wuding in Chuxiong in Yunnan.

Aside from concerns about the survival of specific kinds of Yi alcohol and alcohol-related culture, the recognition of commodities and practices associated with consumption as heritage is attractive to local entrepreneurs because of the branding and marketing opportunities it creates. The idea that the alcohol and alcohol-related culture of ethnic minorities in the Southwest could constitute a component of what is seen as their 'rich tourism resource base' has existed since at least the late 1990s (He & Wu 1999: 240). The oat wine of Huidong had already been commercially produced, but recognition as intangible heritage offered further opportunities for local companies to develop and market the product. Irrespective of whether their product has been formally included on heritage lists, large numbers of small grain wine breweries and distilleries in villages in Liangshan now advertise that they use 'the most ancient handcraft brewing techniques' – as seen at a grain wine brewery in the village of Haitang in Ganluo County in northern Liangshan. Many other enterprises use similar formulations.

There are direct links between the academic study of Yi heritage and the commercialised promotion of it. Jidi Kangshi's 'Yi drinking songs' album for example, credits Feng Yuanwei 冯元蔚, a Nuosu from the Anning River valley who was an early graduate of and academic at Southwest University for Nationalities and has been heavily involved in the collection and translation of Nuosu oral and written heritage.

The incorporation of consumption and consumer goods into heritage raises questions when the consumption is also the subject of debates concerning the commodity's impact on consumers' physical, mental, or economic health. This is especially true for indigenous peoples, for whom consumption of commodities understood to be dangerous is the subject of an enormous amount of scientific research and popular discourse, in most parts of the world including China. The celebrated importance of alcohol consumption for Nuosu society and identity sits uneasily alongside medical and development-work discourses that blame alcohol consumption for many problems facing Yi groups today. One study of Han and Nuosu rural people in Liangshan conducted in 2000, for example, found that while the percentage of Nuosu who drink at least once per month (36.92 per cent) was only slightly higher than the percentage of Han who did (33.5 per cent), more Nuosu were heavy drinkers, consuming an average 16.87 (±15 per cent) litres per year, compared with 11.02 (±12 per cent) litres for Han drinkers (Li, Wang, Heng, Luo, Xu, Wang, Zhang & Zhang 2000). The researchers also concluded that nearly twice the percentage of Nuosu had what they considered to be alcohol related 'mental disorders' (*jingshen zhang'ai*) as Han (23.36 per cent of Nuosu having such a problem versus only 12.23 per cent of Han), with 11.50 per cent of Nuosu classified as 'alcohol dependent'. The researchers also concluded that Nuosu were more likely to suffer what they classified as alcohol-related physical disorders (14.67 per cent of Nuosu versus 9.51 per cent of Han). There is clearly scope for further investigation: how exactly were subjects classified as 'alcohol dependent'; and to what extent should alcohol be blamed for these problems, as opposed to other social factors? Lines of causation between substance dependence and other problems are notoriously difficult to establish. Much research supports the hypothesis that economically and politically marginalised groups are more vulnerable than others to substance dependence (King, Smith, & Gracey 2009; Alaniz 2009).

In popular and political discourse, medical researchers' findings that Yi are more likely to have physical or mental problems related to alcohol are generalised to broader – and less substantiated – claims that the Yi have a problem with alcohol that other *minzu* do not, or that alcohol is responsible for Yi poverty in a way that it is not in other *minzu*. Qumu Wuniu曲木伍牛, writing as the acting county magistrate (*daili xianzhang*) of Xide, lists several reasons for Nuosu poverty, one of which is that Nuosu 'ideas about consumption are backward' (*xiaofei guannian luohou*) (2006). The chief consumption problems, according to Qumu are: the stress on alcohol in Nuosu society; the view that drunkenness is pleasurable and honourable; the view that 'alcohol you have today might as well be consumed today'; and excessive spending (on alcohol, as well as meat and cigarettes) for guests and *bimo* (priests) invited for ritual occasions. Nuosu alcohol consumption is a common component of such lists: Hou Yuangao侯元高, a Nuosu researcher who has frequently commented on Nuosu health issues, suggests in an interview with a Han journalist that youths struggle to find jobs in cities because they 'lack fluency in Chinese, lack skills, love drinking alcohol, and are clannish and ill-disciplined' (Tan 2016).

Heritage as Problem or Solution?

When alcohol is seen as an indelible part of Nuosu culture, something that characterises Nuosu-ness, and is recognised by provincial and national agencies as a formal part of Nuosu intangible heritage – worthy of protection and promotion with the resources of the state – and yet is simultaneously seen by agents of the state as a major source of problems for the physical, mental, and economic health of Nuosu people, it is reasonable to ask about the cultural dynamics of this contradiction. The accusations from researchers and state officials that alcohol is a cause of ill-health and poverty seem to have made very little impact on the popular celebration of alcohol as an aspect of Nuosu identity and heritage. But concerns about Nuosu drinking are not new. As the next section of this chapter shows, Nuosu were banned from drinking alcohol in many frontier towns and market places in the late nineteenth and early twentieth century, which raises the question of how prohibition has turned into celebration of drinking, despite the development of medical and development professions that continue to blame alcohol consumption for a range of social problems. This chapter argues that a major part of the reason has to do with the sorts of historical narratives that have become associated with Nuosu alcohol heritage.

The contradiction between the state's formalisation of alcohol as a part of heritage alongside a state discourse that casts alcohol as a potent danger to Yi health does not go unnoticed. One participant in a discussion on *Yizu ren wang* suggests that drinking habits might harm the promotion of Yi alcohol heritage: 'You can drink, get drunk, but don't go crazy. Otherwise there'll be no way of making more people appreciate our drinking songs and liquors' (Anji 2012). Discussions of alcohol heritage often seek to reconcile the notion of an Yi drinking problem with their celebration of alcohol traditions, often by claiming that 'ethnic minorities' (*shaoshu minzu*) of the Southwest historically lived in extremely un-commercial societies, and therefore their consumption of anything was very limited, so the celebration of alcohol never had the potential to do serious harm in the past (He & Wu 1999: 239). 'Excessive consumption' of alcohol in the present-day can thus be cast as the result of a rapid increase in availability, at a pace that has outstripped the capacity of 'value systems' (*jiazhiguan*) to adjust.

There are two historical theses here, at least one of which could be tested empirically: i.e., that Nuosu society in the past could not have produced or purchased the quantities of alcohol that Nuosu drink today. The problem with this claim is that historically Nuosu society was highly stratified. Consumption among elite Nuosu was modest and restricted to a narrow range of basic goods, but for things the Nuosu produced themselves or bought from nearby Han settlements it is not clear that levels of consumption were lower than poor Nuosu today, or so low as to preclude consumption of large amounts of alcohol. Travelling in Liangshan in the 1950s, Alan Winnington met a man from an elite family, who told him that he used to drink 'a couple of bottles of corn spirit a day' but had had to cut down to one, thanks to his new station in life as a low-level government functionary on what was, from the man's perspective, a meagre wage (2008: 86). Many accounts of pre-1949 Nuosu society emphasise Nuosu alcohol consumption. In the case of Chinese writing, this might be a reflection more of Chinese writers' sense of curiosity or disapproval at unfamiliar norms of consumption – such as female drinking. But some Nuosu also wrote about what they saw as the high incidence of problem drinking among Nuosu in the 1930s and 1940s (Leng 1988: 129). In remote communities and among poorer Nuosu, material circumstances likely did prevent habitual heavy drinking, but the notion that this applied to all Nuosu seems wrong. Even for lower status *quho* Nuosu, the idea that 'value systems' have not changed in the same way that material culture has raises difficult theoretical problems. This interpretation relies on a separation of 'economy' from 'values', hence distinction between a society's material culture and non-material attitudes and impulses. There is little theorisation here of the relationship of 'values' to 'economy', but the implication of the argument is that just as the transformation of the economy owed little or nothing to native agency, so too will external guidance be necessary in order to bring 'values' up to speed with the economic change.

A slightly different line of thinking, prominent in Nuosu society, suggests that it is precisely the loss of Nuosu alcohol-related heritage that is the cause of contemporary problems with alcohol. Drawing on Nuosu proverbs and interview subjects, Thomas Herberer argues that 'problem drinking' among the Nuosu is a new phenomenon caused by the breakdown of traditional social restraints that worked to mitigate excessive consumption (2007: 204). One interviewee points to the impact of the Han habit of downing a cup in one shot (now widespread, but not, apparently, traditional), as well as declining respect for elders, and the spread of alcohol consumption beyond key social ceremonies and rituals. Herberer interprets a proverb that labelled drinkers of more than three cups per session as dogs as a sign of an historical culture of drinking in moderation. This interpretation raises the question, however, of why Han drinking habits are blamed for the corruption of Nuosu drinking culture, but discussion of problem drinking in Liangshan focuses overwhelmingly on the Nuosu: if Han drinking habits are so bad, why are they not the ones with the perceived 'drinking problem'?

The interpretations share the idea that changes of the present-day have transformed a heritage of non-problematic consumption into a culture that is conducive to drinking problems. This differs in that outsiders tend to see problems emerging from the difficulty that ethnic minorities face navigating what is seen as a huge gulf between the 'extremely limited commercial economy' of their past and a much more commercialised present, whereas the Nuosu are more likely to blame Han cultural influence. The two narratives are often combined, as when Hou Yuangao comments that: 'the arrival of modern commercial products [in Liangshan] broke down the older economic structure based on self-sufficiency, [...] in the past people drank local alcohol they brewed themselves, now they drink beer and *baijiu*' (Tan 2016). This begs the question of why those forms of alcohol are apparently so bad for the Nuosu but not the Han who invented them – but implicitly suggests that the protection and promotion of the older forms of alcohol that Nuosu brewed themselves may contribute to solving the drinking problem that Hou sees in Nuosu youth. Thus, part of the reason why contemporary concerns about Yi drinking have not proved much of a deterrent to the incorporation of alcohol within formalised Yi heritage is that a powerful thread of interpretation suggests that problems result from present-day changes to drinking culture, not the inheritance from the past, understood through dichotomous contrast with the present, and thereby freed from its problems.

Historical Discourses on the Consumption of Alcohol and the Danger of the Frontier

Contemporary narratives about alcohol culture are supported to some extent, but also complicated by the pre-twentieth century Nuosu textual record. The main textual sources for Nuosu history are poetry in a range of genres including epic, origin narrative, lyric, proverb, and songs for weddings and funerals, the custodians of which were *bimo*, Nuosu priests, who perform them on various ceremonial occasions (Bamo 2001: 453-479). These were initially oral compositions, but were written down, probably beginning at some point during the Ming Dynasty. Writing did not fix the words, and they underwent subtle shifts and additions in ways that reflected changes in Nuosu society. Some poetry refers to things such as potatoes and tobacco, which only arrived in the eighteenth century (Bender 2008: 37). Related versions of the poems are found throughout the broader Yi cultural area – indeed Bamo Qubumo argues that the poems are one of the things that unifies Yi culture across its many and diverse regional variants.

One genre of Nuosu poetry is the *bbopa*, or origin narrative; there are *bbopa* for almost everything familiar to the Nuosu, including humans, ghosts, fire, institutions such as marriage, the different kinds of plants and animals known to the Nuosu, and also for different sorts of produce, including alcohol ('Jiu de qiyuan' 2006: 149-156). Although called 'origin narratives', the scope of most *bbopa* is broader than this gloss suggests. 'The Origin of Alcohol' *bbopa* gives a mythic account of the creation of alcohol, then describes preparation methods and lists the many social functions of alcohol (emphasising along the way that young women and servants also drink). It finishes by describing the difference between 'those who can drink' and 'those who cannot drink', and the lines that 'when great men drink, they become greater heroes / when small men drink, they make fools of themselves'. The idea that alcohol makes great men even greater is stated earlier in the *bbopa* too: 'When *ndeggu* [Nuosu mediators or arbiters] drink, their settlements of cases are fair' ('Jiu de qiyuan' 2006: 151). Alcohol is thus critical for social purposes, the outcomes of which are seen to be improved by its consumption. Consumption does not always bring good results, but the *bbopa* casts the negative physical effects that can accompany drinking as a reflection of the drinking ability and type of person that the drinker already is, rather than as something that might be experienced by anyone. The sentiment, observed by Herberer in the present, that being able to hold one's liquor is celebrated in Nuosu society is not a new development.

One of the key complaints in the present-day is that Nuosu drinking has become more problematic because of the way it has been influenced by Han drinking habits. Some epic poetry, as well as local government documents give insight into historical views of alcohol consumption on the Han-Nuosu frontier. *Hnewo Teyy*, loosely translatable as 'the book of origins' is a set of epos collected from the Nuosu area in Sichuan, one of which is called 'Where the Nzy live', which narrates the migration of the Nzy (a group of high caste Nuosu) around Liangshan.

> There, at Galumobbo,
> Where the sons of the Nzy enter the binding house,
> Where the daughters of the Nzy take letters
> Where the liquor pipe is vulgar
> Where the young ladies speak the Shuo language [Chinese]
> Where the capable ones wear government hats
> This is no place for the Nzy to stay
> I'll not build my house here (Feng & Qubi 1978: 96).

Galumobbo (which is called Leibo 雷波 in Chinese) is a town in eastern Liangshan, on the west banks of the Jinsha (Yangtze) River. Since the military campaigns of the early eighteenth century led by the Yongzheng emperor's general Ortai, the territory on the eastern bank had been subjected to a greater extent than what is now the Nuosu heartland in Liangshan to the rule of appointed Han or Manchu officials. From the perspective of the aristocratic subjects of the epos, the cultural influence and political power of the Han (or 'Shuo' – a derogatory term for Han) made Galumobbo an unattractive place to settle. Besides political arrangements, the danger of imprisonment, and the use of the Chinese language by young Nuosu women, the other indicator of undesirability here is that 'the liquor pipe is vulgar (*zho*; '*zhot*' in Northern Yi *pinyin*). Elsewhere in the same epic, *zho* is used for places that have been sullied (polluted) through unnatural forms of consumption: the consumption of human flesh by black horses and dogs, and breathing of smoke from funeral pyres by crows. The '*zho*' liquor pipe of frontier Galumobbo suggests that there were normative ways of consuming alcohol which were not upheld there.

While this might demonstrate the existence of exactly the sort of social controls on drinking behaviour that Herberer suggests, it also shows that the role of alcohol consumption as a site for the construction of a boundary between Han and (elite) Nuosu is very old, as are Nuosu concerns about the impact of Han drinking behaviour on their culture. Nor was it only the sort of Nuosu who shunned Han society like those in this section of *Hnewo Teyy* who worried. In 1861, Jiang Wenfu 姜文富, a 'native official' (*tuzhi*) wrote to the Mianning 冕宁 county magistrate suggesting a ban on alcohol shops in the settlement where Jiang was based (Zhongguo shaoshu minzu … 2009: 238). 'Native official' titles in this context were bestowed by the Qing government in an *ad hoc* and unsystematic manner on locals, generally Nuosu, who had standing in Nuosu society and were deemed by the government to have some ability to administer local Nuosu, or at least mediate between the state and Nuosu communities. Jiang's being identified with a Chinese name in communications with a Han magistrate does not suggest that he was not also a man of prestige in Nuosu communities. Jiang blamed robberies committed by Nuosu on their alcohol consumption: their 'snatching of merchants' property and robbery of local residents, is all the result of over-indulgence, without restraint, of alcohol' (Zhongguo shaoshu minzu … 2009: 238). The Mianning magistrate agreed, and banned the sale of alcohol to Nuosu in the area. Clearly Jiang's concerns about Nuosu alcohol consumption were somewhat different from those in the *Hnewo Teyy*: the latter seems to have been concerned with the spoiling of proper Nuosu alcohol etiquette; while the Jiang felt that commercial supply of alcohol to Nuosu led to over-indulgence and crime.

Mianning was not the only town that restricted either the sale of alcohol to Nuosu, or imposed other sorts of restrictions on Nuosu drinking. Zhaojue 昭觉 in the centre of the Nuosu heartland became the seat of a new Chinese county administration in 1910 as part of an effort to bring the region under state control and integrate it more closely with China. The new county published a set of rules governing Yi-Han interaction, one of which prohibited Nuosu (but not Han) from consuming alcohol in the marketplace (*Zhaojue xian zhi* [1911] 1992: 297 [38a]). Similar sorts of restrictions were maintained throughout the Republican period. The bicultural and bilingual local paramilitary leader Deng Xiuting 鄧秀廷 (Di Keddi, as he was known to the Nuosu) banned Nuosu from drinking alcohol in a market town called Daxingchang in a set of rules published in 1931 ('Zhiling shiyi lü lüzhang Yang Qingquan' 1931: 28-34). Like Zhaojue's regulations, the text targeted Nuosu drinking in particular, ironically, given that the same set of rules also prohibited 'discrimination' (*qishi*).

Jiang's petition did not identify the ethnicity of the sellers of alcohol, nor did Zhaojue's regulations mention the suppliers of alcohol in the marketplace. A well-established stereotype of the Han *jian* ('traitor', or more broadly 'deviant') characterised Chinese-language discussions of the Qing empire's Southwest. Deviant Han were often blamed for either corrupting the natives by introducing them to the worst habits of Han society, or exploiting them and causing them to rebel. Some of the accusations levelled at the rhetorical trope of the Han *jian* in this context are demonstrably false: it is claimed that Han *jian* introduced opium to Liangshan in order to avoid the late Qing anti-opium campaign that curtailed poppy cultivation in Sichuan in 1910, but in fact opium was widely grown in Liangshan before then. Readers of Jiang's petition might well have assumed that the alcohol sellers were Han *jian*, but this is not indicated in the text, and it is noteworthy that the danger – both in Jiang's petition and the regulations established by Zhaojue County – is associated with commercially available alcohol and spaces of commerce.

Even though regulations at Zhaojue, Mianning, and other places specifically targeted Nuosu alcohol consumption, in the nineteenth and early twentieth century the drinking habits of other ethnic communities in mixed settlements and marketplaces were a source of anxiety as well. In the 1930s, Qiu Shuling 邱述鈴, an official in the warlord Liu Wenhui's 劉文輝 Xikang regime wrote reports from Gyaisi (Chinese: Jiulong), an area inhabited by Tibetan, Han, and Nuosu where the northwest edge of Liangshan meets the Tibetan lands. In more than one report, Qiu blamed locals' alcohol and opium consumption for a range of problems (Qiu 1938:23; 1939: 40). One of the oddities of the present day is that the influence of Han drinking habits is blamed for what is otherwise cast as a particularly Nuosu problem. This idea seems to come from a now-past context in which both Nuosu and Han alike worried about the consumption habits of mixed settlements and frontier towns. Curiously, reports written by outsiders criticised Han drinking and opium smoking, but chided the Nuosu for drinking only: famous for growing opium, Nuosu seem not to have consumed much of it themselves. For reasons that have to do with later history, notions about the character of Han settlers have changed substantially since the 1930s and their drinking habits are no longer seen by Han as problematic. Nevertheless, the old anxiety about consumption in market-towns and mixed settlements still shapes the narratives about the recent history of Nuosu drinking.

Just as there is a long-standing anxiety about drinking in mixed settlements and the sale of alcohol, so too is there a long-standing recognition – on the part of government agents, as well as the Nuosu – of the ritual significance of alcohol consumption in Nuosu society. Many Qing documents mention that agreements between Qing and Han groups and Nuosu headmen had been consecrated with the consumption of *xiejiu* 血酒 – alcohol mixed with (animal) blood (Zhongguo zhaoshu minzu ... 2009: 211). Indeed, the phrase 'drinking blood alcohol' came to be a way of saying 'making a treaty'. The most heavily propagandised moment in post-1949 narratives of earlier history has been a 1935 meeting of members of the Communist Party on the Long March and Nuosu from the Ggojjy clan. The two groups, who were both then engaged in fierce struggles against the other enemies, made a loose pact, famously sealed by Communist military commander Liu Bocheng 劉伯承and Nuosu chief Ggojjy Yodda (referred to in Chinese as Guoji xiao Yuedan 果基小约旦). The event has been memorialised numerous times and most depictions concentrate on the image of Liu and Ggojjy drinking together. A giant statue of the pair drinking stands at the centre of Xichang, the seat of the Liangshan Yi Autonomous Prefecture's administration. There is another at the 'Yihai alliance memorial site' near where the pact was made, and celebrated artist Wang Weizheng 王为政 chose the same image for a painting to commemorate the Communist pact with the Ggojjy. The effort to memorialise and propagandise a moment of friendship between the Nuosu and the Party has led to a profusion of images of Nuosu ritual consumption of alcohol and literally built drinking into the landscape of Liangshan's towns. The more sacred Nuosu alcohol consumption is understood to be, the more credible is the pact between Ggojjy Yodda and Liu Bocheng – and vice versa, and discussion of 'Yi alcohol culture' in the context of heritage work frequently mentions this episode. To an extent, alcohol heritage is, by association, revolutionary heritage.

None of this disproves the notion of an historical pattern of drinking behaviour that was disturbed, with detrimental consequences, by 1) growing Han influence and the breakdown of established social controls associated with alcohol and/or 2) the commercialisation of Liangshan and a corresponding increase in the availability of alcohol. However, these cases from the nineteenth century demonstrate that if this process has happened, then it has happened over a relatively long time period. They also show that contemporary concerns about the corruption of Nuosu drinking practices are part of a long-established discourse of worrying about the impact of Han culture and commercialisation on Nuosu drinking – worries shared by the Nuosu as well as Han – but which have been balanced by recognition of the ceremonial role of alcohol in pacts made between Qing (and Republican Han) military leaders and Nuosu clans. All of this raises the question of whether present-day narratives that juxtapose a valuable heritage of alcohol in Nuosu social life with anxiety about the impact of commercialisation and Han influence on Nuosu dinking are a reflection more of present-day trends in Nuosu drinking, or of the persistence of a set of ideas about Nuosu drinking over a long period of time.

Conclusion: Alcohol in History and Heritage

Discourses about heritage tend to imagine heritage work as a mission created in the present day to save meaningful things and knowledge from the past that would otherwise vanish under the pressures of contemporary developments. But heritage discourses are not conjured into being fully formed by a present that is newly conscious of a duty to preserve, and neutral in its selection of what to save. Heritage work has its own histories, and is contingent upon accounts of history that also have histories of their own, which powerfully shape practice of the present.

Even though health researchers and government officials often blame Yi poverty on Yi alcohol consumption, Yi have been successful in establishing the idea that their alcohol culture should be protected and promoted as an important part of their heritage. To an extent, this move is contingent on narratives that cast contemporary drinking problems as the result of very recent transformations in Yi drinking due to either Han cultural influence or the commercialisation of Yi society. These narratives suggest that these changes have happened so rapidly and recently that attitudes toward alcohol among the Yi have not had time to adjust properly. Yet the spectre of the Yi drunk or the Yi who drinks badly has inhabited the Yi-Han frontier for a long time. This spectre bears resemblances to stereotypes from other parts of the world: many studies have found that economically and politically marginalised people are more vulnerable to substance abuse – and, just as Yi alcohol consumption is seen as a reason for Yi poverty, dominant communities often highlight substance abuse problems among minorities as a way of explaining problems of poverty, much as lines of causation also run in the other direction. In Liangshan, the Yi have long been participants in discourse that problematises alcohol consumption on the frontier and in marketplaces; and it is perhaps due to their participation that Yi have been able to frame discussions of alcohol and alcohol-related problems on their own terms – in terms that, in the present, allow for the framing of an alcohol heritage that is seen as separate from 'problem drinking' of the present, is worthy of protection and celebration, and may even serve as a cure for contemporary problems.

References

Alaniz, M. L. (2009), 'Migration, Acculturation, Displacement: Migratory Workers and "Substance Abuse"', *Substance Use & Misuse* 37 (8-10): 1253-1257.

Anji, M. 安吉米克 (2012), Post on 'Yi ren lun tan 彝人论坛' at Yizu ren wang 彝族人网, 20 February 2012. [Online]. Available from: http://bbs.yizuren.com/archiver/?tid-57029-page-4.html (accessed 14 January 2016).

Bamo, Q. (2001), 'Traditional Nuosu Origin Narratives: A Case Study of Ritualized Epos in *Bimo* Incantation Scriptures', *Oral Tradition* 16 (2): 453-479.

Bender, M. (2008), '"Tribes of Snow": Animals and Plants in the Nuosu *Book of Origins*', *Asian Ethnology* 67 (1): 5-42.

Cai, F. 蔡富林 & Mi W. 米伍作 (2014), *Dangdai Liangshan Yizu xueyuan jiazhi chuantong xiguan fa yanjiu* 当代凉山彝族血缘家支、传统习惯法研究. Beijing: Minzu chubanshe.

Feng, Y.冯元蔚 & S. Qubi 曲比石美 (trans.) (1978), 'Hnewo tepyy / Lei'e teyi 勒俄特衣', in Y. Feng & S. Qubi (eds.), *Liangshan Yi wen wenshi ziliao* 凉山彝文文史资料, 95-121. Chengdu: Xinan minzu xueyuan.

Harrell, S. & Y. Li (2003), 'The History of the History of the Yi, Part II', *Modern China* 29 (3): 362-396.

He, M. 何明 & M. Wu 吴明泽 (1999), *Zhongguo shaoshu minzu jiu wenhua* 中国少数民族酒文化. Kunming: Yunnan renmin chubanshe.

Herberer, T. (2007), *Doing Business in Rural China: Liangshan's New Ethnic Entrepreneurs*. Seattle: University of Washington Press.

Jia, Y. 贾英忠 (ed.) (2014), *Zhongguo Yizu fei wuzhi wenhua yichan gailun* 中国彝族非物质文化遗产概论. Beijing: Minzu chubanshe.

Jidi, K. 吉狄康帅 (2002), *Yizu jiu ge* 彝族酒歌'. Chengdu: Sichuan yinxiang chubanshe.

'Jiu de qiyuan 酒的起源' (2006), translated by Aji, L. 阿吉拉则 in Dajiu M. 达久木甲 (ed.) *Zhongguo Yiwen dianji yi cong* 中国彝文典籍译丛 vol. 1, 149-155. Chengdu: Sichuan minzu chubanshe.

King, M., A. Smith, & M. Gracey (2009), 'Indigenous Health part 2: The Underlying Causes of the Health Gap', *Lancet* 374: 76-85.

Leng, G. 嶺光电 (1988), *Yi wangxi: yi ge Yizu tusi de zi shu* 忆往昔：一个彝族土司的自述. Kunming: Yunnan renmin chubanshe.

Li P. 李沛亨, Wang Y. 王耀华, Heng K. 衡克礼, Luo Ming 罗明, Xu H. 徐厚才, Wang G. 汪国群, Zhang Y. 张月良, & Zhang H. 张华寿 (2000), 'Han, Yizu nongmin yin jiu qingkuang diaocha 汉、彝族农民饮酒情况调查', *Lin chuang jingshen yixue zazhi* 临床精神医学杂志 10 (5): 270-272.

Liu Y. (2001), 'Searching for the Heroic Age of the Yi People of Liangshan', in S. Harrell (ed.), *Perspectives on the Yi of Southwest China*. Berkeley: University of California Press.

Mahei, E. 马黑尔惹 & Li, F. 李富根 (1994), 'Yin shi wenhua: 'tuotuo rou' yu 'suancai tang' 饮食文化：'砣砣肉'与'酸菜汤', *Liangshan wenshi ziliao xuanji* 凉山文史资料选辑 12: 285-294.

Qiu, S. 邱述鈴 (1938), 'Xikang san da minzu suoying 西康三大民族缩影', *Kangdao yuekan* 康導月刊 1 (3): 19-28.

Qiu, S. (1939), 'Jiulong jingji jianshe zhi yantao 九龍經濟建設之研討', *Kangdao yuekan* 2 (1): 40-46.

Qumu, W. 曲木伍牛 (2006), 'Liangshan Yizu diqu pinkun wenti yanjiu 凉山彝族地区贫困问题研究'. Liangshan Yizu Zizhizhou yi gong dai zhen bangongshi 凉山彝族自治州以工代赈办公室. [Online]. Available from: http://lsygdz.lsz. gov.cn/gztt/gztt601.htm (accessed 31 December 2015).

Sichuan sheng wenhua guan 四川省文化馆 (2015), 'Sheng zhengfu gongbu Sichuan sheng disipi fei yi daibiaoxing xiangmu 省政府公布四川省第四批非遗代表性项目'. [Online]. Available from: http://www.scc.org.cn/detail-2665.aspx (accessed 19 December 2015).

Suomaecho (2011), Post on 'Yi ren lun tan 彝人论坛' Yizu ren wang 彝族人网. [Online]. Available from: http://bbs.yizuren.com/archiver/?tid-57029.html (accessed 11 January 2016).

Tan, W. 谭万能 (2015), 'Hou Yuangao: Liangshan wenti de genyuan he chulu 侯元高：凉山问题的根源和出路'. *Fenghuang* 凤凰, 12 August. [Online]. Available from: http://news.ifeng.com/a/20150812/44410849_0.shtml (accessed 10 January 2016).

Winnington, A. (2008), *The Slaves of the Cool Mountains*. London: Serif.

Zhaojue xian zhi 昭觉县志' ([1911] 1992), in *Zhongguo difang zhi ji cheng, Sichuan fu xian zhi ji* 中国地方志集成，四川府县志集, vol. 69. Chengdu: Bashu shushe.

'Zhiling shiyi lü lüzhang Yang Qingquan wei zhuan cheng yiwu zhihui Deng Wenfu banli Daxingchang Han Yi liantuan qingxing yi an wen 指令十一旅旅長羊清全爲轉呈夷務指揮鄧文富辦理大興塲漢夷聯團情形一案文', *Bianzheng* 邊政 8 (1931): 28-34.

Zhongguo shaoshu minzu shehui lishi diaocha ziliao congkan xiuding bianji weiyuanhui 中国少数民族社会历史调查资料丛刊修订编辑委员会 (2009), *Sichuan Yizu lishi diaocha ziliao, dang'an ziliao xuanbian* 四川彝族历史调查资料、档案资料选编, 2nd ed. Beijing: Minzu chubanshe.

About the Author

JOSEPH LAWSON is a lecturer in Chinese history at Newcastle University. He is the author of *A Frontier Made Lawless: Violence in Upland Southwest China, 1800-1956*, and the translator of Mao Haijian, *The Qing Empire and the Opium War*.

11   'Ethnic Heritage' on the New Frontier

The Idealisation and Commodification of Ethnic 'Otherness' in Xinjiang

David O'Brien and Melissa Shani Brown

Abstract

This chapter aims to explore conceptually the commodification of 'heritage' in 'ethnic' tourist sites, focusing upon a so-called 'traditional Kazakh village' commercial tourist attraction near Tianchi Lake in the Xinjiang Uyghur Autonomous Region (XUAR). Taking an interdisciplinary approach which combines ethnographic methods with theoretical analysis, we consider tourism's role in representing the cultural heritage of ethnic groups, but simultaneously consider how such representations also tie into wider social discourses in which ethnic groups are themselves represented as 'heritage' in being associated with 'traditional cultures' rather than modernity. Drawing on a 'toolbox' of theoretical concepts, we consider the village as a depiction of idealised/idyllised ethnicity, how it functions as a visual 'sight/site', and how Said's concept of 'imagined geographies' might also encompass 'imagined ethnicities'. We finish with a discussion of this tourist site in relation to Michel Foucault's concept of 'heterotopia'.

Keywords: ethnic heritage, ethnic tourism, Xinjiang, imagined geographies, heterotopia

Introduction

This chapter aims to explore conceptually the commodification of 'heritage' in 'ethnic' tourist sites, by focusing upon a so-called 'traditional Kazakh village' commercial tourist attraction near Tianchi Lake in the Xinjiang Uyghur Autonomous Region. Taking an interdisciplinary approach which combines ethnographic methods with theoretical analysis, our aim here

Ludwig, Carol, Linda Walton, and Yi-Wen Wang (eds), *The Heritage Turn in China: The Reinvention, Dissemination and Consumption of Heritage*. Amsterdam: Amsterdam University Press 2020
DOI: 10.5117/9789462985667_CH11

is to consider tourism's role in representing the cultural heritage of ethnic groups, but simultaneously to consider how such representations also tie into wider social discourses in which ethnic groups are themselves represented as 'heritage' in being associated with 'traditional cultures' rather than modernity. Beginning with a background discussion of the official social discourses which define 'ethnicity' within the Chinese context, as well as other scholars' work around the intertwining of tourism and commodification, we go on to explore this particular site through a number of theoretical 'lenses'. Drawing on a 'toolbox' of varied scholars' work, we consider the village as a depiction of idealised/idyllised ethnicity, how it functions as a visual 'sight/site', and how Said's concept of 'imagined geographies' might also encompass 'imagined ethnicities'. We finish with a discussion of this tourist site in relation to Michel Foucault's concept of 'heterotopia'.

Tourism itself might be understood as a process of commodification, making people, places, 'culture', purchasable as 'experiences to be had' and also through being rendered into objects as souvenirs (including through the process of photography). But such tourist sites necessarily operate within social contexts, one in which official discourses (such as State definitions of ethnicity, as well as social policies), as well as more mainstream media discourses (from film to news), represent and reiterate 'ethnicity' in particular ways. To situate this in Foucauldian terms, such ethnic identities are constructed and reaffirmed through the various discourses in society, discourses which define such identities are thus 'technologies' of power (Foucault 1977). The idea of (what it is to be) a particular ethnicity – or indeed, to be situated as a 'minority' (*minzu*) within a Han Chinese majority country – is thus mediated; by this we correlate the meaning of 'media' to 'medium', anything which is a representation is thus 'media', and all identities are mediated through their representations. It is within such representations that certain contrasts are reified: ethnicity as 'other', exotic, simpler, less 'advanced' in a Social-Darwinian/Maoist sense. This also situates ethnicities as inseparable from their heritage, defined by it and representing 'the past' in a generic way. Exploring this otherness is the theme which runs through this chapter.

Tourist sites are interactive media through which images of 'ethnicity' are represented, commodified, and consumed. Commodification through tourism dovetails into the 'mediation' of ethnicity, depending upon and reinforcing particular tropes. Our intention here is to consider not only how ethnicity is depicted within this particular site, but also how tourists are actively encouraged to participate. This occurs both through engaging in imaginative role play, but in particular through photography, both of which

implicate tourist participants in the active reiteration of these idealised depictions. Later in this chapter, we use Foucault's concept of 'heterotopia' as a lens
through which to explore this site as highly ambivalent, both an *imagined
geography*, but one which is *grounded in an actual location*; which (re)presents
ethnicity as heterochrony (eternal and unchanging, but experienced only
transitorily), and one which also mediates contradictory representations of
ethnicity – from the safe and picturesque to the dangerous and potentially
violent, from 'ethnic harmony' to what the Chinese government terms the
'three evil forces' of separatism, terrorism and religious extremism.

Practices of Defining 'Ethnicity' – History and Narrative (of Progress)

In contrast to the Soviet Union, which established a system based on federal
republics with a theoretical right to secession, the PRC instituted a system
of limited territorial autonomy to manage ethno-national differences
(Clarke 2011). The CCP had adopted Stalin's definition of ethnic groups as
'an historically constituted, stable community of people formed on the basis
of a common language, territory, economic life, and psychological make-up
manifested in a common culture' (Stalin 1953: 307). A key task during the
early years of the PRC was the classification of its varied population into
clearly defined ethnic groups, a process achieved through the deployment of
ethnographic teams throughout the country. In Xinjiang this process resulted
in the official recognition of thirteen ethnic groups (*minzu*) – Uyghur, Han,
Kazakh, Manchu, Kyrgyz, Hui, Mongol, Xibo, Tajik, Russian, Uzbek, Tartar,
and Daur (Clarke 2011; Benson and Svanberg 1988; McMillen 1979).

Regional autonomy for ethnic minorities aimed to give them certain
economic, administrative and language privileges but any discussion of
self-determination was strictly and rigorously prohibited. As Matthew
Moneyhon has written 'the CCP essentially offered its left hand to sustain
minority culture, while its right erased any hope for true autonomy or
self-determination' (Moneyhon 2002: 133). Many scholars have argued that
in fact, very little political autonomy actually exists in the XUAR (McMillen
1979; Moneyhon 2002; Stein 2003; Bovingdon 2010).

From the 1980s Beijing policy towards its minority regions was very much
focused on economic development. Any conflict, ethnic or otherwise, was
understood as the result of economic disparities between minority areas
and the developed areas. Propaganda work therefore revolved around the
argument that economic development of the minority areas would solve

any such problems (Becquelin 1997). The 'Opening up the West' campaign which began in 2000 has seen a significant increase in the amount of central government money flowing into Xinjiang. While it is prosperous relative to other western provinces, it is as Nicholas Becquelin has written still very much a peripheral area:

> Xinjiang's economic structure fits the picture of a peripheral area, whose main function is to supply the core with raw resources and industrial products, while most of its manufactured goods are imported from the more developed parts of the country (2004: 362).

Like its predecessor the Qing, the CPC saw Han settlement in Xinjiang as a key to gaining control. Unlike the Qing however they have proved much more successful in actually getting Han settlers to stay in Xinjiang. From a low of 7 per cent in 1953; by 1964 they comprised 33 per cent of the population. A decade later, at the beginning of the Chinese economic reform in 1978, they numbered 40 per cent. In the most recent 2010 census, the Han figure was still hovering around the 40 per cent, while the number of Uyghurs, the largest ethnic group in Xinjiang, had fallen significantly to 42 per cent, down from over 80 percent when the CPC came to power. The Kazakh ethnic group now numbers 6.5 per cent of the population of Xinjiang, with the majority living in the north of the province (Toops 2004; Xinjiang Statistical Yearbook 2012). Kazakhs have long lived as nomads in the mountains around the Tianchi Lake although since the mid-twentieth century the numbers living there have declined greatly. Today many of those that remain are involved in tourism, especially in renting yurts to overnight visitors.

For the CCP, stability trumps all other concerns in Xinjiang. While the region has shown rapid economic development, it has also witnessed numerous violent incidents. The 2009 riots in Urumqi were the worst outbreak of social unrest in China since the Tiananmen Square protests in 1989. They have had wide-ranging repercussions for local and national governments (O'Brien 2015). Chih-yu Shih writes that the study of ethnic consciousness in China is, 'a study of the relationship between the small numbers of ethnic minority people and the vast majority of Han Chinese' (Shih 2002: 4). In Xinjiang however, the Han are (just about) a minority, but a minority who occupy the position of elite. Peter Jenkins (1994) has argued that the distinction between internal and external definition is primarily analytical and in the complexity of day-to-day social life, each is chronically implicated in the other. Or as Kleinpenning and Hagendoorn (1993: 25) put it, '[t]he categorisation of "them" is too useful a foil in the identification of "us"'.

Fredrik Barth's (1969) famous conceptualisation of ethnicity emphasises that it is the ethnic boundary that defines a group, rather than the inherent cultural attributes. An ethnic group can only be defined and structured from within, and only these 'objective' differences considered significant by the actors themselves are taken into account. Barth asserts that 'categorical ethnic distinctions do not depend on an absence of mobility, contact and information but do entail social processes of exclusion and inclusion' (Barth 1969: 10-14). It is not so much who we are, rather who we are not.

The representation of the Han as 'normal' and 'un-exotic' is critical for understanding the construction of present-day Chinese identity (Gladney 1994). This sense of the 'normal' and 'exotic' is directly related to the official portrayal of Han and minority groups in the PRC. By defining and representing minorities as exotic and primitive, it homogenised the majority as united, mono-ethnic and modern (Gladney 1994; Bhattacharya 2003). As Dru Gladney puts it:

> The Han are frequently represented as somewhere near the modern end of a Marxist historical trajectory upon which China's minorities must journey. Much of this derives from a continued commitment in Chinese social science to the study of minorities as 'living fossils' indicating the origins of 'primitive communism'. Matrilineality, communal living and property holding, and even extramarital sexuality among the minorities all become 'proofs' of how far the Han have come' (Gladney 1994: 99).

To consider Gladney's point further, this situates ethnic minority groups and their cultures as intrinsically 'heritage' – not only that their cultural practices are part of their traditions and histories. This also situates these groups as a kind of 'national heritage', embodying *history* and not 'another cultural modernity' alongside others. To adapt Edward Said (1978), it is a process of 'internal orientalism' which defines the Han as 'us' and the minority as 'other.' The ethnic signifier of being Han was fashioned in 'relational alterity', or through identifying 'Otherness' in the non-Han peoples of China (Gladney 1994).

Tourism and the Commodification of Ethnicity

For Åshild Kolås (2004), highlighting the perceived 'backwardness' of minority nationalities has produced an effect of distinguishing each group according to specific ethnic markers, such as dress, arts and crafts, architecture, typical livelihoods, festivals and religious practices; these markers become 'stereotypes [which] are currently being commodified for the sake of tourism, through the making of ethnic arts and handicrafts products, the creation of staged ethnic tourist performances, marketed locally and in ethnic theme parks and tourist villages' (2004: 281). This commodification of ethnic cultures is also visible throughout China from airport departure lounges selling ethnic dolls, to the 'ethnic restaurants' found in most major cities where (usually Han) girls in colourful 'traditional costumes' wait on tables and sometimes sing and dance, to the markets of Lhasa where largely Hui and Han merchants sell every imaginable 'authentic' Tibetan souvenir. In 21st century China to be ethnic is to be something simpler, from another time, something which can be experienced – at a price – as an antidote to the pressurised modern Han world of competition, pollution and overcrowding.

Tim Oakes (1997) argues that the minorities now play a role in the construction of a modern Chinese identity, an identity which is created as evolving from a past under the guidance of the benevolent nation state. It is a romance of a simpler, purer people, often less sexually restrained who have lives free of the cares of the world and whose music and dancing demonstrates a happy primitiveness. In discussing the China Folk Culture Villages theme park in Shenzhen, Oakes argues that it attempts to offer 'a coherent vision of modernity consistent with the fixed certainty of the nation state' (1997: 54) and that it conveys 'the side of modernity which seeks to order and regulate through standard categories and essential abstractions' (1997: 57). At sites like the Kazak village at Tianchi Lake this romantic vision can be experienced with all the modern conveniences at hand, toilets and instant noodles and ice tea, rendering 'history' and 'ethnicity' as simultaneously exotic, yet unchallenging.

In a recent article Agnieszka Joniak-Lüthi (2015) describes visiting the 'Park with Mysterious Trees' (Chinese: *Shen mu yuan*), a tourist site located two hours from the Xinjiang city of Aqsu. Here trees which are between 500 and 1000 years old have been bent by the strong winds into bizarre shapes. Predominantly Uyghur guides are employed in the park to provide tours, in Mandarin, to the mostly Han visitors. The guides name and invent stories about the trees to entertain the guests:

> Every tree was thus given its own name in Han language. There is a 'Lovers' tree', an 'Ethnic unity tree' (an apricot and mulberry tree that have grown together) and a 'Crouched dragon roaring to the sky tree', among many others. Tourist guides tell stories about what one can reportedly identify in

the twisted trunks: the head of Mao Zedong, the profile of Deng Xiaoping, a horse head, the letter "A" for Aqsu. Groups of Han tourists visiting the park drink from the water spring and hang strips of cloth with Chinese wishes, like 'Bon voyage' (yi lu ping'an) or 'Let everything go smoothly' (yiqie shunli), on the surrounding trees (Joniak-Lüthi 2015: 10).

In fact the reality of the site could not be more different. The tourist site now named the 'Park of the Mysterious Trees' is in fact a graveyard surrounding the *Mazar* (tomb-shrine) of an early Islamic missionary, Qirmish Ata. Each of the trees has been planted on a grave in the Uyghur tradition. It seems likely that many of the Han visitors taking pictures at the 'Lovers' Tree' would be uncomfortable if they knew it actually marked a grave. Such a re-interpretation of a space to render it more 'touristic' raises important questions regarding the idea that tourism easily functions as a means of 'preserving heritage' through rendering it more consumable (and therefore profitable). This reimagining of a space with a very specific cultural meaning into something quite different (and more acceptable to tourism) is happening throughout Xinjiang as the authorities aim to promote the region to Han tourists from inner China. These spaces are being reimagined as something exotic but familiar. A familiarity which can be captured by camera or smartphone: the trees may be mysterious, but they look like Chairman Mao, the traditions of the minorities may be different, but they are comforting in their simplicity. As Joniak-Lüthi writes '[t]he transformation of the Qirmish Ata *mazar* as a new feature of tourist geographies demonstrates that the modernising space of today's Xinjiang is a composite of various spatial layers generated by numerous actors: the Uyghur and Han individuals, the predominantly Han tourist companies, the Chinese central government, and the local governments that stand between them' (2015, 11). However, the meaning or story that develops as these layers build up usually eclipse the true origins (Bai 2007); particularly evident in this case, where the construction of the *mazar* as a tourist site superimposes 'mysteriousness', names, and stories, in such a way which obscures history rather than depicting it.

This particular example raises the important question of 'authenticity', a recurring issue of debate within academic studies of tourism. While it has been variously argued that all tourists search for 'authenticity' (Mac-Cannell 1973), or that there may be multiple forms of 'authenticity' (Pearce and Moscardo 1986), or that 'authenticity' is not a stable category but is in constant negotiation (Cohen, 1988; Squire 1994, Zhu 2012), the purpose of our engagement with the 'traditional Kazakh village' is not to primarily explore the extent of its 'authenticity'. While we identify the extent to which this village represents an 'idealised' depiction of 'traditional Kazakh life' (which necessarily implies a level of 'inauthenticity'), to a large extent we intend to side-step some of these debates, while acknowledging that all tourist sites constitute a negotiation with the 'authentic'.

The Tourist Site as an Idealised Representation of Ethnicity

The Kazakh village is a mandatory stop on most tours of the Tianchi Lake which is located in the foothills of the Tian Shan about two hours north of the Xinjiang provincial capital Urumqi. Billed as an 'authentic Kazakh village' it promises visitors the opportunity to 'see the ethnic people in their natural environment'. Visitors enter through large plastic gates designed to look like wooden stockades, past camels upon which they can have their picture taken for an extra fee, and into a 'village' divided into different sections each displaying a different aspect of Kazakh culture. Recorded music plays and throughout the small theme-park village there are a number of different dance troupes performing. Other performers rest in the shade of trees, while attendants and tour guides urge each tour group to keep walking a designated route. Concrete paths and signs take visitors past yurts where 'traditional Kazakh customs' like weaving and tea making can be seen and photographed. There is a 'Tunnel of Love' under which all must pass and where all visitors have their photograph taken with a young woman in 'traditional Kazakh costume'. An attendant then attempts to persuade them to purchase the photo. Lambs and other petting animals can be held or fed, while 'traditional Kazakh clothes' can be tried on for photographs, all for a fee. Many of the yurts have been cut in half allowing visitors to see inside where mostly elderly performers are drinking tea or spinning yarn. These half-moon yurts are 'living dioramas' which allow the visitor the opportunity to watch but not to engage – although some visitors during our visit did jump over the small barriers to have their picture taken with the performers. Throughout the village there are numerous performers both male and female, dancing in bright sequined costumes clearly made from polyester and held together with Velcro.

Jane Desmond (1999) notes that live performance and bodily display are very common within tourism (in Urry and Larson 1999). These examples involve what MacCannell (1973) terms a 'reconstructed ethnicity' and a 'staged authenticity'. While tourists are encouraged to take their picture with the performers there seems very little interaction beyond this and no real attempt to explain the significance or history of the performances. Much of what was on display is clearly problematic in terms of Kazakh culture, authenticity is as Yujie Zhu points out neither objective nor subjective, but rather performative (2012), and the majority of our fellow visitors did seem to get into the spirit of things and seemed to be enjoying their visit.

For the visitor, authenticity can be a projection of the tourists' own beliefs, expectations and stereotypes (Zhu 2012), an issue we will be exploring further later in this chapter through the concept of 'imagined geographies'. Writing about performance and the eroticisation of ethnicity among the Tai (Dai) in Xishuangbanna Dai Autonomous Prefecture in Yunnan, Sandra Teresa Hyde (2001) stresses the distinction between social representations of the Dai and actual cultural practices. She argues that because Han migrants and tourists both claim to appropriate Tai culture, ethnicity becomes an especially malleable category: 'it is precisely this Han representation of Tai women as beautiful, sexualized, and at home in their tropical paradise that makes Banna a desirable travel location ... Here the logic of internal colonialism takes root because the Tai are constructed as other and as sexualized in the Han imagination' (2001: 333).

Dru Gladney (1994: 108) has written that 'the repression and control of sexuality among the Han, and its open representation among the minorities ... demonstrate the important role eroticization of the engendered minority "Other" plays in the Han construction of the self.' At the Kazakh village this eroticisation is on display not just in the dancing and the 'Tunnel of Love' but also in an attraction which allows visitors, for an extra fee, to take part in a 'traditional wedding ceremony' where the 'bride' and 'groom' are serenaded in song and music before being escorted to the wedding night yurt with much hilarity and photo taking.

Gladney writes that enforced prudishness and controlled fertility among the Han, as opposed to represented minority sensuality, serve the state's national project of emphasising Han solidarity, civility and modernity (1994: 108). This eroticisation can be seen throughout 'ethnic China', a mural in Lhasa airport (Figure 11.1) and another in an Urumqi hotel (Figure 11.2) being examples. These images are also striking when contrasted to the 'Project Beauty' campaign which has been running in Xinjiang since 2013. 'Project Beauty' discourages local Uyghur women from wearing veils and men from sporting beards and has been the cause of much controversy in the region (Ghosh 2013).

As well as being eroticised, minority women are also depicted as pastoral and nurturing, tending to lambs and picking fruit. Louisa Schein (1997: 92) has argued in a paper on Gender and Internal Orientalism in China that '[t]he

Figure 11.1   Mural in the departure lounge of Lhasa Airport

Source: David O'Brien and Melissa Shani Brown

Figure 11.2   Mural in Urumqi Hotel

Source: David O'Brien and Melissa Shani Brown

chain of significance that linked ethnic to female to rural to backward served in effect to encourage a derogated subordinate positioning of minorities, women and peasants in Chinese society.' Throughout the Kazakh village young women in 'traditional costume' feed baby animals or arrange the harvested fruit. Indeed, most minority depictions are of young women or older men. Where young men are depicted they are often dancing or playing musical instruments, situated as non-threatening. A stark contrast to the other stereotypes of Xinjiang minorities of violent often urban young men engaged in criminality.

Tourist Site as Sight

The physical structuring of much of this 'village' demonstrates the intertwining of tourism and photography, in effect rendering this as much a construction of a tourist 'sight' as 'site' (a theme widely explored by other scholars, perhaps most famously in Urry and Larsen's 'The Tourist Gaze' (2011 [1990]). The village was structured so as to move visitors from one location to the next, with each 'attraction' being a focal point to be viewed, and mediated through photography (be it through the plethora of smartphones, or the widespread Canon IOS). In 'On Photography' (1979), Susan Sontag discusses photography in tourism as on one hand serving to document and 'verify' the experience to absent others, 'the trip was made ... fun was had ... sequences of consumption carried on [...]' (1979: 9); but also as being a means of controlling an otherwise potentially anxious interaction with the unfamiliar: 'Most tourists feel compelled to put the camera between themselves and whatever is remarkable that they encounter. *Unsure of other responses, they take a picture*' (1979: 10; emphasis added). We might argue here that photography has become so habitual not only to tourism but indeed to many people's daily life through the banality of smartphone photography that such anxiety is unlikely to be conscious. Most tourists are unlikely to debate 'whether to take a photograph' or what else they might do, because taking pictures in tourist locations 'is what is done'. But there is something pertinent in Sontag's description here, namely that the possibility of other responses is elided in such mediated engagements. Any other form of engagement with the actual people – be they 'authentic' 'ethnic' 'others', or 'performers' – is not what this 'tourist experience' is about. To return to the village, it was not merely a site which *might* be mediated into souvenir images, but was constructed *to be made* into such.

An example of this is the 'living dioramas'. We use this term because it highlights the presentation of a particular scene, such as one might encounter in a museum, with the exception that in this case the scene itself was being performed, rather than merely represented by manikins. The 'staging' of this is present not only in the removing of one half of the yurt – thus opening the interior, and the women and their spindles, not merely to view, but also to be more easily photographable: exposed to open daylight, and also on a raised platform rendering the seated women approximately the same height as those photographing them, thus rendering a closer view on what they were doing, and also making 'selfies' easier. The cement paths also looped across the open part of the diorama, enabling larger numbers of people to gather around without blocking the view.

Most of the tourists' engagement with the site focused upon either photographing the sights, or photographing themselves in this milieu; this was precisely the response being elicited by the site itself, such as the 'Tunnel of Love' through which everyone had to pass, with the costumed young woman waiting under the arch, precisely to 'be photographed with'. The staged marriage ceremony likewise was performed in order to be filmed/photographed, and was arrayed to be 'captured' from a particular vantage. The 'lovers swings' also were set up (with photographs alongside demonstrating how they were to be used) as props for tourists not only to use, but to be photographed using, in the same way also the animals existed as props. There was no encouragement to linger, to engage with any of the 'Kazakhs' through any kind of contact beyond photography and spectatorship.

This rendering of the 'natural environment' of the Kazakh village distills the culture and ethnic heritage of this group into a number of clichés – dancing girls, young men playing instruments, and pastoral setting – and one which is strikingly not that distinguishable from other ethnic groups except for the key signifier of clothing. In this the varied heritages of many of the ethnic minorities is reduced to distinctions in 'how they appear' – rather than any engagement with differences in belief, or other forms of intangible cultural heritage.

Imagined Geographies / Imagined Ethnicities

Sontag refers to photography turning the world into 'a museum-without-walls' (1979: 110), a concept that we have gestured towards also with the 'living dioramas'. As with a museum exhibit, what is presented is an idea (an idealisation) of 'typicality', that each scene is representative of a type (stereotype). The living diorama of the women spinning thus represents 'ethnicity', 'handicrafts', 'traditions', conflated into a single scene. The homogenisation of 'the other' implied in such stereotyping was also evidenced in our tour-guide's instruction to the tourists upon entering the village, namely that 'minority names are difficult to remember, so you can just call all the girls "Guli" (a common Sinicised Uyghur girls name).' The question of 'authenticity' in regards to the living dioramas, and other sites, is not the focus here, but rather to contemplate the image they represent, and the images that are produced of them. Our step away from the question of 'authenticity' here is in part to shift away from the concept of such photographs being 'inaccurate' (after all, they are photographs of an 'actual' location, 'real' people), but rather to consider what they create. Urry and Larsen (2011) discuss the creation of 'imaginative geographies' through tourist photographs, namely they function to create an idea of the place, and those who inhabit it (2011: 167). The term 'imaginative geographies' is borrowed from Edward Said (1978), describing the stereotyped conception of the 'Orient' in the 'Western' imagination. Thus the engagement with such photographs is simplified if it focuses only upon the (in)authentic, since such images are not simply representative, but are generative: '[...] "objective" not in the sense of mirroring the represented places' complex lived realities, but because they reflect and reinforce stereotypical western imaginations of these worlds' (Urry and Larsen 2011: 169). In this context, it is not a 'western' imagination which is being catered for, nor is it being generated through tourists 'seeking out' an 'authentic snap-shot' – while Urry and Larsen (2011) are focusing on the construction of 'imaginative geographies' through tourist photographs, we might argue here that they are likewise constructed through such tourist sites which actively present a particular 'image of ethnicity', and the 'actual images' generated through photographing them.

Entwined in such imaginative travel as implied by 'imagined geographies' is the pleasure of engaging with such idealised depictions of 'other (simpler) lives' taking place in 'other (simpler) times', theme-park excursions which '... ask spectators to engage with them "as if" they were real: to suspend disbelief and instead dream into their pictured heavens as if in a theatre or cinema' (Osborne 2000 in Urry and Larsen 2011: 176). As with other media forms, there is a blurring between 'fantasy' and 'stereotype' inherent in such 'imagined geographies'. Through the ability to 'dress up' in 'traditional clothes', engage in the staged weddings, or to render any parts of the village as a prop, tourists are invited to participate with the site, and the imagined space it creates. Through this entertaining 'play', and the evident enjoyment of capturing it on camera, the tourists are active participants with this 'pictured heaven', and with the dissemination of further images of it. Tourist sites, and photographs generated through them are thus also media, and mediating particular 'images of the world'. But when considering imagined geographies – and in this case, ethnicities – we must consider the representation, and commodification of these identities, as more than 'mere entertainment' – particularly for those on whom this potentially has an impact. Ethnicity as represented at this site is simultaneously marked as 'other', and also 'safe', and at a safe distance. Performers were largely young, or older women, they were friendly and smiled but made no attempt to speak or engage with the tourists themselves beyond posing to be photographed, and many were separated by clear boundaries – either the edge of the dioramas, or the stage. An idealised representation of both ethnicity, and also the past with which it was conflated.

Heterotopian Ethnicity

The theorist and historian Michel Foucault uses the term 'heterotopia' to refer to 'spaces of otherness' in his lecture 'On Other Spaces' (2008 [1967]). 'Otherness' in this context refers to 'difference', that which is contrasted to the 'normal', even if this otherness is recognisable, even familiar. Originally a radio talk delivered in 1966 on the theme of utopia and literature, then a lecture to architects in 1967, the transcript was published in 1984 with Foucault's permission but without his review (De Cauter and Dehaene 2008: 13). In his work on 'Thirdspaces', Edward Soja writes of heterotopias that they are 'frustratingly incomplete, inconsistent, incoherent' (1996: 162). His alliterative accusation is made while acknowledging that 'Of Other Spaces' is compiled of lecture notes, and possibly constituting 'just an early, preliminary sketch' (Soja 1996: 154). Despite – or possibly because of – the 'sketchiness' of Foucault's concept, using Foucault's 'heterotopias' as a starting point for further contemplation is precisely also the approach taken by numerous other scholars, including those focusing on tourism and heritage such as Ravenscroft and Matteucci (2003), Andriotis (2010), Kahn (1995), Dickenson, Ott and Aoki (2006), as well as the works compiled in Dehaene and De Cauter's (2008) edited collection.

Dehaene and De Cauter (2008) contemplate the spatial/conceptual positioning of heterotopias as existing at the intersection between different poles: neither the imaginary 'no-places' of utopias, nor the 'commonplaces' of society, heterotopias are ambivalent. They describe them as: 'aporetic spaces that reveal or represent something about the society in which they reside through the way in which they incorporate and stage the very contradictions that this society produces but is unable to resolve' (2008: 25). It is precisely the ambivalence of heterotopias – perhaps an ambivalence in 'otherness' itself – which we find useful for our discussion of this particular site.

Our reason for using the concept of heterotopia in this context is that it facilitates our exploration of ambivalent otherness, both conceptually, but also 'grounding' this in a particular location. In engaging with heterotopias in this chapter, we take several characteristics which Foucault situates as central to this concept as focal points. Some characteristics, such as being bounded (being both 'isolated' and yet 'penetrable' (2008: 21)) conforms to the structure of the Kazakh village – as a bounded tourist site, with a fee to enter – but while this might allow us to posit this space as heterotopic, it does not necessarily further our analysis. To this end, we will focus upon three particular aspects which Foucault touches upon: heterotopias' relationships with time (heterochrony), to utopias, and to the rest of society (functioning in compensation).

Dehaene and De Cauter's (2008) describe heterotopias as: 'aporetic spaces that reveal or represent something about the society in which they reside through the way in which they incorporate and stage the very contradictions that this society produces but is unable to resolve' (2008: 25). Concerning this village, in regarding it as a heterotopia, we argue that the imagined space it represents in concrete form is precisely a 'staging', through which it is possible to read the 'contradictions' produced yet unresolved by the social context of which this tourist site is a part. Thus we choose to use heterotopias as a lens through which to focus our further discussion of this site, by focusing upon the concept of 'heterochrony', the relation between heterotopias and 'utopia', and finally the concept of heterotopias functioning 'in compensation' to their social context.

Heterotopias bear a particular relation with time, the 'other time' of this 'other space' being termed 'heterochrony' (there is a question of translation from the French heterochronie, Miskowiec suggests 'heterochrony', Hurley 'Heterochronia'; Dehaene and De Cauter describe 'heterochrony' as 'the most logical option', but nevertheless go with 'heterochronism' 'for the sake of fluency' (2008: 26). We find 'heterochrony' easier, in terms of fluency and logic, and so go with this (2008: 20). Foucault discusses two potential types of heterochrony, the first being one which encloses 'in one place all times, all epochs ... a place of all times that is itself outside of time, and inaccessible to its ravages' (2008: 20), his example here including a museum. The second heterochrony is a space of 'transitory' 'festive' time, his example being holiday fairgrounds (2008: 21). Yet Foucault situates also the possibility that both heterochronies might coincide in one place, his example being 'Polynesian vacation villages', being simultaneously transitory spaces (for those visiting them), yet also 'primitive and eternal' (2008: 20). We interpret this same coincidence in the Kazakh village. The village functions as a heterotopia for the tourists as a space of leisure, separate from whatever is quotidian. Its relation in this case to holiday travel, the 'fairground' of a themepark, also situates it as a heterochrony – a place functioning in (and for) a particular time. This space of leisure is also a space of pleasure, and play – if we consider the rentable costumes, as well as the staged wedding. For Foucault, heterotopias may often be such spaces of fantasy, of imaginative travel. In the original radio talk given in 1966, he described the 'localised utopias' created by children 'at the bottom of the garden ... a forest where one can hide or a zone of titillating pleasure' as an introduction to the 'heterotopias' of the adult world (Boyer in Dehaene and De Cauter 2008: 53). But is also this more 'abstract' (fantasy) dimension which situates this village as heterotopic – and heterochronic – in other ways also, by virtue of being situated ambivalently in relation to the past and history, 'other times' rendered also as 'eternal', displaced from change (specifically, 'modernity'?). In this Kazakh village we might perceive the acting out of this representation of both ethnicity, and the past, grounding the idea of ethnic harmony (both within, and between ethnicities) into this actual site.

Its conflation with the past, 'living fossils' – ethnicity as heterochrony – the 'heritage-ing' of 'being an ethnic minority' and the idealisation of ethnicity comes to bear on Foucault's situating of heterotopias in relation to utopias. From the beginning of this work, this is a relation of contradiction: utopias 'are fundamentally unreal spaces' (2008: 17), whereas heterotopias are 'real ... places that are written into ... society itself' (2008: 17). Despite the insistence on the 'reality' of heterotopias there remains also a sense that these spaces function simultaneously in terms of being physical places as well as imagined spaces – it is the conception and attribution of difference, as well as the physical demarcation of it, which coincide in such spaces. A shatter-point between heterotopias and utopias may be what Foucault terms a 'heterotopia of compensation': 'another real space, as perfect, as meticulous, as well arranged as ours is disorderly, ill construed and sketchy' (2008: 21). This theme brought to the fore in Dehaene and De Cauter's description of all heterotopias as 'aporetic spaces [which] stage the very contradictions that this society produces but is unable to resolve' (2008: 25). In heterotopias we can perceive the ambivalence of 'otherness', an ambiguity present also in the eclectic-ness of Foucault's concrete examples, and also in his preoccupation with 'fantasy', and 'dreams'. In enacting heterotopias, perhaps, the question of 'authenticity' is circumnavigated in favour of the enactment (and emplace-ment) of an idea, a utopia – in this case of an idealised ethnicity. The village is utopic in its representation of an idyll of a 'traditional Kazakh village', and in the idyll of leisure and convenience as presented for the tourists' consumption. But a 'realized utopia' is precisely a heterotopia (2008: 17), a contrast to the 'real world' in which contexts are more complex than any picture-perfect harmoniousness. A heterotopia of compensation, 'as well arranged as ours is disorderly, ill construed and sketchy' (2008; 21), in which 'ethnicity' is aesthetic, religious tensions absent, and 'ethnic harmony' is mediated through consumerism.

Conclusion

The ambivalence of heterotopias is the ambivalence of 'otherness' – while being 'othered' may be everything from dehumanising to merely frustrating, so too is a denial of difference, or a refusal to engage with the multiple, contradictory or the complex. Such tourist sites, and other forms of commodifying ethnicity, simultaneously represent 'ethnicity' as 'other' and 'desirable' – at least to purchase, or to be experienced conveniently. This is perhaps intrinsic in the very process of commodification: to be purchasable requires the product to be simultaneously novel (exotic), desirable, safe. This raises questions when that which is being commodified is an identity category. But the structuring of the site around such commodification, so as each engagement comes at a price be it petting the lambs, or trying on a costume, also reinforces a particular distribution of economic power, and the presumption that consumerism will promote stability.

In her description of visiting the 'Park with Mysterious Tress' (Chinese: *Shen mu yuan*) which we have cited previously, Agnieszka Joniak-Lüthi mentions two trees growing together, and thus named the 'Ethnic Unity' trees (2015: 10). As with this village, the desire for stability and harmoniousness is both 'grounded' into these sites, and mediated through how tourists variously interact with them. It might be possible to situate tourism as being a positive force, not only potentially in bringing more capital into the region, but also being a means of fostering engagement – both the *mazar* and the 'authentic Kazakh village' depict 'harmony' in a context of uncertainty. However, in both cases these appear to eclipse actual engagement with either 'authentic' histories or 'actual minority cultural practices', or indeed their daily lives likewise unfolding in a modern contemporary context.

Our discussion of this tourist site has sought to interpret it as a 'grounding' of an imagined geography into a concrete form, and a form which both commodifies this particular representation of ethnicity and actively encourages particular interactions on the part of its tourist visitors. These interactions delimit the engagement of tourist visitors as spectators, and their participation with the site largely serves as a reiteration of its imagined geography. An exploration of the image of ethnicity being represented at this site not only allows us to consider the 'othering' of ethnicity through stereotyping, but simultaneously to consider 'the other side of the coin', namely the way in which the constructing of a 'modern' Han identity is implied through these tropes.

References

Andriotis, K. (2010), 'Heterotopic Erotic Oases – The Public Nude Beach Experience', *Annals of Tourism Research* 37(4): 1076-1096.

Bai, Z. (2007), 'Ethnic Identities under the Tourist Gaze,' *Asian Ethnicity* 8 (3): 245-259.

Barth, F. (ed.) (1969), *Ethnic Groups and Boundaries: The Social Organization of Culture Difference.* Boston: Little Brown.

Becquelin, N. (1997), 'Trouble on the Margins: Interethnic Tensions and Endemic Poverty in the National Minority Areas', *China Perspectives* 10: 19-28.

Becquelin, N. (2004), 'Staged Development in Xinjiang', *The China Quarterly* 178: 358-378.

Benson, L. & I. Svanberg (1988), 'The Kazaks in Xinjiang', in L. Benson & I. Svanberg (eds.), *The Kazaks of China: Essays on an Ethnic Minority*, 1-106. Uppsala: Almquist and Wiksell International.

Bhattacharya, A. (2003), 'Conceptualising Uyghur Separatism in Chinese Nationalism', *Strategic Analysis* 27 (3): 357-381.

Bovingdon, G. (2010), *The Uyghurs: Strangers in their own Land.* New York: Columbia University Press.

Boyer, C. (2008), 'The Many Mirrors of Foucault and their Architectural Reflections', in M Dehaene, M & L De Cauter (eds.), *Heterotopia and the City: Public Space in a Postcivil Society,* 53-75. New York: Routledge.

Clarke, M. (2011), *Xinjiang and China's Rise in Central Asia 1949-2009: A History.* London: Routledge.

Cohen, E. (1988), 'Authenticity and Commoditisation in Tourism', *Annals of Tourism Research*, 15 (3): 371-386.

Dehaene, M. & De Cauter, L. (eds.) (2008), *Heterotopia and the City: Public Space in a Postcivil Society,* London: Routledge.

Dickinson, G., Ott, B. & Aoki, E. (2006), 'Spaces of Remembering and Forgetting: The Reverent Eye/I at the Plains Indian Museum', *Communication & Critical/ Cultural Studies* 3 (1): 27-47.

Dikötter, F. (1992), *The Discourse of Race in Modern China.* London: Hurst & Co.

Desmond, J. (1999), *Staging Tourism: Bodies on Display from Waikiki to Sea World.* Chicago: University of Chicago Press.

Foucault, M. (1967), 'Of Other Spaces: Utopias and Heterotopias'. in M. Dehaene & L. De Cauter (eds.), *Heterotopia and the City: Public Space in a Postcivil Society*, 13-29. London: Routledge.

Foucault, M. (1977), *Discipline and Punish: The Birth of the Prison*. London: Penguin Books.

Ghosh, P. (2013), 'Project Beauty: Chinese Officials Pressure Uighur Muslim Women in Xinjiang to Drop their Veils, Men to Cut Beards', *International Business Times* [Online] 27 November 2013, Available from: http://www.ibtimes.com/project-beauty-chinese-officials-pressure-uighur-muslim-women-xinjiang-drop-their-veils-men-cut (accessed 18 January 2016).

Gladney, D. (1994), 'Representing Nationality in China: Refiguring Majority/Minority Identities', *The Journal of Asian Studies* 53 (1): pp. 92-123.

Gladney, D. (1998), *Ethnic Identity in China: The Making of a Muslim Minority Nationality*. Fort Worth, TX: Harcourt Brace.

Hyde, S.T. (2001), 'Sex Tourism Practices on the Periphery: Eroticizing Ethnicity and Pathologizing Sex on Lancang', in N. Chen, C. Clark, S. Gottschang, & L Jeffery (eds.) *China Urban: Ethnographies of Contemporary Culture*, 143-164. Durham, NC: Duke University Press.

Jenkins, R. (1994), 'Rethinking Ethnicity: Identity, Categorization and Power', *Ethnic and Racial Studies*, 17:197-223.

Joniak-Lüthi, A. (2015), 'Xinjiang's Geographies in Motion', *Asian Ethnicity* 16 (4): 428-445.

Kahn, M. (1995), 'Heterotopic Dissonance in the Museum Representation of Pacific Island Cultures', *American Anthropologist* 97 (2): 324-338.

Kleinpenning, G. & L. Hagendoorn (1993), 'Forms of Racism and the Cumulative Dimension of Ethnic Attitudes', *Social Psychology Quarterly* 56 (1): 21-36.

Kolås, A. (2004), 'Tourism and the Making of Place in Shangri-La', *Tourism and Geographies* 6 (3): 262-78.

Li, Y. (2010), 'Ethnic Tourism and Cultural Representation', *Annals of Tourism Research* 38 (2): 561-585.

MacCannel, D. (1973), 'Staged Authenticity: Arrangements of Social Space in Tourist Settings', *American Journal of Sociology* 79 (3): 589-603I

McMillen, D. (1984), 'Xinjiang and Wang Enmao: New Directions in Power, Policy and Integration?' *The China Quarterly* 99: 569-593.

Moneyhon, M. (2002), 'China's Great Western Development Project in Xinjiang: Economic Palliative, or Political Trojan Horse?' *Denver Journal of International Law and Policy* 31 (3): 491-523.

Oakes, T. (1998) *Tourism and Modernity in China*. London: Routledge.

O'Brien, D. (2015), "If There Is Harmony in the House There Will Be Order in the Nation': An Exploration of the Han Chinese as Political Actors in Xinjiang,' in:

A. Hayes & M. Clarke (eds.), *Inside Xinjiang: Space, Place and Power in China's Muslim Far Northwest,* 32-52. London: Routledge.

Osborne, P. (2000), *Travelling Light: Photography, Travel and Visual Culture.* Manchester: Manchester University Press.

Pearce, P. & G. Moscardo (1986), 'The Concept of Authenticity in Tourist Experiences', *The Australian and New Zealand Journal of Sociology* 22: 121-132.

Ravenscroft, N. & X. Matteucci (2003), 'The Festival as Carnivalesque: Social Governance and Control at Pamplona's San Fermin Fiestas', *Tourism Culture & Communication* 4 (1): 1-15.

Said, E. (1978), *Orientalism.* New York: Pantheon Books.

Schein, L. (1997), 'Gender and Internal Orientalism in China', *Modern China* 23 (1): 69-98.

Shih, C. (2002), *Negotiating Ethnicity in China: Citizenship as a Response to the State.* London: Routledge.

Soja, E. (1996), *Thirdspace: Journeys to Los Angeles and Other Real-and-Imagined Places.* Oxford: Basil Blackwell.

Sontag, S. (1979), *On Photography.* London: Penguin.

Squire, S. (1994), 'Accounting for Cultural Meanings: The Interface Between Geography and Tourism Studies', *Progress in Human Geography* 18 (1): 1-16.

Stalin, J. (1953), *Collected Works of J.V. Stalin, Vol. II.* Moscow: Foreign Languages Publishing House.

Stein, J. (2003), 'Taking the Deliberative Turn in China: International Law, Minority Rights and the Case of Xinjiang', *Journal of Public and International Affairs* 14: 1-23.

Toops, S. (2004), 'The Demographics of Xinjiang', in S. Frederick Starr (ed.), *Xinjiang: China's Muslim Borderland,* 264-275. Armonk NY: M.E. Sharpe.

Urry, J. & Larsen, J. (2011), *The Tourist Gaze.* London: Sage.

Xinjiang Weiwu'er Zizhi Tongjiju (2012), *Xinjiang Tongji Nianjian 2012 [Xinjiang Statistical Yearbook 2012].* Beijing: Zhonguo Tongji Chubanshe.

Zhu, Y. (2012), 'Performing Heritage: Rethinking Authenticity in Tourism', *Annals of Tourism Research* 39 (3): 1495-1513.

About the Authors

DAVID O'BRIEN and MELISSA SHANI BROWN combine their respective backgrounds in ethnography and critical theory to offer interdisciplinary analyses of contemporary China. Their research has focused upon Foucauldian analyses of official discourses in Xinjiang, as well as ongoing research into Chinese tourists' photographic practices.

Afterword

Historicising and Globalising the Heritage Turn in China

Carol Ludwig and Linda Walton

The policies of economic reform and openness initiated by Deng Xiaoping in 1978 drew China into the global economy, and with economic expansion came the need to reposition China in the world diplomatically, politically, and culturally. One result of this was a significant shift in how the Party and state viewed (and instrumentalised) the past. By the 1980s, the Communist Party had dramatically shifted its perspective on heritage, realising that 'complete demolition of traditional fabric is a reckless way to drive the country forward' (Chen & Thwaites 2013: 49). This shift in thinking and policy represented a significant turning point for heritage conservation and management in China, the unifying theme of this book. Beginning with the Introduction, we historicise this turning point, showing not only how ideas about heritage evolved in the context of a modernising China, pre- and post-revolutionary, but also how conceptions of heritage were part of the political and cultural fabric of premodern China. In addition to setting the methodological stage for the disciplinary lens of anthropology, Chapter 1 places its subject in the context of evolving discourses of traditional folk culture beginning in the early twentieth century. Chapters 2 and 3 trace the development of historic sites of Confucian cultural heritage as they began to be viewed as political resources and economic assets well before the heritage turn, contextualised in the unfolding political history of the twentieth and twenty-first centuries. Chapter 4 both historicises and globalises the Great Wall as a cultural heritage site, tracing visual and textual representations and usages of the Wall by foreigners as well as Chinese, past and present. Exploring the uses of history and nostalgia, Chapter 8 brings out the colonial past as an element used in the creation of contemporary cultural heritage in urban settings. Focusing on an entirely different topic of intangible heritage among non-Han minority peoples, Chapter 10 makes use of pre-twentieth century textual records to provide context for recent discourses on Yi culture and heritage.

Ludwig, Carol, Linda Walton, and Yi-Wen Wang (eds), *The Heritage Turn in China: The Reinvention, Dissemination and Consumption of Heritage*. Amsterdam: Amsterdam University Press 2020
DOI: 10.5117/9789462985667_AFTER

In contrast to most recent work on heritage conservation and management in China, two chapters offer comparative perspectives that frame China's (re)invention, dissemination, and consumption of heritage in a global context. Chapter 1 compares the Swiss institutional structure for heritage preservation with that of China, showing similar tensions and conflicts among stakeholders. Chapter 5 is directly comparative, focusing on the topic of an open-air museum in the UK and two historical theme parks in China. Although none of the chapters explicitly addresses the topic of China's numerous World Heritage Sites, the globalisation of heritage is everywhere embedded in how Chinese cultural heritage is (re)invented, disseminated, and consumed. The 'global hierarchy of value' (Herzfeld 2004) shapes the valorisation of places, things, and practices for domestic consumption as well as for potential global audiences, most notably through UNESCO's 'magic list of global status' (Askew 2010). Using themes addressed across all the chapters – instrumentalisation of heritage, sanitised heritage narratives and the commodification of heritage – the following sections provide some reflections on the heritage turn in China and its global setting.

The Instrumentalisation of Heritage

In the ideological vacuum created by the erosion of faith in Marxism among the vast majority of the Chinese population, the Party-state has been able to instrumentalise a sanitised form of heritage to justify its rule based largely 'on its delivery of consistent economic growth' and 'the maintenance of public order', as well as the cultivation of morality (Shepherd & Yu 2013: 19). Beginning in the 1980s, for example, Confucianism was increasingly instrumentalised as a vehicle not only for the (re)clamation of a shared Chinese identity (with the potential to unify the Chinese people and engender a shared sense of pride and belonging) but also to encourage a 'harmonious' society benefitting from 'moral education', and potentially global recognition of Confucian humanistic values. Indeed, after attacks on Confucianism in the twentieth century, along with the mass destruction of religious and historical sites during the Cultural Revolution, little appeared to remain of China's cultural heritage. Attacks on the Confucian and 'feudal' past, coupled with the economic reforms of the 1980s and a rapidly growing market economy that undermined Marxist economic principles and thus Marxism as a whole, left the Chinese people with little to believe in, other than making money. Newfound emphasis on capitalist competition and the sanctity of the marketplace also yielded negative consequences with social impacts, including the lowering of standards in food processing, negligence of consumer safety, and forms of corruption such as stealing and cheating to maximise profit.

By the 1990s government leaders saw an urgent need to restore faith in the Chinese Communist Party and to regulate individuals' behaviour by rebuilding moral standards embedded in Confucianism, a cultural tradition emphasising self-cultivation for the good of society and moral codes of behaviour. Confucianism re-emerged as a topic of public intellectual discourse, and interest in Confucian ideas and practices was also encouraged among the population at large (Billioud & Thoraval 2015). This development took place in tandem with increasing government emphasis on the management of China's cultural heritage both to promote a shared national identity and to achieve global recognition. The Party-state also recognises the value of built heritage as tourist attractions with both economic and cultural/political benefits. Government leaders see the contribution heritage assets can make to city branding and place identity and thus have a renewed focus of attention on safeguarding such built heritage. Since the early 1980s China's approach to heritage conservation has begun to align more and more with the longer established Western system (the compiling of inventories of heritage assets, establishment of laws for cultural heritage protection, etc.), although Chinese conservation laws and plans have at times been heavily criticised for their lack of control and purpose, their lack of community input, and their seemingly narrow target audience (Harrell 2014). While acknowledging the impact of Western influence on China's conception and practice of heritage conservation, like Harrell (2014) we argue that China's current use of heritage should be understood from the perspective of its own historical experience and shifting political strategies. The latter align with both domestic and international priorities: to promote nationalism among the Chinese population at home and to elevate China's status as a nation in the global community. In contrast to Western heritage authorities' fixation on the 'authenticity' and 'genuineness' of heritage, for example, Chinese state authorities' understanding of heritage focuses more on the 'purpose' or the broader role that heritage is intended to serve as an instrument to promote national interests at home and abroad. From a variety of perspectives, the chapters in this book have shown how heritage is selectively cultivated and interpreted by Chinese authorities at national, regional, and local levels, disseminated to both domestic and international audiences, and how heritage as defined by these authorities is received, contested, and modified by stakeholders.

A Sanitised Heritage Narrative

Heritage has become internationally recognised as a key part of the 'territorial capital' of a place (Sykes and Ludwig 2015: 9), and for China this relatively recent realisation has revolutionised the discourse of heritage conservation and management in China. The potential of both World Heritage Sites and nationally designated cultural heritage sites as tourist destinations and thus economic assets is now deemed an essential resource for promoting patriotism as well as for producing profits. Indeed, while heritage has played a key role in China's growing tourism industry over the last three decades, it is crucially also still an important part of a wider political project (Blumenfield & Silverman 2014; Denton 2014). In the post-reform era, China's Communist Party has had to adapt Marxism to new historical conditions and redefine itself. To justify its continued rule the Party has had to create a new narrative of the past, which is carefully controlled and erases uncomfortable truths (such as the Party's former ideological focus on revolution and class struggle). Instead the Party reconfigures history in order to portray itself as saviour of the nation and its past, an organisation of patriots committed to 'a collective national struggle' against enemies of the Chinese people, both internal and external. In other words, the historical narrative depicted is a selective one: 'liberation from an exploitative past' with a clear emphasis on 'patriotism, national unity, and a strong China standing up to take its place in the world' (Shepherd & Yu 2013: 20-21).

Focus on national unity also enables a clear, strong story line to be told in newly opened or restored provincial museums, at all heritage sites, and at the Ming-, Qing-, and Republican-era 'old towns' across China (Shepherd & Yu 2013: 25). Government control of the dissemination and consumption of heritage, however, raises important questions about the many dissonant and alternative conceptualisations of heritage that appear to be closed down, marginalised and/or discredited simply because they sit outside the Party-approved, sanitised version of the past, such as the subjugation and silencing of non-Han ethnic heritage or its manipulation for the purpose of tourism development in a Kazakh village in Xinjiang (Chapter 11). These and other cases replicate Smith's (2006) criticisms about the negating or erasing of subaltern heritage in her detailed work examining the Authorised Heritage Discourse (AHD) in practice and represent the 'homogenizing tendencies of the state' (Byrne 2011: 146) operating within the global hierarchy of value (Herzfeld 2004).

As noted in the Introduction, in China the great diversity of institutional and non-institutional heritage definitions and approaches might best be understood as an 'assemblage of AHDs'. The national government has taken a leading role, spearheading a campaign for the protection (and exploitation) of heritage in an attempt to cultivate a shared cultural identity, promote public pedagogy, foster bonds of nationalism and achieve global recognition. This can be seen in chapters 2 and 3 on the promotion of Confucianism through the restoration of ancient sites, and likewise in chapters 6 and 7 on the construction of public museums to build a sense of shared history and common cultural identity. Meanwhile, officials at the local level have capitalised on cultural heritage for city and village branding, formulating and asserting distinct place identities, both urban and rural, as demonstrated in chapters 8 and 9. It has also been shown here that local elite uses of history, nostalgia and heritage – their historic economic heritage branding schemes geared towards creating a distinct place identity and economic benefits – have made important contributions to the AHD. Moreover, as demonstrated in Chapter 8, regional officials in Shanghai and Wuhan have capitalised on the city's colonial heritage, diverging from the revolutionary narrative of the past that the national government aims to promote. Different representations of the past are articulated by rural villagers, ethnic minority groups, media professionals, etc., or imagined by consumers or entrepreneurs of entertainment business that are not necessarily in line with what was/is intended by national government agencies. Several chapters focus precisely on such 'unauthorised' heritage, such as the theme parks in Chapter 5, or the performances described in Chapter 1. These 'historic' theme parks include a selected collection or reconstruction of remnants of the past for entertainment and were not intended to be part of China's AHD assemblage. Yet, having been well-received by the general public and perceived as sites of education and promotion of intangible heritage, they have eventually become representative of the cultural identity of the place or region: in other words the commercial non-AHD has become part of the AHD. Likewise, the drinking culture among the Yi ethnic minority in Chapter 10 or the heritage-making process in a rural setting in Chapter 9 share a similar trajectory. While the campaign for heritage conservation has therefore been driven and orchestrated by the national government to promote cultural pride and support its own political legitimacy, non-state actors at all levels across China, along with some regional and local officials, are very much involved in the heritagisation process and in the constant evolution of the AHD assemblage for China (Madsen 2014; Zhang & Wu 2016).

The Commodification of Chinese Heritage

The current political leadership in China recognises that the construction and maintenance of a shared cultural (and national) identity is critically important, not only for the continued acceptance of the CCP, but also for the continued economic development of China and consequently its global standing and competitiveness. It has been argued in many of the chapters in this book that heritage is being used in China as a vehicle for soft power (Nye 2004). Indeed, a sanitised, deeply embedded shared history and heritage has led to a Chinese identity that can be 'sold' not only to the Chinese people, but crucially also as a form of urban branding, making China and its cities attractive to foreign and domestic investors, as well as international tourists. In rural as well as urban spaces, China embraces cultural heritage to portray itself not only as 'a civilization that has influenced other countries and cultures' (Winter 2014a: 328) and can continue to do so, but also as a global superpower with a rich history and culture. China's deployment of 'cultural display' (Albro 2012) is therefore useful for diplomatic relations, geopolitical influence and in the cultivation of a global reputation as a leader in growing areas of international interest, such as, *inter alia*, sustainable and eco-development and innovative technology, architecture and urban design.

The increasingly business-like approach to heritage management and use in China may be criticised by many for damaging the real purpose and the true meaning of heritage, an argument central to the heritage industry critique that played out in Britain as far back as the 1980s (Hewison 1987; Wright 1985). Yet such a strategy could equally be recognised as a realistic means by which heritage can be promoted, saved and economically justified (Harrell 2014). A Chinese interpretation of authenticity presented in the Hangzhou and Kaifeng theme parks, for example, shows that 'the subjective, "experience-centred" notions of tourist authenticity' have completely overpowered 'the objective, "object-centred" modern notions of heritage authenticity' (Guttormsen & Fageraas, 2011; González Martínez 2017:56; Wang 1999; Zhu 2015). The formal designation of the two theme parks in Hangzhou and Kaifeng as demonstration sites for intangible heritage in fact serves to rejuvenate and bring back to life dying cultural heritage (Zhu 2012). Moving beyond a Eurocentric conception of authenticity in China involves more than the practice of 'experiential' (or 'existential') authenticity, however. One Chinese scholar, Wu Zongjie, has proposed an indigenous approach to the meanings of 'heritage' and 'authenticity', arguing that both concepts are produced through discursive practices that are culturally inflected. Wu draws on a distinctive form of historical narrative as well as subaltern voices to demonstrate the possibilities of alternative understandings of both (Wu 2014).

The (re)awakening of interest in the conservation of China's heritage by its leaders over the past 30 years marks a significant development not only for China but for the world. Recent Chinese historical experience and current political exigencies dictate a distinctive approach to cultural heritage that should be understood in its own context both as a response to global influences and as a contribution to global discourse on heritage (Maags & Svensson 2018). Indeed, the Chinese leadership has been very successful in extracting value from its heritage to serve both domestic and global political, diplomatic, and strategic interests (Winter 2015). China has also reacted expeditiously to contemporary shifts in the international heritage discourse, embracing the notion of Intangible Cultural Heritage, as defined by UNESCO (2003) and using the separation of the material from the symbolic to its advantage. In contrast, many nations remaining overly concerned with the Western understanding of heritage and its authenticity often struggle to find ways to safeguard their heritage or to justify its validity/legitimacy (and thus retention) if it lacks the more rigid, pre-defined tangible scientific evidence required to satisfy the conservation 'experts' (Ludwig 2016).

Together, the chapters in this book demonstrate that not only has China experienced a clear (re)awakening in relation to its appreciation and value of heritage, but also this heritage is being (re)invented, disseminated and con-sumed in alternative ways; some of which sit firmly outside the conventional, accepted and/or authorised versions traditionally upheld by 'the West'. For instance, Chinese heritage has been rebuilt (sometimes in a completely dif-ferent place) or retold (differently or selectively, for instance through digital, temporary and/or entertainment media) without affecting its legitimacy or heritage status. This approach clearly aligns with the ideas underpinning current heritage discourse that heritage is a set of changing values, accessed and consumed in the present (Ludwig 2016) rather than the traditional, deeply engrained understanding of heritage as a fixed, expert-defined construct. Moreover, the role and purpose of heritage (re)invention, dissemination and consumption is expanding into newfound areas. These relate both to the economic and public pedagogical value of heritage as well as to fostering bonds of national identity, purifying and strengthening the 'spirit' of citizens and cultivating cultural nationalism. Further still, heritage has become a useful geopolitical strategy for wider international diplomacy and power relations on the world stage. China's leaders strategically deploy these new modes of heritage governance to serve national needs and international ambitions, while its citizens alternately embrace and challenge these aims.

References

Billioud, S. & J. Thoraval (2015), *The Sage and the People: The Confucian Revival in China*. Oxford: Oxford University Press.

Blumenfield, T. & H. Silverman (2014), *Cultural Heritage Politics in China*. New York: Springer.

Byrne, D. (2011), 'Archaeological Heritage and Cultural Intimacy: An interview with Michael Herzfeld', *Journal of Social Archaeology* 11 (2): 144-157.

Chen, F. & Thwaites, K. (2013), *Chinese Urban Design: The Typomorphological Approach*. Farnham: Ashgate Publishing Ltd.

Clark, P. (2008), *The Chinese Cultural Revolution: A history*. Cambridge: Cambridge University Press.

Denton, K. (2014), *Exhibiting the Past: Historical Memory and the Politics of Museums in Postsocialist China*. Honolulu: University of Hawai'i Press.

González Martínez, P. (2017), 'Urban Authenticity at Stake: A New Framework for Its Definition from the Perspective of Heritage at the Shanghai Music Valley', *Cities* 70: 55-64.

Gruber, S. (2007), 'Protecting China's Cultural Heritage Sites in Times of Rapid Change', *Asian Pacific Journal of Environment and Law* 253 (10): 253-301.

Guttormsen, T. S. & K. Fageraas (2011), 'The Social Production of 'Attractive Authenticity' at the World Heritage Site of Røros, Norway', *International Journal of Heritage Studies* 17 (5): 442-462.

Harrell, S. (2014), 'China's Tangled Web of Heritage', in T. Blumenfield & H. Silverman (eds.), *Cultural Heritage Politics in China*, 285-294. New York: Springer.

Herzfeld, M. (2004), *The Body Impolitic: Artisans and Artifice in the Global Hierarchy of Value*. Chicago and London: The University of Chicago Press.

Hewison, R. (1987), *The Heritage Industry: Britain in a Climate of Decline*. London: Methuen.

Lew, C. (2009), *The Third Chinese Revolutionary Civil War, 1945-49: An Analysis of Communist Strategy and Leadership*. London: Routledge.

Ludwig, C. (2016), 'From Bricks and Mortar to Social Heritage: Planning Space for Diversities in the AHD', *International Journal of Heritage Studies* 22 (10): 811-827.

Maags, C. & M. Svensson (eds.) (2018), *Chinese Heritage in the Making: Experiences, Negotiations, and Contestations*. Amsterdam: Amsterdam University Press.

Madsen, R. (2014), 'From Socialist Ideology to Cultural Heritage: The Changing Basis of Legitimacy in the People's Republic of China', *Anthropology and Medicine* 21 (1): 58-70.

Shepherd, R.J. & Yu, L. (2013), *Heritage Management, Tourism, and Governance in China: Managing the Past to Serve the Present*. New York: Springer.

Sykes, O., & Ludwig, C. (2015), 'Defining and Managing the Historic Urban Landscape: Reflections on the English Experience and Some Stories from Liverpool', *European Spatial Research and Policy* 22 (2): 9-35.

UNESCO (2003), *Convention for the Safeguarding of the Intangible Heritage*. Paris: UNESCO.

Wang, N. (1999), 'Rethinking Authenticity in Tourism Experience', *Annals of Tourism Research* 26 (2): 349-370.

Winter, T. (2015), 'Heritage Diplomacy', *International Journal of Heritage Studies* 21 (10): 997-1015.

Wright, P. (1985), *On Living in an Old Country*. London: Verso.

Wu, Z. (2014), 'Let Fragments Speak for Themselves: Vernacular Heritage, Emptiness, and Confucian Discourse of Narrating the Past', *International Journal of Heritage Studies* 20 (7-8): 851-865.

Zhang, Y. & Z. Wu (2016), 'The Reproduction of Heritage in a Chinese Village: Whose Heritage, Whose Pasts?', *International Journal of Heritage Studies* 22 (3); 228-241.

Zhu, G. (2012), 'China's Architectural Heritage Conservation Movement', *Frontiers of Architectural Research* 1 (1): 10-22.

Zhu, Y. (2015), 'Cultural Effects of Authenticity: Contested Heritage Practices in China', *International Journal of Heritage Studies* 21 (6): 594-608.

About the Authors

CAROL LUDWIG is a Chartered Member of the Royal Town Planning Institute (RTPI) and Honorary Research Fellow at the University of Liverpool. Her research interests include the theorisation of heritage, the cultural process of identity formation, and community mobilisation in local conservation planning processes.

LINDA WALTON is Professor Emerita of History at Portland State University and Visiting Professor at Hunan University Yuelu Academy Research Institute. A historian of Song and Yuan China, especially academies, she has recently been studying the revival of Song-era academies in contemporary China and their role as sites of cultural heritage tourism.

Index

 **Publications / Asian Heritages**

Ana Dragojlovic: *Beyond Bali. Subaltern Citizens and Post-Colonial Intimacy*
2016, ISBN 978 94 6298 064 8

Carolien Stolte and Yoshiyuki Kikuchi (eds): *Eurasian Encounters. Museums, Missions, Modernities*
2017, ISBN 978 90 8964 883 9

Christina Maags and Marina Svensson (eds): *Chinese Heritage in the Making. Experiences, Negotiations and Contestations*
2018, ISBN 978 94 6298 369 4

Yujie Zhu: *Heritage and Romantic Consumption in China*
2018, ISBN 978 94 6298 567 4